A HANDBOOK | *for*

Parents *in* Ministry

A HANDBOOK | *for*

Parents *in* Ministry

TRAINING UP A CHILD
while ANSWERING THE CALL

DOROTHY KELLEY PATTERSON
and | ARMOUR PATTERSON

BROADMAN
&HOLMAN
PUBLISHERS

Nashville, Tennessee

0–8054–2786–4

Published by Broadman & Holman Publishers
Nashville, Tennessee

Dewey Decimal Classification: 253
Subject Heading: MINISTERS' FAMILIES

1 2 3 4 5 6 7 8 9 10   10 9 08 07 06 05 04

Dedication

For Charles Seymoure Kelley—devoted husband, loving father, affectionate grandfather, loyal soldier, benevolent businessman, caring citizen, faithful to God, dutiful to church, considerate of those in need, steadfast in character. Papa, in all your days under the sun, from the strength and passion of youth to the glory of twilight, you have been, and are, all that a man should be. This volume we dedicate to you with love, honor, and gratitude.

Contents

Foreword

It wasn't easy growing up as a son of Billy Graham. His long crusade trips seemed forever to a little boy, but how I vividly recall those moments when he returned home. Daddy would sweep me up in his big arms and toss me in the air. He made the most of his time at home, spending every moment he could with us, and those times together carried us through when he was away. Mama is a strong lady, and her tender, yet tough, love held down the home front while Daddy was ministering around the world.

I know the stresses and strains that ministry can place on a family, and I was delighted when Paige told me that his wife, Dorothy, and son, Armour, were writing this book. My parents are exceptional folks, and I thank God for the way they handled their ministries, in the home and in the world's stadiums and arenas. But I have seen many less fortunate families. I have met Christian leaders who sadly focused their entire beings on their "career" ministries, to the neglect of their spouses and children.

Handbook for Parents in Ministry brings a balanced approach, realizing that God's calling in a minister's life is first to his family. Dorothy and Armour bring a wealth of experience and creative insights and ground them in Scripture. The result is a solid and balanced way for God's people in ministry to tend their flocks, while learning how to "train up a child in the way he should go" (see Proverbs 22:6). *Handbook* is a practical help for families in ministry.

I pray that, as you read this book, God will bless you with understanding and wisdom, so that in His Church and in His homes, we "should be to the praise of His glory."

Franklin Graham, President and CEO
Billy Graham Evangelistic Association and Samaritan's Purse

Preface

ARMOUR AND I have determined to share with our readers—whether memories or our respective convictions—the lessons we've learned and challenges we've faced in our own ministry home. Although primarily written to parents, we have also shared helpful words with kids. Neither of us is a kid, but Armour is a lot closer to his childhood, bringing a perspective sometimes different from his aging mother's. We may remember things differently; nevertheless, you will hear from both of us and hopefully glean help in your own choices. For your convenience and clarity, when speaking as individuals, we have used two different typefaces—bold for Armour and italic for Mom.

Being a PK thrusts a unique set of challenges, obstacles, and hardships upon a child or young adult. Is this fair? No, but neither is life. To think you can eliminate all difficulties and create a PK utopia is unrealistic. If you could make everything perfect here, then Jesus would not have had to go elsewhere to prepare that special place for you. You can take an introspective look at how one ministry mom and dad deal with the problems and challenges inherent in rearing children, while carrying out the Lord's sacred call to ministry, as well as how their kids responded. A minister is a minister to all whom God brings across his path, including, first and foremost, his own family (see 1 Tim. 5:8). Provision reaches far beyond material necessities.

Some would argue that I am the perfect choice to write about the subject, suggesting that I have yet to "grow up," let alone figure out

what I'm going to do when I reach that point. As a PK myself, I have known and associated with many other PKs and their parents.

Believers must take seriously the calling of the Lord to walk in His ways, to live by His precepts, and to minister to His children, while still meeting family needs. Mom and I will try not to take ourselves too seriously. Every parent needs sharp senses, beginning with a sense of humor.

I approach the subject as a PK not too far removed from the current generation of young adults and children but, hopefully, far enough away to look back through a lens with some objectivity. In addition to drawing from my own experience, I have included testimonies of others, adding another dimension to the quest for bridging gaps of frustration, misunderstanding, and fracturing among families. I make no claim that the principles herein are the only, or even the best, way. If you see a different path that works for you, great!

We will adhere to the precepts of Scripture as best we can understand and interpret God's Word. Our goal is not to achieve complete agreement but rather to prompt thought, challenging you to think in ways you have not considered before. From that can flow greater understanding, discernment, and freedom for meaningful dialogue and interaction.

Acknowledgments

MANY PEOPLE CONTRIBUTE to a writing project. For Dorothy Patterson, gratitude goes to Chris Thompson, Special Assistant to the President, who manages Pecan Manor and its many ministries at Southwestern Baptist Theological Seminary in Fort Worth, Texas. Bobbi Moosbrugger, Beth Hernon, Gene Palanciuc, and Maurice Ahern each contributed by keeping hospitality and other ministries running smoothly. Jason Duesing and Summer Johnson also offered encouragement and support as needed, but no one carried the load as did Women's Studies researcher Candi Finch. She typed the manuscript, checked documentation, and made corrections in multiple drafts.

Armour and I are also indebted to Rachel, Armour's wife and my daughter-in-love, who has read and offered suggestions, and to the Big Daddy, whose awesome shadow falls across these pages as it has across our lives over the decades.

CHAPTER | *One*

The Gift of a Child

THE FAMILY IS God's first institution, established at the heart of His creative activity and recorded in Genesis, the book of beginnings. For whatever reasons, God chose to reveal Himself through the metaphor of the family and the relationships therein. He identifies Himself as Father, you as His child, heaven as home, Jesus as the Bridegroom, the church as the Bride. No one who studies the Bible can doubt that children are significant. The psalmist puts into perspective the place of a child in the divine economy (Ps. 127:3).

Who Is Watching the Kids?

How often do parents forget what blessings their children bring! Since the 1970s, a child's time with his parents has been declining year by year by about ten hours per week,[1] and more than half of the children born in America today will spend at least some of their childhood living apart from one of their parents.[2] For teenagers, as well as children, these circumstances have been devastating, resulting in more depression, homicide, suicide, drug usage, and a pregnancy rate out of wedlock twice that of any other developed nation.[3]

Children increasingly are spending more time with a child care provider than with their own parents. Researchers study, evaluate, and argue about the effect of substantial non-parental care on a child. In 2001, 61 percent of preschoolers regularly received some form of non-parental care. For children between kindergarten and eighth grade, 51 to 52 percent received some measure of non-parental care. Older children tend to care for themselves. Youth beyond eighth grade are not even included in the survey since they are presumably looking after themselves.[4]

Some ministry parents use their church's daycare for oversight of their children, overlooking that even the best church program is institutional care. While a loving environment with care providers who espouse Christian tenets is a plus, for ministry kids to spend more time within the walls of the church under non-parental supervision than with their own parents can have some long-lasting repercussions. The same possibilities for disaster are now extended beyond the activities of the church to most of the child's waking hours. Some caregivers look upon children of ministerial staff as off limits for enforcement of routines, rules, and discipline. Others use ministry children as a scapegoat or to "get at" the minister. Whether extending favoritism to or prejudice against ministry kids, the consequences can be grave.

Ministry parents may tend to push their children into the background to be retrieved for leisure enjoyment or to be put in the category of optional responsibilities. Sadly, these parents never learn God's purpose in parenting, nor do they accept the demanding task of understanding a child's role in the divine economy. To assume the primary responsibility of molding a helpless baby into a godly, courageous, confident, and creative one-of-a-kind person is truly an awesome task. Even in the dark hours every child is a symbol of hope for the future.

Some ministry parents may reject the opportunity for continuing the generations with the mind-set that their high and holy calling precludes the distraction children bring to life. Although most pursue parenthood with enthusiasm, even godly parents, busy with important spiritual ministries, are sometimes too eager to push their children into a world of responsibility to function on their own and free their parents for more ministry.

Ministry parents are usually underpaid, with little in their austere budgets for babysitting and child care. They assume that living in a godly home will pass to their children godly character traits and equip them with a working knowledge of values. Bowed under the burden of trying to help a congregation—many of whom are struggling from the results of living in dysfunctional homes—and playing a leadership role in propelling the postmodern community in a God-honoring direction, ministry parents often just don't seem to have the energy or the patience needed to pour out more tender loving care, not to mention patient instruction in biblical principles and meticulous training in living God's way, to the offspring awaiting them at home. In short, they can be overwhelmed with the unimportant, because wrong ideas coming from the influence of a worldly culture inevitably overtake the right principles found in heavenly principles.

Ministry kids should not be expected to know the biblical way by osmosis. Rather they must be carefully taught and motivated to walk in the Lord's way. The marketplace of ideas offers two mutually exclusive worldviews—living according to the absolute truth found in God's Word, that is, the Bible, on one hand, and, on the other hand, imbibing in the postmodern choice of establishing your own truth base, that is, "situation ethics" or deciding what is right and wrong according to personal experience.

Ministry parents should be more committed to the task of rearing their children in the nurture of the Lord, preparing them for the world where they will encounter an assault upon their faith and spiritual commitments. As young apologists, these children must be equipped to stand against the wiles of the devil—however winsome, logical, and relevant these enticements might be—and determined to measure every temptation against the pure and true Word of God. Sometimes this task is more challenging in a ministry setting because your children spend most of their time around Christians. C. S. Lewis spoke perceptively: "Christians are the best arguments for *and against* Christianity."[5] Nothing hurts your vulnerable child any more than shallow or pseudo-Christianity. Knowing this danger should help you encourage your children to put their focus where it needs to be—not on Christians but on CHRIST!

While children are struggling in ministry homes to meet the expectations of their parents and often the congregation as well, they are not only expected to mature without the instruction and training given to the congregation their parents serve, but also they have a behind-the-scenes look at the respected pastor and his spouse. The example before ministry children is not the carefully presented façade of a spiritual leader paraded before the congregation—an answer to every problem and a calm spirit in the midst of storms. Rather, a minister's children see him clearly, warts and all, in his hour of despair and in the moments when he loses it all— often at their expense! Ministry parents could save themselves a lot of grief if they viewed parenting as ministry—and ministry with a double benefit. Not only does serious and responsible parenting give your own kids a better shot at knowing and serving the Lord, but also your example for the families in your congregation will be more effective than a thousand sermons on the subject. The influence you have on producing another godly generation who will honor and serve the Lord can take a gargantuan leap forward.

Children Demand Time

No evangelical minister would dare question the value of a child, and most want children themselves and would grieve if an infertile womb were to make that impossible. However, too few understand that with blessings and opportunities come responsibilities and accountability. What costs you nothing is worth just that.

During the conservative resurgence in the Southern Baptist Convention, my husband—and our family—experienced some dark hours. Friends refused to speak to us in public; we were excluded from certain gatherings; my husband's integrity was questioned; his motives were judged; his reputation was maligned. Most of these personal attacks came from Christians—even from leaders in our denomination. Some even believed as we did and quietly encouraged our stand behind the scenes, but they did not want to be seen with us publicly. During this decade of great hurt in our lives the single most important human escape for us was the personal friendship, genuine love, and sensitive ministries of our children. Armour and Carmen, aged ten and eight when the movement began, not only sensed our hurt and discouragement and responded with tender loving care on every level—physical, emotional, social, and spiritual; but they also caught a vision of our mission. Without our verbal invitation, and certainly without any coercion, they decided to join us! They attended conventions; they fielded telephone calls and located people; they ran errands and planned meals. But more important than any of these tasks, they distracted us from pressure and made us laugh, hugged and held us when we were hurting, stood with us when we felt alone.

Children demand both quantity and quality time. That time has its dividends. However bad a day (and the bad day of a preacher is often compounded by the bad days of all who come to tell him about their bad days), whatever burdens are on your shoulders, you can escape for just a moment when your child greets you with a welcoming hug and words of love.

Parenthood is a lifetime investment. God chose parenthood as a metaphor for His loving care for all who believe and trust Him. They become His children, and to all who call Him Lord He is Father with tender affection and firm discipline through a program of discipleship that never ends. The starting point before ministry parents, as they enter parenthood, might be expressed in this way:

- Do you consider your child an appendage to ministry, an extra hand in doing the work of the church, one drafted by you to pursue your kingdom ministries at any cost?
- Is your child an afterthought, part of your model for the congregation but sometimes an inconvenience in your plans for serving the Lord?
- Is your child the apple of your eye—a precious treasure entrusted to your care by God Himself—not a hindrance or enhancement to ministry but an opportunity for extending the generations with godly seed?

Whose Job Is It?

For fathers and mothers, family—including children—is your first and foremost ministry. Never underestimate the importance of the centrality of the family with children for communities and nations as well as for the kingdom of Christ. Contained in the Lord's twofold challenge to the man and woman at the culmination of God's creative activity is the mandate to "be fruitful and multiply; fill the earth and subdue it" (Gen. 1:28). God intended the pristine couple in the Garden of Eden, as well as to those who would follow, to continue the generations through nurturing godly seed. God has entrusted to parents a blessing and responsibility. Rearing your child for those engaged in ministry, as for all parents, is unto the Lord and demands your utmost:

- Parents create the home environment with the right balance in tender loving care and purposeful discipline, guiding their children in the right way.
- Parents offer God-honoring instruction through the teaching of biblical truth and the fashioning of enriching life experiences.

God absolutely forbids the child sacrifices of pagan nations (Deut. 12:31–32). He also forbids sacrificing your children, even in a figurative sense, on the altar of your own ambition or dreams or ministry (Isa. 23:4; Jer. 9:21; Lam. 2:11; 4:10; Ezek. 16:4).

Children are more than the by-product of a biological function. The Lord placed tremendous importance upon teaching children about Himself and training them to walk in joyful obedience to His way (Deut. 6:7–9). Jesus said that a person would be better off dead than to bring harm to a child (Mark 9:42), and He affirmed that your investment in a child is service to Him (Mark 10:42).

The Hebrews pictured rearing children as a building process (Heb. *banah*, "build"). Parents lay a foundation of faith, upon which they build character and inspire service to God and others; and finally they polish their children through fervent prayer and diligent nurturing and lay them as crowns at Jesus' feet (see Psalm 128, often called "The Builder's Psalm"). The cycle continues as their children select godly mates, establish Christ-honoring homes, and build their own sons and daughters.

How is this task magnified in the home of a minister? Because the minister is the spokesman for God, the shepherd leading the flock, an example of biblical patterns before the people—he is to take the time and make the effort to establish his own home as a lighthouse and to model for other parents biblical patterns for parenting. Far better than a sermon from the pulpit will be the lessons learned from observing the minister who is actually rearing his children according to divine patterns. The loving commitment to which husbands and wives are called is catapulted into the next generation when they have a model of God's plan for marriage lived out before them by their own mother and father.

Passing Your Faith

Passing faith to your children demands far more than attending church, listening to family devotions, and following pious platitudes. A deeply rooted faith will insulate your child from the tentacles of a secular society without isolating him from the world. Genuine faith will fortify him with answers and magnify the biblical standard without nullifying his identity, stifling his questions, or belittling his struggle.

How do ministry parents create a "hothouse" environment that will cultivate and sustain even the weakest and most fragile pilgrims?

Actions produce more than words. Children are observant. The Lord seized upon lifestyle instruction when He gave the Israelites His Law. He didn't assume they would know how to pass along this vital information about Himself. Through His spokesman Moses, the Lord instructed parents to use every conceivable time, position, and occasion to teach His commandments to their children (Deut. 6:7–8). The demonstration of a lifestyle of faith must be integrated into every facet of life, so that God's truth is not merely taught in purposeful encounters but also caught as you move through the daily events of life. Lifestyle teaching will fill in the gaps beyond years of sermons and formal instruction.

Nothing was any more important for my children than developing a time of personal intimacy with the Lord beyond corporate worship and family devotional time. How delightful to observe during their teen years well-marked Bibles not only at church and at home but even on family vacations! How did they develop this habit? Not through lectures and assignments, but by watching this discipline at work in the lives of parents and grandparents! My children will not remember the words of wisdom I've passed along over the years, nor will yours remember the good advice you've given. However, etched in their minds and planted in their hearts is a permanent picture of who you are and how you've lived before them. Even if a child strays far from the faith carefully taught to him in his childhood and youth, God may use the picture of godly parents to bring him home—not just to parents but to the Heavenly Father as well. The life you live before your children is not in vain. Every parent has some regrets—careless words, inappropriate actions, ungodly moments, costly mistakes. These inconsistencies come and go but are seldom erased from memory. Your children will note flaws in your character. However, if you acknowledge mistakes, seek forgiveness, and renew your commitments, these mistakes and resulting consequences can be another classroom for your child. Intuitively a child knows and his experience confirms that you are not perfect. What he needs is consistency. He needs a pattern for what to do when you mess up. When you fail, if you ask God's forgiveness, begin anew, and refuse to abandon seeking the Lord with your whole heart, your child will have a marvelous, tested-and-proven-faithful blueprint for his own pilgrimage of faith. Whatever his detours, he has the best map for finding his way back.

Back to the Bible

Basic biblical principles for rearing children include:

- *Parents are to demonstrate God's pattern for Christian marriage (Titus 2:1-5). For mothers and fathers to love one another and demonstrate that love not only gives their own children a picture of God's design for this most intimate relationship, but also this living love becomes a lesson for other children and, in the case of ministers, for parishioners who can see biblical principles at work. Even a limited picture will always be more effective than unlimited words. A lifestyle example will go far beyond the most eloquent sermon.*

- *Parents are responsible for teaching their children biblical truth (Ps. 78: 1-8). A minister who sees the church education program as more important than the training of his own children is defeated before he begins. To allow his children to remain untaught and undisciplined in spiritual matters will become a tool of Satan to undermine all he does in the church (1 Tim. 3:4). The minister must have a vision for teaching children as well as adults; Christian education is vital in the building of a great church. The most effective way to accomplish that goal is to place alongside the innovative programs in your church your own personal example of training your children and overseeing that spiritual nurture. I do not suggest nor does Scripture say that a minister with rebellious children should resign and leave the ministry. Every individual is ultimately accountable to God for his choices. Israel's King David, a man after God's own heart, made some unwise choices. His children suffered consequences. David's son Solomon, who succeeded him on the throne, sought the Lord's wisdom during much of his life; his son Absalom sought to kill him in order to get the throne. God holds parents accountable (and spiritual leaders have clear standards in Scripture) for understanding the importance of parenting and the responsibility for doing it God's way.*

- *Parents are responsible for helping their children go God's way by using loving but consistent discipline—the ultimate tool in discipleship (Heb. 12:5-8, 11). Discipline is not limited to punishment for wrongdoing. Just as important is a parent's responsibility to walk alongside his child, leading him in the right way, gently pulling him back from the edge of the precipice to the center, giving him a map and noting landmarks along the right path.*

Parents must prayerfully define boundaries and set goals for their children. They must be clear and specific in communicating expectations. Parents can be firm while still sharing respect for their child. They must be clear and specific in communicating expectations. Even a parent's voice and demeanor should exude confidence so that the child will listen and obey. To admonish a child "to be good" is too vague and nebulous to send a meaningful message. Ridicule and sarcasm have no place in rebuking your child, nor should disciplinary action be preceded by an escalating degree of threats, suggesting that your child need not listen until your voice reaches the pitch indicating action is imminent.

Many pastors have ignored the home in their preaching; they have acted as if family time were unimportant in their ever-burgeoning programs; they have dismissed their own home responsibilities affirming their indifference to the importance of family. Nothing will undercut the kingdom any more than spurning God's handiwork in the creation order, thereby impeding His sacrifice in redemption.

Ministry families have a wonderful opportunity to magnify and lift up the importance of the home—not in the sense of being derelict of their responsibilities to the corporate body (a pastor has a work to do) but with the commitment to model the principles given in Scripture for establishing a home that builds sons and daughters, who in turn will continue a godly influence unto the generations.

Father Time—It Works!

A study reported in the *Journal of Marriage and Family* concluded that conservative evangelical fathers are more likely to read with their children, eat dinner with them, and engage in outside activities together. Although some greet this phenomenon with surprise, genuine evangelicals understand that a father's commitment to invest in a significant way in the lives of his children is the natural result of his commitment to the biblical paradigm for the family.

On the other hand, some estimate that 88 percent of the teens attending evangelical churches will forsake their churches, and perhaps even their faith, by the time they reach the age of eighteen. These same researchers affirm that this rate seems to be the same among the children of pastors.[6] Certainly nothing brings weariness and discouragement to ministry parents any more than to lose their own children to the kingdom. When children see their fathers only in the pulpit, they can indeed vent their anger toward the Lord, whom they may see as robbing them of a father. This anger may develop into an unhealthy bitterness and their abandoning corporate worship, even if their faith in God remains intact.

May it never be that pastor fathers consider growing a church more important than rearing their own children in the Lord. The same principles for discipleship and mentoring in the church should be first used in the home through the faithful and sacrificial commitment of fathers and mothers to discipling their own children.

Even though mothers usually spend more time with children, fathers are also absolutely essential in the development of a child. In ministry homes, the church and its ministries sometimes are elevated above family responsibilities. The father immerses himself in ministry, losing perspective on the responsibilities he has to his family, who become less important to him than the congregation. Fathers become so preoccupied with work that mothers are left to rear the children.

Many fathers begin their ministries with devotion to their families, but one interruption leads to another until they become caught up in a rat race every bit as destructive as the tailspin of the corporate world. Training your children is an essential ministry in itself. God will not be pleased if a ministry couple pours their time and energy into kingdom discipleship to the exclusion of making disciples of their own children.

There is no greater joy than watching your children embrace a biblical worldview and commit themselves to incorporating godly principles into their own lives. Scripture commands fathers to train their children (Eph. 6:1-4; Deut. 6:6-7; 11:19). Training goes beyond verbal instruction to include persuasion, warning, and correction. Of course, mothers are also involved significantly in this process but never to the exclusion of the father. The church's program of spiritual nurture for children is also important; but God's setting for primary spiritual instruction of children is the home, and parents are ultimately responsible for this training.

Biblical instruction was not confined to a "home" classroom. Moses made clear that this instruction was not only to be woven into daily life but also to be incorporated into times of rest. In fact, he describes the process as including *repetition* every day *integrated* into life so that a child sees God as central to his family, to his relationships with others, and to his work and play whatever the circumstances might be—happiness or sadness, blessing or tragedy, feast or famine. Only through integration of faith and life can a child see his faith as applying to the whole of life—not merely regularly scheduled meetings within the four walls of the church. Parents are to provide a living *demonstration* of how biblical principles work in daily life. *Repetition* and *integration*, together with *demonstration*, become a living *validation* for a faith that works because it is woven into the tapestry of life (see Deut. 6:6-9).

The same children who sit in the pew and hear their father proclaim the truths of Scripture must watch him live his life according to those principles. If the father is not consistent in harmonizing his life with his sermon, his children will believe that their father has no integrity or that the Bible he proclaims is not relevant for governing life or that a person can choose what principles he wants to embrace and what he wants to ignore. A father's consistent application of God's Word is the surest way for his children to find their way to the faith of their father.

The Lord shows in another way how seriously He holds ministry fathers accountable to their family responsibilities. A minister who does not accept his duties to wife and children does not meet the biblical qualifications for kingdom ministries. A pastor *must manage his own family well . . . and see that his children obey him with proper respect* (see 1 Tim. 3:1-7). A minister father must provide spiritual training for his children, investing whatever time is necessary to disciple his children. He not only provides what is needed for the spiritual nurturing of his children but also models for his congregation an important responsibility given by the Lord to husbands and fathers.

Training a child to honor his father and mother is his prelude to a lifetime of honoring and glorifying God with his obedience. A child who enjoys the loving care of his father and learns how to respond in obedience to his father will more easily relate to his Heavenly Father, to whom he has been introduced in Scripture through anthropomorphic language. When an earthly father is distant and uninvolved, his child will have more difficulty relating to his Heavenly Father.

Both sons and daughters need their father—not just as pastor of their church but as father in their home. Fathers should be shepherds and spiritual leaders in their homes. No one in ministry has as much time as he would like to have with his family. However, by commitment to right priorities and careful scheduling accordingly, the time you have will be enough.

For a man in ministry to give himself effectively to a congregation—loved and admired for the way he shepherds his flock—

without taking seriously his responsibility for spiritual leadership in his own home is a tragedy for which he, as well as his wife and children, will inevitably pay dearly. On the other hand, a father who models spiritual leadership in his home will enhance and augment all he does in his congregation. The congregation is made up of families; and if each of those families has a warm and caring spiritual father/leader, the congregation itself will be stronger and more vibrant.

Fathers in ministry must provide for their families. For a congregation not to take seriously its responsibility to pay the pastor a living wage, enabling him to care for his family with food, shelter, clothing, and other necessities (1 Cor. 9:14) as well as some pleasures beyond is sad. Ministers, by virtue of their sacrificial devotion to Christ, dare not become obsessed with monetary demands; however, a minister does have the prerogative to let the congregation know his needs.

Unfortunately, ministry families are often caught up in materialism and may extend themselves beyond necessities to embrace desires and whims as being essential for their happiness. More often than not, these desires are centered on what they feel they must provide for their children—designer clothing, the latest in technological gadgetry, private schooling, even automobiles and sporting equipment. These parents might be surprised at their children's evaluation of what is most important. Surveys have shown again and again that children want the presence of their parents more than the presents parents might give to assuage their guilt by providing happiness through things.

Children want loving affection woven into their daily routines; they want the security of seeing their parents loving each other and living in harmony; they want to be accepted; they want parents to listen, hear, and respond to their questions with straightforward honesty; they want help in identifying their own strengths, weaknesses, and giftedness. No one is better than a parent for encouraging and helping a child do his best. Ministry parents are in the "equipping" business; they develop their parishioners in spiritual disciplines; they identify and give opportunities to potential leaders.

What a tragedy to know the gifts and skills of people in your congregation and not identify the abilities and talents of your child.

Provide, Protect, and Lead

Provision actually begins with your presence, more desirable than any things money can buy. Your presence begins with babies and toddlers. Bonding occurs early through the sound of your voice and your touch regularly and consistently. Significant conversation begins with isolated words long before your child can make sentences and participate in dialogue. Meaningless chatter will move to meaningful conversation much faster than you ever dreamed possible if you take the time to listen.

Ministry fathers have the assignment of protecting their children in expected ways, that is, providing a safe shelter where children can relax. Fathers must protect the minds of their children by supervising television and computer and by screening literature to be sure those in their care are not exposed to pornography or undue violence. This protection extends to introducing children to books and television programs or documentaries or videos that educate and entertain in wholesome ways.

Ministry parents must also be active participants in their children's activities. The tendency is to bypass this responsibility lest it appear you are favoring the church age group to which your child belongs. You were probably a parent before you became a pastor. You are the only father your child has; whereas there are spiritual leaders in a church other than you as the pastor. You must be committed to supervise and interact with the friends and activities of your child as a father rather than only as pastor. Never assume the babysitter or caregiver from your congregation is safe. Check carefully anyone to whom you entrust your child. Be sensitive to changes in your child's behavior or attitude and evaluate any information coming from your child about a sitter. There is really no substitute for your personal attention and supervision.

Ministry fathers have an added dimension to their assignment to protect their offspring from undue and inappropriate scrutiny of the congregation, neighborhood, and community. Because of the public leadership role engulfing their parents, ministry kids seem to be "open season" for every detractor of the minister, not to mention being the target of the devil himself. To cause a preacher's kid to stumble is a double whammy of hurt and sorrow. When the child of ministry parents makes a wrong choice, the child is hurt by the consequences from his choice; his parents are grieved because they want the best for their child and know tragic consequences are coming his way; beyond that, the congregation and the kingdom of Christ suffer.

People tend to hold parents responsible for the actions of their children or young adults; and they hold ministers to an even higher standard. The minister's child lives in a glass house. Everyone knows who he is and whose he is; everyone feels free to give him advice or correction; all eyes are watching and reporting. Preachers tend to find their best sermon illustrations in the lives of their children, which adds to their public notoriety. Some parishioners rejoice when the pastor's child is rebellious because his perceived failure as a father justifies failure in anyone else.

What Is a Ministry Family to Do?

When ministry kids fail, people immediately want to chant relentlessly, "Those biblical principles sure didn't work for the preacher." Ineffective parents, whether or not they have tried God's way, whether or not the preacher himself has used biblical principles with his children—none of these facts matter, because people seize upon every opportunity to say biblical principles are inadequate and out-of-date.

- Ministry parents accept the responsibilities of leadership and work harder at practicing the principles they teach. They must go to Scripture for answers to their challenges in parenting.
- They must not jump to conclusions and assume their child has erred just because someone has accused the child, for ministry kids are often falsely accused. Let your child tell his side of the story, talk to as many witnesses as possible; as you would with someone else's kid. Move heaven and

earth to find out what really happened before you pass judgment.

- When the matter has been adjudicated and you feel you have all the facts, if your child has erred—however much or little—hold the child accountable and administer punishment as appropriate; but most important, walk with your child through the mistake and help him to learn so that he can make better choices the next time. Give your child a chance to fail. Don't have unrealistic expectations. Your child's disobedience is a family matter between you and your child—not a matter for the church. Affirm your unconditional love for your child. Be sure your child knows you are more concerned for him than for how you look before others. Damage control may be necessary, but not without keeping in your own heart the need to restore your child and bring him back where he ought to be spiritually. You should not expect your child to hold to a standard of behavior because he is the preacher's kid; rather, you expect your child to maintain a Christ-like lifestyle because you and your family represent Christ. Christ is the reason and focus for all you do. Your child's choice to serve Christ must not be prompted by familial heritage but by his own personal commitment to follow Christ.

- Help your children meet and establish a relationship with another spiritually mature mentor who can be available when a child wants accountability and guidance outside the family. Inevitably young adults go through a cycle of seeing their parents as not only fallible but also as wrong about virtually everything. Instead of feeling loved and needed, parents may feel unloved and unnecessary. Instead of wanting your presence, your child may go through a time of ignoring you and suggesting you are not needed or wanted in his life. While you must keep on loving and trying to do the right thing—praying for your child, being available, ministering in ways you can, you also want to do everything you can to encourage your child to establish friendships with those who might stand in your stead when necessary.

Fathers are also called to be servant leaders, and never is this role any more important than in a ministry home. This leadership begins with a regular and consistent time for family worship. Whether in conjunction with a meal or an appointed family gathering after a meal or before bedtime, the time should include prayer and Scripture. Songs and hymns, prayer requests, testimonies, messages of spiritual formation can be added. The father who leads the congregation in worship must also lead worship in his own home.

Since my husband is a born teacher, our times of family worship included instruction in one form or another. My husband would ask the children questions to be used as a springboard for teaching truth, but he did so in an entertaining way. Frequently, he would direct his light inquisition to a visiting student or friend, fully intending his instruction to be primarily for our children. The children would delight to see some enterprising young theologue stumped by a question and then would receive the answer more eagerly. Also, they saw they were not the only ones to need their father's instruction.

As ministry parents set the tone in the home by not speaking in a critical way of others in ministry or of erring people in the church, they can help their children learn to be discerning, using wisdom with understanding. Children in a ministry home will be exposed to the problems of others more than most children. You can and, especially in early years, should protect your children from the hypocrisy and tragedies woven into the life of the church. Nevertheless, when your children see these inconsistencies for themselves and, especially when you are mistreated, they will tend to take up an offense for you.

No child wants his parents to suffer and certainly not unjustly. Bathed in prayer, you must often help your child understand the devastation of sin and the sorrows left in its wake. Your child must learn that all Christians will suffer and that through suffering they can become more like the Savior.

On the other hand, you must consciously exhibit a spirit of joy, even in the midst of trials. You must look for good in others—even those who make themselves your enemies. You must use Scripture to teach your child how to deal with the adversities of life. You must magnify the times of fun and fellowship within the body of Christ so that when the times of sorrow come, your child can put all in perspective.

Mother—the Heart of a Home

Ministry mothers certainly have challenges that thrust them above and beyond the call of duty. A penchant for order, an inclination toward cleanliness, and a proclivity for stewardship of resources are important since most mothers and wives in a ministry setting are forced into making-do and reusing, while at the same time living under scrutiny of those who expect "the best" from the minister's wife. A combination of frugality and creativity with a large dose of determination will help her cope with the challenges of keeping her home, helping her husband, and nurturing her children.

Motherhood is demanding for all who take its responsibilities seriously, and sometimes its rewards are slow in coming. Nevertheless, as with the ministry father, a ministry mother has the opportunity not only to disciple her own children, but she also has an open door to touch the lives of their friends and the entire congregation through her maternal nurture and loving care. While she may be pivotal to the woman-to-woman ministries within the church, she will be observed as a role model in her relationship to her own husband and children.

As with fathers, a mother must have consistency in character and lifestyle. Her children must see her faith possessing her, and her commitment to the Lord will be fleshed out in how she honors and cares for her family. Ministry mothers have a unique arena in which to abandon personal rights and embrace a servant's heart.

Often ministry mothers must miss fellowship and activities with their husbands to supervise their children. The many meetings of the church, coupled with conventions and conferences and professional gatherings, sometimes extend beyond what a mother can do and still meet the needs of her offspring. This balancing act is part of the challenge.

When my children were young, we took them along more often than most parents. They adapted well to the adult world and seemed to enjoy being included in our activities. We drove more often than flying. Even when flying, we often sacrificed in order to purchase tickets for our children. We enjoyed being together as a family. Our children attended annual meetings of the Southern Baptist Convention during more than a decade of their childhood and youth. Taking them along sometimes altered our schedule and occasionally called for a sacrifice; but we have never regretted this integration of them into our world.

Our grandchildren are enjoying the same experience as they, too, often accompany their parents, who are also in ministry, to conventions. This choice on the part of their parents is especially delightful to me since I can add another rendezvous to our limited opportunities for connecting. However, for my daughter this decision often becomes a sacrifice when she has to bypass some activity or meeting. I, as well as Abigail and Rebekah, am grateful for her unselfishness, which enables our darling granddaughters to be more a part of the lives of us and of their parents.

Ministry moms can indeed make a difference in their own families as well as in their ministry sphere. The key to maximum influence rests in a mother's determination to establish the right priorities. Maintaining her own personal relationship with the Lord is first, followed closely by helping her husband and nurturing her children. Beyond sustaining her own walk with the Lord and her family responsibilities, she will invest in church ministries. I have always struggled with getting everything done even according to priorities! A wonderful "spiritual mother" in my life shared her secret with me:

- Do the next thing.
- Begin with what only you can do.

Only you can be the mother of your children, loving them unconditionally, comforting them in their hurts, knowing their unique needs and being willing to do whatever it takes to meet those needs. You may have a ministry to which you give your time and influence; but your main ministry and foremost passion must be your family. Your children ought not to crowd out your husband, but helping your husband includes nurturing the children whose heritage you share in a special way.

The seasons of life are also seasons of the family, and your priorities will not change, but what is required to meet those priorities will change. What you can do in ministry with preschool children is quite different from what you can *do when the nest is empty. The highest priorities cannot always be scheduled with accuracy. Of course, the boundaries encircling your priorities help you to apportion your time appropriately. In looking back, I should have scheduled twice the time I thought I would need in order to allow for interruptions, that is, some neat but unscheduled experiences along the way.*

"When mama has a headache, all the family had better take aspirin!" Mothers set the attitude for the family. In a web poll reported by *Today's Christian Woman,* women were asked "Who's had the greatest impact on your life?" Thirty-three percent of the respondents named Mom, a percentage equal to husband, grand-parents, and Dad combined (14 percent, 10 percent, 9 percent respectively). A joyful spirit breeds happiness and delight; a sour disposition produces pessimism and grumbling. God loves a cheerful giver—of service as well as of money. Nowhere should there be a greater reflection of the unconditional love and gentle care of Jesus than in motherhood. A mother's love is exceeded only by the love of God Himself. Her love seems to grow along with her child. However, her love is neither measured by the success of her child nor diminished by his failure. A mother's love should remain unselfish, immutable, protective, tender, forgiving—a forever love from a cup that remains full no matter how much is poured out.

Ministry moms will honor the Lord when they exhibit a positive attitude in the midst of criticism and disappointment. Perhaps a bit of creativity can overcome the harshest criticism and a dash of humor override the most bitter disappointment. Anything positive that happens in ministry should be noted with appropriate praise to the Lord and humble gratitude as a family for the blessings of God.

Events that seem to produce negative results should be greeted as an opportunity to ask the Lord's help—not only to remove what is hurtful but also to remind your children that God will walk with your family through trying times (Isa. 43:1–2). A mother's presence will cover a multitude of hurts and woes. Socrates described himself as a "midwife of ideas." The greatest ministry for any mother should be that of sculpting her children into the image of Christ.

Canadian psychiatrist Elliott Barker identified obstacles to nurturing: lack of time, inadequate preparation, inappropriate consumerism, increasing materialism, and the low value society places on childrearing.[7] All can easily creep into ministry homes, together with pseudospirituality. A mother can be so wrapped up in church ministries that she does not meet the needs of her own children. She becomes obsessed with kingdom work and assumes God will "cover" her children while she pursues a "high and holy purpose." Instead of being approachable, patient, and interested in her children, she is preoccupied, disinterested, and too busy for the mundane task of nurturing her children.

The best parenting and a committed ministry setting are not enough to produce children who will be spiritually responsive any more than the best witnessing will ensure a convert. This fact does not minimize the ministry parent's responsibility to give time and effort to discipling a child. Recognizing that only God can possess a child's heart in such a way as to ensure his making the right choices and pursuing godliness, mothers must put forth their best efforts, coupled with earnest and persistent prayers for their children.

A ministry mom must not assume that because her child has been born into a home dedicated to God and is then offered to God, the child will pursue godliness. Nothing can be left to chance. With a mother's prayers must come the commitment to strive earnestly "to put skin and flesh on God" as she lives her life and responds to her challenges. She must weave into the warp and woof of life stories of God's protective care of His people and of her own family. She must keep before her children the wonderful Bible stories that tell of God's faithfulness to His people. She should pray openly before her children, taking burdens and petitions to the Heavenly Father while giving Him praise. She should sing the hymns of Zion and hum gospel tunes. She must find ways to integrate Scripture into the lives of her children, keeping the Lord's wisdom continually before them. I have selected and placed appropriate Scripture accessories throughout our home as carefully as any piece of furniture, setting the Word of God before us in a natural and winsome way.

No ministry mom dare belittle the impact of her motherhood upon her own offspring and through her maternity on the kingdom of Christ. The more you invest, the more will be your yield. The fallen world makes the path your children will follow much more difficult. Therefore, they need your time, energy, creativity, and spiritual nurture.

The Despair of Feeling Useless

Ministry moms face discouragement in unique ways. For example, many are gifted and equipped to do a variety of kingdom ministries. Because of family demands, these women often walk away from rewarding ministry pursuits. Sometimes that separation is painful; but as you pour your life into your children, healing comes, together with new interests and opportunities. The real challenge often comes years later when your children become adults. They leave for the university and/or marriage, and only return to the childhood home for brief visits.

The talents, skills, and consuming work of this passing season of life are no longer needed. These mothers have been too busy for personal pursuits or ministry opportunities, but suddenly the job that put everything else on hold seems to be done; and even worse is the feeling that you have not really made a difference in your child or a contribution to the world.

How well I know this feeling! When my older child entered middle school, I realized that even a limited speaking schedule and occasional joint ministry with my husband would not work. My husband's heavy schedule of commitments frequently took him out of the city. I needed to be at home and available to my son and daughter every day during these critical years. I walked away from the public platform, canceled engagements, eliminated trips with my husband except when we could take the children. My husband supported me in this decision, but he did warn me that I would never regain these opportunities bypassed and engagements declined. He encouraged me to count the cost of walking away from a blossoming ministry to women. Although I never looked back, I did shed some tears and I especially missed the ministries with my husband. However, God gave me peace and happiness during those years of immersing myself in the lives of my children.

The day came when my younger child moved across country to attend university. I was alone much of the time and feeling quite sorry for myself until I decided to return to using my giftedness and resources as the Lord opened doors. I began traveling with my husband again, and I immersed myself in a demanding publication project. Again the invitations started to come. I can hardly remember a bump in that transition. My priorities became even more firmly established. I enjoy ministry to women, and I have more opportunities than ever before; but I have learned to harness these ministries within the boundaries demanded by my family priorities. As I waited on God to open doors, I meditated on the fact that no ministry is worth distorting the purposes of God. I had no time to mourn my losses or a change in assignment, but I had the responsibility to move forward into the work of the future—never losing sight of the commitments I made to home and family when I chose to marry.

Ministry moms, please don't let your children become "semi-orphans," described by the distinguished scholar Jacques Barzun as children who spend so many hours home alone that they need surrogate homes. These children are bereft of parental guidance and supervision for hours or extended periods almost every day. Their lack of home ties leaves these children adrift, struggling with their own identities and without any pattern of family life. This sorrowful state is not acceptable just because the child's parents are involved in kingdom ministries.[8]

Your Presence—The Heart of the Day

Mothers in ministry homes have the wonderful opportunity to reestablish home as more than shelter—a place set apart for comfort, security, loving care, and warm acceptance. Home is where each family member is a very important person. What a difference would come in churches and communities if those in leadership would model Christ-centered home life! This kind of mothering takes time and energy. That investment should be quality time, but quality time cannot be planned and confined to a few hours in a day. You need to relax and go with the flow, letting each day unfold with your presence as the heart of the day. Make memories, listen to your children, and immerse yourself in their lives. Love your children with caring actions as well as endearing words. Home is never really done. Revive its interior, redo the acts of love, reuse your energies and creativity day in and day out; reprise the familiar principles from Scripture that will maintain a sure foundation.

A mother has no more important function than to provide food in due season (Ps. 104:27). In a busy ministry home, mealtime can and should be an oasis from the difficulties and sorrows of the outside world. Preparation for meals is

*in vain without an ironclad commitment to make it happen! A sales job is essen-
tial—first with her minister husband (who could easily fill every meal with
kingdom responsibilities) and then with her children (who are only too quick to
acquiesce when interruptions come or to concoct a few diversions of their own).
Family mealtime will not happen in a busy ministry home if the interruptions
of the outside world—however worthy these may be—are allowed to trump
every family gathering. There are genuine emergencies to which the entire
family must arise at least to pray for the minister father as he is called to a tragic
situation. However, the real attack on mealtime is more likely the "nibbling of
the minnows"—little interruptions of telephone, door bell, or one more thing to
be done.*

*Our family has discovered a simple solution for insulation from the outside
world. We eat outdoors unless weather and insects make this plan unworkable.
Inside we fight the usual barrage of interruptions, especially since my husband
never has allowed answering machines. Nevertheless, we taught our children
polite ways of answering the telephone, including how to protect their father—
that is, he cannot come to the telephone, or he is not taking calls now. May
I take a message; would you mind calling his secretary at the church?*

*Mealtime is worthless if rushed. Mothers may not see this event as worthy
of a real investment, because no one takes time "to smell the roses" or the soup.
Perhaps they should call forth creativity and a bit of energy to make this family
gathering one that every member of the family anticipates and hates to miss. A
menu mixed with old favorites and enticing new delectables, a table setting that
is unique and diverse (different sets of dishes, ethnic decorations, items from
throughout the house arranged in unusual ways, candles, even unexpected
locations for your surprise meal), and always an atmosphere of love and caring
with meaningful conversation.*

Ministry parents must remember that their children take great
pride in talking about the fun within the parsonage. The Lord will
multiply the time and creativity invested by ministry moms in their
own families just as surely as He did the loaves and fishes. Other
homemakers in the church are learning that mealtime is special,
even in the busy parsonage. They learn the importance of gathering the family around a table laden with more than food. They, too,
will catch the vision of feeding the spirit of the family and ministering to the needs of their hearts.[9]

What's a Ministry Parent to Do?

Parenthood is an awesome opportunity and overwhelming challenge to link hands with the Creator God to fashion and mold another generation to serve and glorify Him. This opportunity and challenge should be enhanced within a ministry setting. Despite unique challenges and difficulties, the parsonage or manse offers correspondingly extraordinary opportunities and open doors for giving your children the best in spiritual nurture and bringing to them the world and its wonders. The key is what you as ordinary parents will do with the help of an extraordinary God to give your freshest energies and finest creativity within your ministry setting to developing kids who also want to honor the Creator God and serve His creation in whatever professional pursuits they may follow.

You begin your task as any Christian parent with devotion to Christ and commitment to go His way yourself and with the determination to do everything within your power to make your children disciples of Christ.

- Honor Scripture and set it apart as your guide to faith and practice. You can read portions daily and, as a family, have communion with the Lord beyond a brief blessing before meals. You have an added unction to model spiritual leadership because you are calling for such leadership in the homes of your congregation. *Your daily walk must match your pulpit talk!* Your children will hold you accountable.

- Lead your family to participate in corporate worship. Your commitment to the local congregation is not only expected by your congregation, but it is also a given with your children. You dare not present this assignment as drudgery or routine. You have an added impetus to make the Lord's Day special and to present your praise to the Lord from a heart of joy. To live "two lives" is almost certain to assign your child to damnation. While you must have personal and family time away from your responsibilities in the church, your observing the Lord's Day is essential to prepare your children for their own commitments to corporate worship. What they see in your attitude toward worshipping the Lord with the congregation will prepare them for establishing their own habits.

• Accept gratefully a wonderful venue for using a servant's heart. As you serve members of your congregation and those who seek your help, you can model in an intimate setting the rewards that come from serving others. The many interruptions and demands coming to ministry parents can be put in perspective, according to the example of Jesus, by humbly putting others before yourself and treating everyone with lovingkindness and gentleness, being careful to encourage and build up. You can introduce them to Christian ministry in what becomes your family's contribution to the kingdom of Christ. You can also show your children unique love for them by setting biblical priorities and appropriate boundaries that protect family time.

• Embrace your home as a wonderful setting for teaching your children to express gratitude for every kindness. Ministry parents often receive extra blessings from members of the congregation who bring food and gifts or offer service and help to the family of God's anointed. They can make telephone calls or write notes of gratitude. Often ministry kids get more practice at this grace gift, which has almost vanished even from the Christian world.

The first Saturday morning Mr. Wilson (a retired widower in our church family) appeared at our door we were rolling out of bed. He was loaded with groceries (assorted meats—even pastrami; eggs; milk; and ice cream—items we could not afford to buy on a regular basis), and we insisted he join us for brunch (our special breakfast with several courses was always late on Saturdays). From that day until he died, every Saturday we were in town Mr. Wilson joined us for brunch (He did start arriving a bit later). Every week we sent him a thank-you note for his precious ministry to our ministry family, taking turns expressing gratitude—a delightful opportunity instead of a dreadful chore!

- Teach your children to be content with what they have and to be willing to share that freely with others. Many families who are in kingdom service do not have salaries commensurate with their educational preparation and the specialized services they offer; few are receiving what comparable professions offer their contemporaries; and some barely exist with wages that are below the poverty line. *This sad fact is even more true among those who give their lives to equipping future Christian pastors—many of whom will receive salaries surpassing their professors in their first pastorates. Parents in ministry have the opportunity to teach their children about the goodness of the Lord. Times of difficulty and shortages can be used to teach your children lessons lost in the materialistic age in which we live.*

- Help your children adopt a biblical work ethic. Ministry parents are not paid for every task done in ministry; and often when you are paid, the amount is a pittance for what you have done. Yet you should have the spiritual maturity to know that ultimately God is keeping the books. Your children can observe your faithfulness in completing a task in a timely and efficient way without asking for a check in advance. They learn that a "Well done, thou good and faithful servant" from the Lord surpasses monetary compensation. They also learn that "a workman is worthy of his hire," since lessons can come from negative positions as well as positive. How proud you can be when your children sit on a pew and do their part in seeing that their future pastors are well cared for!

Ministry parents have the opportunity to teach their offspring valuable and rare character traits, such as standing for what is right even when you are alone; learning discretion and confidentiality; exercising self-control when you have been treated unjustly; being a peacemaker when your enemy has wronged you; assuming a gracious spirit when others are mean-spirited and selfish.

Ministry homes are generally more public than private, even when the house is not a church-owned parsonage. Your children learn the discipline of keeping the home neat and clean, especially the rooms where you welcome unexpected guests. They also have the privilege of participating in family hospitality.

Ministry parents have an additional shield in protecting their children. All children make mistakes; but you must expect the best of your children and establish a relationship of trust with them. Avoid framing your expectations in light of your position in the church or some other ministry. Expect and lead your children to the highest standards, because they are made "in the image of God." God is the one to whom they owe ultimate allegiance, and you must challenge them to walk the narrow way of truth and obedience because they represent the God of the universe, not just the pastor of the local church. Your children will learn that God has given them a position of honor and leadership by virtue of the home in which He placed them.

A testimony of word and deed can honor the Lord or hurt His kingdom work. However, your children cannot be guided by the entire congregation. Build a hedge about your children to protect them from unjust criticism as much as is possible. When they do fail, you deal with your child. You can listen respectfully to the reports of others, but you must give your child an opportunity to present his side. Then you must adjudicate the matter as fairly as possible. On the one hand, your child should not be immune to punishment when he is guilty any more than he should be held accountable for something he did not do. The children of ministry parents need consistency in the routine of daily discipline as would any child.

What are the most valuable gifts you can give your child to be enjoyed over a lifetime?

- Overwhelm your child with tender affection, including hugs and kisses. Be sure your child *feels* loved. Look your child in the eye again and again and say "I love you. You are special to me."
- Establish a godly heritage of faith in the heart of your child. Let your child know that God is your fortress and help. Introduce your child to Jesus early and tenderly instruct him in the way of the Lord. Teach your child to

fear the Lord and help him to understand the importance of adding discernment to wisdom. Saturate your child's mind and heart with Scripture.

- Incorporate gentle but firm discipline in the life of your child early and teach your child the joy of absolute obedience.
- Create traditions and rituals and weave these into your ministry lifestyle. Make ministry responsibilities fun; learn to laugh and relax even in the midst of serious responsibilities.
- Be involved in the life of your child not only in your home but in school, church activities, and community events. Know your child from A to Z, what makes him tick, what his strengths and weaknesses are, what he likes and doesn't like, and who his friends are.
- Allow your child to make mistakes. Be willing to forgive and restore. When you err, be quick to ask forgiveness as well.
- Inspire your child to make your home a welcoming place where people can come for comfort and loving acceptance. Don't limit hospitality to members of your congregation, and don't always segregate children from adults. Your child needs to have interaction with adults as well as his peers. Plan special events for your child; invite his friends to your home.

CHAPTER Two

Growing Up

HOW, IN THE COMPLEX WORLD of parent-child relationships, do you "train a child in the way he should go" (Prov. 22:6)? Ministry parents wrestle with this question more than their parishioners because they seem to inherit not only the challenges of rearing their own children but also those of parents in their churches.

This verse is not merely a decreed guarantee of success for godly parents who take their duties seriously. The principle coming from the wise Solomon must also be noted as a general guideline for parents in their nurturing process. The only guarantees in life are death and taxes, according to Benjamin Franklin, and you could add to that equation at least some trials and hardships. Much can happen for better or worse in between.

Is There a Formula?

Are there promises or guarantees in Scripture? Absolutely! "Whoever will call upon the name of the Lord will be saved" (Rom. 10:9). "Yet those who wait for the Lord will gain new strength" (Isa. 40:31). "God is faithful, who will not allow you to be tempted beyond what you are able" (1 Cor. 10:13).

If you claim these promises, you may wonder then, why you can't view Proverbs 22:6 as merely another promise. The answer lies in the dynamics of the 22:6 equation. The aforementioned biblical promises involve the unchanging, omnipresent, and omnipotent God and the reciprocating heart and mind of an individual believer. Solomon's proverb, on the other hand, includes not only God and the reciprocating believer, in this case the parent, but also the heart, mind, and free will of another human being—the child—as well as the entirety of genetic, circumstantial, and societal differences that constitute that child's experience in life. Many God-fearing parents have endured heartache and sorrows with their straying children, while simultaneously feeling abandoned by God to whose service they have devoted themselves sacrificially and unendingly.

Only God can control the will, thoughts, and desires of another; yet He will not do so arbitrarily. The Lord desires that you come to Him of your own free will. As in a game of poker, you play the hand you are dealt, and your child's free will puts a wild card in the deck. Fortunately, the poker analogy ends here.

Parents who follow the precepts of Scripture and seek to emulate Christ in their daily sojourns have much more control over the development of their child's character and the outcome of his life than does the poker player over his game. "Train up a child in the way he should go," and in the great majority of cases, the adult who emerges will ultimately continue in the faith of his father and mother. "Train" (Heb. *chanak*, that is, more literally "putting something in the mouth") suggests careful tutoring along the way. The Hebrews used this verb to describe the breaking of a wild horse by controlling the horse with a rope in its mouth to bring the horse into submission. Midwives used the term to describe the process of stimulating a newborn baby to suck the mother's breast for needed nourishment. They crushed dates, dipped their fingers into the mixture, and then massaged the gums of the baby. Training went beyond teaching of facts or transferring knowledge and added the dimension of discipleship. A parent in essence "makes disciples of his own children."

Although some interpret "way" as God's way or the way of wisdom, others feel that parents should seek the child's "natural bent." The latter interpretation is a potentially dangerous trap for ministry parents, because their children are often so enmeshed in a godly atmosphere that they have few choices that are not good. Parents can easily be lulled into feeling their youth are spiritually sound because they are making some right decisions.

The same ones who make right choices as children choose foolishness as young adults. The interpretation that seems most hermeneutically sound considers the verse as both a promise of reward for faithfulness and a caution not to lose heart along the way, especially when you meet the willfulness of the child head on. The verse may be paraphrased, "Train up a child to go *his* way, and when he is old, he will not depart from going *his own way*" (italics mine). Of course, you dare not break the child's *will*, for the *will* provides his volition to do good or evil. Rather you harness the child's *will* so he can be led in the right path.[10]

The effort and commitment of parents will be blessed by the Lord, even in those cases where the child, as an adult, chooses to travel another path. The assurance is not simply that "he will not depart from it" or that "he will never waver or stumble" or that "he will honor the Lord from the days of his youth until the day he grows old." If I were an aging parent of a young adult son or daughter who has chosen the wide path that leads to destruction, I might be discouraged, but I would not lose heart or quit the game just yet.

A Word of Encouragement

This verse certainly does offer encouragement to parents who take the task of spiritual nurturing seriously, but in addition the verse trumpets a warning to parents not to take lightly their responsibility for parental disciplining. Ministry parents cannot assume that having their children in church every time the doors are open and having consistent worship as a family in the home will be sufficient for spiritual training in these difficult days. There have been fine Christian parents, who, according to all visible signs, were true to their beliefs and faithful in their lifestyles, making every effort to train their child according to the precepts of Scripture. Yet some of these godly parents have watched helplessly as their child grew to adulthood and chose another way. All parents make mistakes. Actions and behavior can be judged, but when lifestyle actions are consistent with stated beliefs, there is nothing more to judge or say. God alone can know another person's heart.

There is no sure-fire formula or sanctified seven-step method sent from God for training a child. Life is never so simple and, thankfully, not so boring. Each child will be different as will be the circumstances and challenges he faces as he grows to adulthood. Parents will likely witness the good and bad, the ugly and beautiful, the serious and humorous. There is no standard formula, series of steps, or one guaranteed, tried-and-proven method. Rather, there are clear biblical principles from which parents in ministry can equip themselves mentally, spiritually, emotionally, and physically for the long sojourn demanded in training a child and providing tools, knowledge, and understanding based upon the experience of persons from both sides of the relationship. Scripture, common sense, and the needs of children and young adults as they come of age in a society that is increasingly unfriendly to the family are also components to consider.

Children See What Parents Do

The most effective tool parents have in training a child is personal example. As James Baldwin noted, "Children have never been very good at listening to their elders, but they have never failed to imitate them." The most effective tool is also potentially an Achilles' heel. All tools, principles, and methodology you acquire will be for naught if children and young adults do not see in your lives consistency in action that matches words, instructions, and admonitions coming from your mouths.

A parent who leads by example will not have to say as much as one who takes the "Do as I say, not necessarily as I do" approach. If a parent is spending an inordinate amount of time explaining and reprimanding older children and young adults, likely his actions are not what they ought to be, and his life is inconsistent with his words.

Whether the task is simple or complex, you learn best by example—usually from a parent or grandparent. After observing examples once or many times over, you do it on your own with your mentor's supervision.

The Axis Around Which Example Turns

The critical axis around which the actions of parental example turn centers upon how parents treat each other. The first and most important step in teaching a child to love and to do good to others is for you to love your spouse and to express that love in appropriate ways. Merely to say that you love your spouse is not enough, for true love, or the lack thereof, is revealed by actions.

A husband who yells at his wife, demeans her, is insensitive to her needs and desires, fails to put his wife's needs above his own, does not show kindness and affection to his wife, or does not listen to her and take time for her is not living in love. On the other hand, a wife who nags or acts disrespectfully toward her husband in public or private, who fails to recognize and follow his leadership, or who fails to be sensitive to his needs is also not living in love. Your children will notice these inconsistencies whether or not anyone else does. A child, having a congenital and spiritual connection to both mother and father does not want to see either parent hurt or mistreated. You, therefore, cannot show full lovingkindness to a child without first showing the same to your spouse—whether you are his mother or father.

In addition, how children see their parents treat each other will usually have a direct effect on how they treat their own spouses. Observing the negative effects of bad or abusive treatment of one parent by another should ensure that a child would pursue the opposite. Unfortunately, statistics and personal observations reveal that children and young adults usually do what they have seen their parents do. Men tend to imitate their fathers and women, their mothers, for better or worse. The power of example reigns, looming larger than life in the ministry home. You not only have the opportunities afforded by position but also the responsibilities invested by way of your assignment for spiritual leadership to model what a home ought to be and how family members are to relate to one another. You have an audience watching what you say in the public pulpit for consistency with what you do in the private home. Mistakes are inevitable, and they will not destroy your example if you acknowledge them, seek forgiveness, and make restitution. Mistakes allow a forum for teaching and yet another "example."

Even divinely inspired words are overwhelmed by the example of Jesus. Through the deeds and deportment of His life, Jesus showed that you can live in love under the statutes and precepts of the Heavenly Father. In the mind and heart of Almighty God, knowing how to live in obedience to Him was important, but to see these principles lived out in the world and under the circumstances all must endure was also necessary.

The Power of Well-Chosen Words

The lone example of a leader may be sufficient in some endeavors, but in most, parenting among them, well-chosen words will be needed at times. If you say something ridiculous in a fit of rage or a time of stress, children and adults will tend to remember those frivolous words longer and more clearly than one hundred wise words you may have uttered.

For Christians, the only worthy foundation for faith and practice is Scripture. Everything you want to know may not be specifically addressed, but all you need to live in righteousness is there. The general application to believers regarding the usage of words in no way lessens the importance of these guidelines in the relationship between parent and child/young adult. Knowing when not to speak can be as important as knowing when to speak and what to say (Eccles. 3:7).

This question of when to use and not use words will most often come at times when tension and wills are high on both sides or in teaching the more difficult lessons and principles of life, which you first contemplate and then learn. Should you ponder deeply the frequency with which you verbally show your love and support of your children? No! The more of that, the better. In correction or redirection, however, more thought and prayer may be needed.

How does a parent know when to speak and when to refrain from speaking? According to Proverbs 12:18, "There is one who speaks rashly like the thrust of a sword, but the tongue of the wise brings healing." Being on the receiving end of the thrust of a sword will not always kill you, but it will ruin your day; and you can just as easily ruin the day of the one doing the thrusting as well. The point is not always to remain silent (Prov. 17:27). The wisdom comes with balance in the context of, "A time to keep silence, and a time to speak" (Eccles. 3:7).

For parents to use their words wisely, they must know and understand their children. Each child will be different. If three children commit the same offense, a parent might conceivably have to admonish or explain the offense in three different ways with varied choice of words and phrases. While stern and clear words might be needed for one child, eye contact and a forbidding silence might be sufficient to correct another.

You cannot know and understand children or young adults without taking an active part in their lives. This consistent interaction with your children means listening to them, talking to them, constantly observing them, watching them perform in the activities important to them—whether sports, music, drama, or whatever else they enjoy—and letting them feel the love you have for them. When children know they are loved, a parent can do and say things to good effect that would otherwise be ineffective.

I hate spectator sports, but my son decided athletic pursuits were going to be a big part of his life. Therefore, I became an enthusiastic spectator. I arrived for warm-ups. I was there when the stadium lights faded. I read books on football and basketball; for track events I sat in the hot sun all day to see my son's fifteen minutes of glory; I planned and prepared after-game meals, which I served to my son and his teammates, punctuated with words of praise and encouragement; I made my own posters and signs to commemorate my son's achievements. I was his adoring fan. No less was this true of our daughter's brief basketball stint. If their games were at the same time, my husband and I each took one. Neither of our kids ever played to an empty house because Mom and Dad would always be there cheering them on.

Parents must also appreciate and understand each situation. To the best of their ability, they should try to know everything that happened in a situation that culminate in a confrontational reprimand or punishment of their child. If you do not know what happened or what is happening, how can you fairly and thoroughly address the situation?

For example, fighting is usually bad. When I got in fights over ego, I got in more trouble with my dad at home than I did with authorities at school. On the other hand, when a guy insulted and harassed my sister without provocation and I "dimmed his lights," Dad gave me a pat on the back and a few pointers. None of the teachers on the scene had intervened, and the men in my life had never been keen on letting the "fairer sex" be insulted.

Parents inevitably must admonish and punish a child (Prov. 6:23; 10:19; 16:21), but equally they must praise and compliment him on what he does well. Keep the balance.

As a six- or seven-year-old, I was having a hamburger with my father. A mentally retarded boy was making some odd facial contortions and trying to speak. His words were loud yet indiscernible. I chuckled. His awkward movements seemed humorous to the eyes and mind of a child.

My dad's expression changed instantly to one of indignation, which seemed like sudden anger. As he closed the distance between us quickly, I saw only his widened eyes dead set into mine, an expression that usually meant I was about to get whipped. "Don't you ever laugh at a child like that again!" His words were low, but intense with a harsh edge. I had gone from good humor to fear to choking back tears all in a few moments. With his tone remaining firm, he explained to me that the boy was born with this handicap through no fault of his own. He would never have the opportunities afforded by the good health I enjoyed. I was put into the world to protect, help, and show compassion for these innocent ones.

My father stopped for a few seconds and let his words sink in. Realizing that he had made his point and that I understood the seriousness of my mistake, he softened his tone and finished with this counsel: "When you see another boy or girl who is handicapped, you first make sure that there is nothing you can do to help. Then you say a prayer to God and give thanks for the blessings and health He gave to you. Except for the grace of God you could have been born with hurts like his, and to whom much is given, much is required." Pray for that one who will have a much more demanding journey than you.

I understood and never made the mistake again. Even though I did not understand my chuckling as inappropriate, Dad's response was right. The harshness and indignation were needed to be sure I understood the seriousness of what I had done as well as the ramifications of related issues. What Dad taught me went far beyond proper etiquette with handicapped people. He used the effective words, delivered the right way, to correct the problem and to teach me other life lessons in the process. He became my "pastor" on the scene, introducing spiritual truth and its application to my life. He was taking time to come alongside me where I was and lead me to where I ought to be. He was not only giving corrections, but he was also offering training in the process.

Words of reprimand, admonition, and instruction are an important part of training a child, but use them only when necessary. A parent's words are somewhat like a soldier's ammunition in battle. If he fires his rounds frivolously and unnecessarily, he may not have bullets left at the critical moment they are needed.

If parents rattle off words without care or restraint in every situation, those words begin to sound the same to a child or young adult. The words lose their impact and become an annoying background noise, like someone's leaf blower on an otherwise placid Saturday afternoon.

The greatest victories you win as a parent come when your children, inspired by your leadership and invigorated by your example, pursue what is right and shun what is wrong of their own volition. When people, young or old, make a decision and follow a path because of their own observations and contemplations, they will be stronger, more stable, and more determined on that path than will those who take a path because of coercion, manipulation, or force.

On the Reading of Books

The reading of books will supplement your example, your words, and Scripture. If a child is going to become an educated, intelligent, and articulate adult, he must be a reader. The sooner he embarks on this journey of books, the better. Whether in public, private, or Christian school, your child's education cannot be left to those who run the academic institutions. Which is worse—that much of the material students in public schools are being forced to read tears down what you are trying to teach them in values and character or that so much good is being kept from them? The constraints of time and the selection of curricula do not allow the wide range of reading necessary for a well-rounded education. Furthermore, truly educated people are those who continue to read widely even after their schooling is over.

Many with earned degrees are educated and intelligent, but they inevitably continue to read, study, and educate themselves beyond their school years. Nothing parents can do guarantees that their children will be avid readers as adults; but if children are not encouraged to read in their youth, almost certainly they will have little interest in books as adults. Conversely, when books are introduced early and children learn to appreciate stories, poetry, philosophical thought, and the exchange of ideas, a parent has opened the door to a journey of books and scholarship for children to pass through and explore.

Many ministry families have a head start on building a private home library, especially if a pastor determines to do exposition from his pulpit. How can a private library enhance the learning experience of your children? Early in our ministry we found a distinct advantage in keeping our library at home, which meant both sacrifices and blessings. Obviously space allotted to library holdings resulted in less space for other family pleasures. A quiet environment for Dad to study can be a challenge for Mom as well as the kids. But our experience turned these sacrifices into blessings. My husband's disciplined time in his study proved an excellent motivation for the development of good study habits by our children. His presence for these extra hours was considered a bonus, although we knew he had to have privacy for study; he managed extra minutes for hugs and interaction with the family. The library proved infectious in opening our eyes to the world and ferreting out our respective interests. Each family member developed his own collection of books within the whole. Now our children have their own homes; however humble the dwelling, each has a library!

Throughout childhood and young adulthood, I was very much absorbed with sports and outdoor activities. My parents encouraged these things, but they made me set aside a couple of hours daily to read for pleasure, when that time was not taken by school homework. Each family member selected books to take on trips as carefully as we planned our clothing. This early balance allowing time for reading has remained a plus in my life.

Social development is an integral and crucial part of growing up. The nature of life and culture ensures that much of what needs to happen in the social development of a child happens in its own time and course; yet parents need to scrutinize some aspects of development. If you homeschool your children, which is a noble and worthy endeavor, you will have to be more aware and active in some aspects of their social development.

Activities involving other children—whether at school, church, birthday parties, camping trips, or field trips—are essential. Those doing homeschool will need to be active and innovative in planning these excursions. Find other homeschooling families and plan activities with their children, while also including activities with children attending public or private schools.

Field trips are valuable, both as social interaction and as experience in learning how society works, regardless of what other schooling a child is receiving. Trips to business offices; local, state, or federal government offices; factories; medical facilities; prisons; the zoo; a practice or concert of the local symphony orchestra (if you live in a large city); a play; a construction site; a working farm or ranch; a major sports facility; military bases; police stations; and universities are all good choices. There are many options, limited only by your resourcefulness as a parent. Plan ahead to have a knowledgeable employee, owner, or official to escort you and explain the inner workings and purposes to the children unless you plan to do that yourself.

Don't neglect including your child in ministry—not in the sense of dragging him along and putting him in front of a video or leaving him to amuse himself. Rather introduce him to staff members and explore with him every nook and cranny of church facilities. A young child will be fascinated by the baptistry; and in showing him where it is and how it is prepared for use, you can teach him about this important ordinance for the church, sharing directly from the New Testament.

These adventures allow children to experience the sights, sounds, smells, and functioning of the many and varied threads that combine to create the diverse tapestry that is their world. They learn not only about a place and what the people who work there do but also why they do what they do and why their work is important. Moreover, through these experiences, children and young adults may discover their own interests. Some things will appeal to them or draw their interest; others will not. Again, there is no substitute for experience, and to get that experience with your own parents is the best yet!

A child's activities should not be limited to those centered around other children. Whenever possible, children should be allowed to take part in adult activities, even when your child may be the only one present. These encounters are an important part of his education and social development. They allow him to expand his knowledge and vocabulary and to conduct himself as an adult.

The World of Adults

Some suggest that children act like children until they are eighteen or in their early twenties, depending on which authority you consult, and enjoy this interaction despite your teaching them to act like adults. This view is dangerous if your ultimate goal is for your children to reach functional adulthood. It is never too early for a child to start maturing and learning to behave as an adult. They can go to pool parties and act like barbarians and troglodytes with their friends. They begin to learn that there is a time for full-contact pool wrestling, but there is also a time to be quiet, listen, converse politely, and retrieve their food.

Parents can best prepare their children for interaction with adults by having frequent and meaningful conversations with their children. Some parents are determined to cast their conversations on what they believe to be their child's level. Worse, some let television, movies, computers, and video games fill that slot, and they make no attempt to have personal interaction with their children.

Although necessary for all parents, this critical point is certainly not to be missed by parents in ministry. Children with parents in ministry will face criticisms, expectations, and gossip to a greater degree then their peers. For this reason, as well as the natural challenges of growing up, parents must keep the communication lines open and be able to have frank, meaningful, and instructive dialogue with their children.

One danger ministry parents face is heaping on their children their own bitterness and disappointment. Too many ministry kids are living far from God because they have "taken up offenses" for their parents. My husband and I have several simple guidelines:

- *We used common sense when sharing our burdens, considering the ages and spiritual development of our children.*

- *We never knowingly lied or misled our children concerning ministry challenges.*

- *We continually expressed the genuine joy derived from kingdom ministry.*

- *We were honest about the challenges and sorrows but careful to put these in context of the fallenness of a sinful world.*

- *Our children are young adults. One is in vocational ministry; one is not; but both children and their spouses are our best friends. They provide fellowship and counsel. I think all of us would say that we have had and do have family ministry we gladly offer to the Lord!*

As a general principle, topics are not to be avoided because they are considered to be beyond a child's comprehension. Children understand much more than they are given credit for. Sometimes younger children will notice things missed by their parents, mostly because their ability and willingness to read eyes and body language has not yet been diminished by the proprieties of social instruction.

Whether you like it or not, you are tempted to make your judgments on people based on their social standing and what they say rather than on what they do and the rudimentary signals they send through their eyes and body language. An elementary examination of the people you follow and those whom you acknowledge as leaders in your lives reveals this principle more clearly than anything else. Never underestimate a child's understanding.

Engage in meaningful conversation with your children but do not stop at that. Children should also be allowed to converse with other adults, to broaden their understanding, knowledge, and social development, and to quicken the development of their maturity.

Bridging the Generations

When I was seven years old, our family was on a Greek cruise ship in the Mediterranean. Because my mom helped with logistical arrangements and my dad did educational lectures, my sister and I were allowed and even encouraged to go along.

On this occasion, I sat on the pool deck next to a middle-aged gentleman whom I had never seen before. He spoke politely to me and introduced himself, and a lengthy conversation followed. Not until much later did I realize the benefit of the wisdom and positive effect of his patience and kindness to me. Although simple enough, what he did is rarely done. I knew subconsciously at the time what he was doing, but I did not fully put it in the proper context until later. This heart surgeon from South Africa was obviously successful in his work. He and I talked at length about surgery, medicine, ships, Africa, wildlife, the Middle East, and much more. He did more talking and I did more listening, for what he had to say captivated me. He brought things and places I had never experienced to life in my young mind. He talked of history, quoting famous philosophers and world leaders, some familiar and many with whom I was not familiar; and in response to my questions, he told me specifics of what he did with the hearts of people who underwent his surgeries.

Interestingly, though, the doctor asked many questions about me—what I liked to do, what I wanted to be when I grew up, what I thought about the cruise. What was incredible to me, looking back, is that he never talked down to me. He spoke to me as if he were speaking to an adult. He used many words that I could understand, but he also taught me some new words. He was careful to define and explain the words I did not understand.

A man of his stature could have easily stopped with a polite greeting and gone about his leisure, certainly a more pleasant course than a long dialogue with an inquisitive seven-year-old. I realized he had taught me much as I walked away contemplating the things we discussed. Looking back, however, I realize that he taught me more than I then knew. Some might counter that not all children are capable of this type of discourse, or that many will not respond to adult conversation the way I did. One thing is certain: They will not if they are never given an opportunity.

A child's grandparents are a great source of this type of interaction, and parents should see that children spend as much time with them as possible. Grandparents generally have the wisdom of years and the experience that children and young adults need to see and hear as they grow. Much of that wisdom, though not all, may be missed or ignored at the time. Amazingly, certain words, phrases, actions, and instruction from grandparents can resurface in the minds of children as they journey through the seasons of adulthood. When I remember my many fishing trips and airplane rides with Papa (my maternal grandfather), or the trips to the Farmer's Market and the ice cream shops with Pateé (my paternal grandfather), the wisdom of their words and deeds are as fresh on my mind as if spoken yesterday.

The association of children with their grandparents is important for another reason. A tragic and troubling trend in our culture is that respect, compassion, and gentle lovingkindness towards the elderly have fallen far from what once was expected. Many young people and families seem to think of their elderly family members as a liability to be handled with as little inconvenience to themselves as possible rather than as spiritual gold to be treasured.

How did we take advantage of the golden opportunities from those in their golden years?

- *We included our preschoolers in senior events when appropriate (Our daughter and son-in-love have continued this custom with our granddaughters, who have enjoyed their first "senior retreat" in Branson, MO).*

- We took the children to homes of shut-ins and to retirement centers and let them talk with the residents or quote a Scripture verse or sing a song, especially during the holiday season.
- We helped our young children write a thank-you note for any gift or kindness extended to them.
- We learned that a busy pastor couldn't do all in his heart for the seniors, but he had wonderful family helpers who could assist in the task.

Activities with grandparents, accompanied by parental instructions as to why they are important, teach children to honor, value, and care for these often-neglected family members. They learn to care not only for their own grandparents but also for any elderly people whose paths they cross. Whether it is a fishing trip with Grandpa or an outing to the store with Grandma, helping grandparents with their daily activities is quality time for children and young adults (Prov. 16:31; 20:29).

Reality Living

An integral part of this association with adults and adult life is the exposure of your children to the difficult as well as the good in life. My parents were very proactive in creating opportunities for me to cross the generational lines. When you train a child, you are preparing him for the good times and the bad. Society has nearly perfected the method of insulating adults and children from the unpleasant parts of life. For adults this insulation can only be effective to a certain degree. Ultimately, you must deal with the harsh realities of life, death, and suffering. To lead children and young adults through the early years of their lives pretending that tough times may never come is of no value.

This reality is more pronounced for parents in ministry than for others. The nature of their calling mandates closer and more-frequent contact with those suffering and touched by tragedy. Children, and even more so young adults, will ask questions about such events, as I did. Parents do well to present candid and honest answers regarding the realities of life.

In childhood and youth, I spent days and nights with family members or friends who were seriously ill or recovering from illness in hospitals or at home. My parents never forced me into such situations.

They explained to me what was needed and asked me to do it. I never said no, and I believe it brought out the best in me and taught me some of life's most crucial, if painful, lessons. My sister and I were honored to give long hours of care to our grandfather Pateé in the final weeks of his life. We did not leave him alone in the hospital, and each took shifts to stay with him and offer comfort and care as he had done for us over the years.

Many times I was there just to comfort the suffering person with my presence. Other times I had to monitor their condition or help them with their most basic needs. This type of experience, though not pleasant, is good and necessary. Children learn through experience to care for others and to help those who cannot help themselves. A ministry home should not only provide more opportunities but also, at the very least, offer training for children who are reared within its circle. You learn servanthood, which Jesus modeled and mandated for His followers (see Mark 10:43). Helping those who cannot help themselves keeps life in the proper perspective, affirming in the minds of children and youth that they, too, will one day go the way of those for whom they may now care.

Suffering and death are not popular subjects in modern culture. The tendency is to keep every vestige of sorrow and pain far from sight and mind. Ecclesiastes is not a favorite text for sermons among most pastors and congregations. Solomon reminded his readers that days in which they would have no delight would come and that they should make the most of their time on earth, for there would not be activity or joy in the grave to which all are going (Eccles. 12:1; 9:10).

Why did Solomon, inspired by Almighty God, think it necessary to keep such obvious and unpleasant facts before his readers? Why should your children and young adults see suffering and sickness, view the dead and attend funerals, volunteer to work with the handicapped or disabled, or be in the room with a dying friend or relative? In short, to get perspective.

When a person keeps before his eyes the day of his own death and the nature of the course of life, knowing that good times, bad times, suffering, and death are all part of life, he will live his life differently than if he focused only on the constant pursuit of pleasure, material gain, and recreation, which have become the obsession of modern culture. I am not suggesting an obsession with death or living with incessant fear of the day when your time will come. Such morbid thoughts would be ridiculous and are far from the example given by Christ and by the great men and women of God in Scripture.

When you keep in mind from whence you came and where you are going, you will use different criteria to make the crucial decisions in life, especially those between right and wrong, good and bad, what is edifying and what is not. A bedrock principle is more profoundly understood if taught from childhood.

Society teaches you to think of everything but the bad times and the harsh realities. The focus is on the pleasure of the moment, and the message goes out that anything is OK if it is good for you and does not hurt anyone else. You cannot make decisions that glorify God based on such shallow criteria. Nor, locked into this mentality, can you prepare for the harsh truths and challenges life will bring. Ministry parents have a perfect venue for "reality" living. The tendency is to get out of balance. Either you are carried away with the blessings of life, ignoring the tragedies and camping on the mountain without learning the lessons of the valleys, or you become so overwhelmed with tragedies and heartaches that you lose perspective on the providence of God that enables you to walk through valleys and again ascend the mountain of joy.

Some will argue that exposing children to these difficult aspects of life will traumatize them into dysfunctional or troubled adults. In childhood and youth I saw suffering, sickness, death from violence and illness, hunger and malnutrition, and poverty. All were terrible and troubling, yet I have never spent any time on a psychiatrist's couch. Furthermore, many children and youth have seen the same and sometimes worse when there was neither the system nor the resources to insulate them from the realities of life. Interestingly, today a higher percentage of children and youth than ever before are on narcotics or prescription drugs, or they are in prison.

Unto the Ends of the Earth

A teaching tool often overlooked yet more effective than any other except Scripture and example is travel. Many ministers travel in their teaching, preaching, and mission work, which sometimes gives them and their families an advantage in using this tool. When time and monetary considerations allow, families, or at least one of their children, can accompany them.

My father preached around the region where I grew up; so I rode along on most of his trips. Many of my peers did the same. It allowed me to see and experience people, places, and events beyond the comfortable realm of my home, church, school, and town.

At some point my parents decided that local travel was not enough and that if God blessed them with sufficient financial resources and opportunities, they would supplement my education with travel to whatever degree possible. Indeed, the Lord's blessings provided abundant opportunity, and I had the privilege of experiencing life in all regions of the United States and in countries on five continents.

My travel experiences have proven to be the greatest and most profound part of my education. My parents' teaching, both of Scripture and principle, and their examples had to come first, for these were the foundation stones. With the foundation intact, however, the family travel provided me the broadest range of learning and understanding about my world. Another advantage came in the extra time I had with my parents. My dad always had heavy and demanding responsibilities. We both relished those weeks away from telephone and appointments and even from televisions and newspapers, during which we had time for extended conversations and learning experiences.

You can read about other places, peoples, cultures, religions, and ecosystems or listen to teachers, professors, or other travelers talk about them and often gain knowledge; yet there is a level of knowledge that cannot be effectively attained in this way. More important, only through the experiences of being in a place, observing its intricacies, and mingling and conversing with its people can you attain genuine understanding.

What can ministry parents do to enhance learning through travel?

- *Be alert to use natural opportunities. If a pastor attends a convention or conference, can a family member be included in the trip? Drive instead of flying; get a room with two double beds or take along pallets. Sharing the bathroom and patiently operating in crowded conditions was worth the sacrifice for our family!*
- *Make it more than travel. When our children attended the Southern Baptist Convention with us, they were expected to be a part of some sessions and to help in our assignments. We always managed a brief family outing before or after as a reward.*
- *Don't forget the ministry. When my husband and I escorted study tours to enable the children to travel with us, each had assignments.*

Understanding via Knowledge

Knowledge is important, and the more you have the better, but knowledge is not equal to understanding. Many who are knowledgeable have little or no understanding. No one has understanding without knowledge, whether by study, experience, or both. Understanding comes when you are able to juxtapose knowledge with observing, association, interaction, thought, and contemplation. Knowledge alone is akin to being able to load a gun without knowing anything else about its function. With some people it is dangerous. With others there is no danger, but neither is there anything of value offered.

Understanding enables you to recognize and solve problems, to maintain an upright and steady course, and to make wise decisions. While a lack of knowledge accounts for some problems a nation faces, a lack of understanding of the issues domestically and internationally has been, and continues to be, devastating. In a world as interconnected as ours, individual decisions affect not only a person and his family but also the nation and the world. Even more is this true in the homes of leaders in government, education, and religion. A ministry home is a worthy setting for moving from knowledge to understanding. The world comes to its doors.

To qualify the virtues of travel as a teaching tool, you need to consider where and how often you travel with your children, and how you do it. Some travel without gaining understanding. To visit another country and stay in westernized hotels serving only American food is of little or no value. If you go to Egypt and see only the pyramids and the Egyptian Museum in Cairo, what have you really learned about Egypt? I remember cruising on the Nile in a small and unsteady sailboat, riding an all-night train from Cairo to Luxor, wandering through the spice market, driving out to Goshen, where it appeared by the response of the people that no American had ever been, and having a visit from a local doctor in his sandals and with his "torch" (which I was relieved to learn was a flashlight) to treat my earache.

Help your child or young adult mingle with the local people, talking with them, asking them questions, and answering their questions. Eat ethnic cuisine and accept invitations to personal homes. By being friendly and open, I have been given these opportunities by local people.

Stay in local homes rather than a hotel when given the opportunity. Observe their customs. Play their games. Study their history, both written and oral. In addition to visiting with the people on the street, talk to business, government, and religious leaders if you have the chance. Go to markets and shops other than the ones frequented only by tourists. In this way you begin to understand other countries, cultures, religions, and peoples.

The morning we visited with Israeli Prime Minister Menachin Begin in his Knesset office, Armour, nine years of age, was escorted by Begin to a window overlooking Jerusalem for an emotional moment when the prime minister with his thick accent said, as he ran his fingers through Armour's blond hair, "Jerusalem will never be divided."

You accept some risk in certain places if you are to experience them in these uninhibited ways. How much you accept for your family is a personal decision. People go to extremes on both ends of the spectrum. Most, it seems, err on the side of obsessive precaution and are unwilling to take any perceived risk, acting almost as if nothing bad can ever happen to them as long as they stay in the USA.

"Nothing risked, nothing gained" was the phrase my dad used with me more times than I can remember. My family and I chose what for us was the sensible middle ground. We went places where bullets might fly, cold steel might clear leather, or bombs might go off, and on a few occasions these things happened. With vigilance, awareness, and a bit of God's grace, the risk was usually minimal. On the other hand, when there was the probability or certainty that bullets and bombs would be involved, we stayed away. My parents and I were in Baghdad shortly before the Gulf War, but we have not returned during the last decade. The education and experiences reaped from traveling with your children is worth some monetary sacrifice and even a degree of risk. As parents you will have to decide where to draw the lines. If you cannot afford to travel, there are still some good things you can do; but let's be clear. When I was younger, my peers and their parents often told me how lucky I was to travel so much. I agreed then and now.

However, I noticed that most of these families had cars newer and nicer than ours. Some had boats and recreational vehicles and big, fancy televisions and stereo systems. They went on ski trips to expensive resorts once or twice a year. We adapted our lifestyle to use our limited resources for the travel my parents believed to be important to our education.

During a visit to Baghdad with my husband and son, we met with Yasser Arafat in a guest house within one of Saddam Hussein's palaces just before the first Gulf War. When three bullet-riddled cars drove up at 9 p.m., my husband suggested each of us host a vehicle so that each car would have a member of our family. I must admit anxiety over being separated from my only son, who had just graduated from college. Each car went a different route, at high speed, but we arrived simultaneously at our destination. I was a bit surprised that Chairman Arafat showed more interest in our son than he did in us!

My parents could have done many things and acquired more possessions, but instead they chose to make the travel they had in ministry open doors for me and my sister to travel as well. To be able to see the world was worth that sacrifice. They had nothing against boats, recreational vehicles, country clubs, designer clothing, the latest appliances, or new BMWs, but they were not interested in having them if it meant that our family could not travel.

Some families, despite living frugally, do not have the financial resources to travel extensively, especially overseas. Considering what things cost now and rising costs for airline travel, options for trips as a family are dwindling. You are unwise to travel if that means using financial resources needed at home, and expensive travel is probably best bypassed altogether.

Who's in Charge of Your Child's Education?

Other things can be done to help your children gain knowledge and understanding about countries and cultures. You cannot count on public or private schools to teach your children what they need to know in any discipline. Testing has proven American students' knowledge of geography to be abysmal, and often a student's understanding of the culture, people, and religion of other countries is even less satisfactory. Parents would do well to oversee carefully what their kids are being taught—not just to protect them morally and spiritually but also to be sure they are getting the academic education they need!

Parents must supplement the reading program of their children and young adults with books about other regions, countries, and peoples of the world. Extra research and effort on the part of parents will be necessary. Whereas parents are wise to be sure their children read about all regions of the world to give them a broad, general base of understanding, both children and young adults should be given leeway and encouragement to concentrate their reading on areas of their own personal interest.

I was fascinated and absorbed with eastern and southern Africa and with the deserts of North Africa and the Middle East, so my parents allowed me to read a great deal about those areas. Mom and Dad purchased books in areas of my interest for my personal book shelves instead of the larger family library. I read about wildlife, tribes and culture, wars, missionaries, geography and ecosystems, and more. I was also fascinated with war and was allowed to read widely on the subject with this provision: For every three books I read, at least one must have nothing to do with war. Dad wanted to be sure that my home education was not one-dimensional. My father kept a close watch on all that I was reading, as parents should do. Normally, he would skim through the book at some point and ask me a few questions to be sure I was learning as well as reading.

A thorough world atlas, such as the one put out by *National Geographic*, is a resource that should be in every home to provide a valuable reference source for parents and children and a teaching tool as well. The atlas with basic information, such as population figures, languages spoken, ethnic breakdown, GNP per capita, area in square miles, principal exports, and religion is particularly useful for reference and teaching.

Be creative and try to make the learning situation interesting and relaxing for your children. Over the course of a year or several years you could combine the atlas information with a bit of research at the local library and come up with basic facts and notes about each country. Then, weekly or more often, depending upon what kind of pace is viable for your family, you can open the atlas to the country that will be the evening's discussion. Mealtime has always been a special time for our family discussions of the world and events of importance.

Once your children have looked at the country and understand its location in relation to their own, you can go through your information with them. Allow them to ask questions or bring home a book or two from the library and help in research if you want to go at a more relaxed pace. Even if you move slowly, you can introduce your children to every country in the world in a few years. This process will give children a general, broad-based knowledge and understanding about the world. They may discover areas of the world in which they are interested, some of which they may want to research more on their own. This same principle can be used with a good atlas of the United States. It would not be sensible to study the world while ignoring the American union of fifty diverse states.

Come up with your own ideas for teaching. You know your children better than anyone else and are best equipped to appeal to them. Be cautious, however, of making these "teaching" sessions too long, unless, of course, your children are still engaging the subject or asking questions. The more enjoyable these sessions, the more children and young adults will take away from them.

Consider the personalities and interests of your children, and do not expect every country or culture to be equally interesting to them. If you have boys, make sure you study Kenya and Tanzania; tell them about the Masai, who drink blood straight from their cattle and who used to kill lions single-handedly with their spears, like Beniah in the Old Testament (2 Sam. 23:20). I thought this was great stuff when I was a boy, and many of your boys will, too. If you have a girl and have been teaching her to cook or sew, she might be interested in how women and girls in other countries make their clothes and prepare their food.

One of my favorite "trip gifts" for our daughter Carmen was a carefully selected doll from each country. I continue to collect the dolls to entertain my granddaughters. Ministry families can find some wonderful overlapping of ministry and learning. I use these dolls in centerpieces and for programs. I purchase ethnic clothing for our family. A look at our family Christmas card pictures is almost a travelogue in itself.

Another tremendous resource you have for teaching your children rests within the population of the United States—long a melting pot and its population now more diverse than ever. Many US citizens and residents were born in other countries, and they have much to offer in teaching us about their respective cultures and providing enriching friendships. Rural areas tend to be more indigenous, but in most metropolitan areas you find a variety of ethnicity.

Get to know these people. Invite them to your homes. They will often reciprocate. If they invite you for dinner, ask them to prepare and serve the meal to you just as they would in their own respective country. Most are more than happy to do so. In this way you and your children can have the same experience you would have if you were visiting another country. Ask questions and encourage them to talk about their countries, their lives, and their diverse heritage. What you will learn from these encounters cannot be taught in classrooms or from books.

Ethnic restaurants are another potential "classroom" for your children. Many, especially Asian and Mexican restaurants, have been anglicized to some degree. Look for smaller, family-owned restaurants that keep their traditions and food as they are in their homeland. To find a small place that smells of spices and where very few people are speaking English, is probably a culinary jewel. Eat the food and get to know those who work there. Ask questions about their food, culture, and country and allow your children to engage in conversation with them as well. You will usually be well-received, and those who run the restaurant will be honored and appreciative of your interest. You may also find these contacts a fertile evangelistic tool. You not only immerse your children in a new culture but let them observe first-hand how you share the gospel. Ministry families experience the satisfaction that comes from leadership and influence, neither of which is reserved only for parents.

Again, be creative. Once you get to know those who own or work at the restaurant, ask them to do a private party. Let your children invite a small group of their friends, together with their respective families, and have the restaurant serve you a full meal in their traditional manner, preparing everything just as they would in their own country. After dinner the restaurateur could give the families a lecture, directed toward the children, about life in his country. He might bring pictures, musical instruments, clothing, or crafts for a bit of show and tell. Anything visual is effective with children.

Teach your children proper etiquette before you go into someone else's home or restaurant. For example:
- **Eat what is on your plate**
- **Don't make faces when something does not taste good to you**
- **Speak respectfully**
- **Listen when being spoken to**
- **No food fights**

If you find a cuisine appealing to your family, buy a book of recipes and assemble the necessary ingredients for a few dishes. Do not hesitate to ask the advice of people in the market concerning the recipe's preparation.

When talking about food, I invariably learn things unrelated to food about the people and their country. Allow your children to help

in the preparation of the meal if they are so inclined. You will learn how time-consuming much of the preparation is. In many countries, especially those outside the Western world, food is still prepared from scratch with fresh ingredients, which takes more time than mixing the ingredients of cans and packages.

In much of the world women are still focused on the care of their homes and children as their prime responsibility. More than their American and Western European peers, they have time to prepare these dishes, which are fresher and more elaborate and in many cases tastier. Employed working women do not have time for such labor-intensive dishes. Thus, the need for, and popularity of, fast food, processed foods, and T.V. dinners has arisen in the West.

I have reveled in devoting my primary energies and freshest hours to my family. I love being first and foremost a homemaker. I concur with Armour's observation. I am indeed a "working" woman, but I am not employed. I love preparing ethnic foods and making mealtime special. Armour may remember the time we decided to have a Mexican theme for Christmas and menu to match. He innocently suggested I prepare tamales from scratch. I happily accepted his challenge. After a citywide search for the exotic ingredients, I began the arduous task. Well, the rest is history, and Armour was the first to suggest gently that we buy our tamales from the Mexican market in the future!

Bringing the World Home

Most evangelicals, especially ministers, come to know missionaries at some point. These traveling ministers are an excellent source of education for your children and young adults. I still remember how missionaries, through their pictures, food presentations, lectures, and conversation brought other worlds and people alive to me. They fueled my desire to know more about other places and to visit them myself if the opportunity arose.

Most missionaries have designated furlough periods when they return home for brief stateside assignments. Get acquainted and invite them to dinner. Plan times for them to speak to your children and show them slides, pictures, and crafts from their adopted country. They may invite you to dinner and serve an ethnic meal. This learning experience is not to be missed. Missionaries generally know not only facts about the country in which they serve but also how the people live. For they live with them, experiencing the same blessings, hardships, and way of life.

Finally, do not forget about the travel opportunities available in your own country. The United States has a tremendous geographical and cultural variance within its own borders. When traveling the United States from north to south and east to west, although politically one nation, you will find this vast country culturally divided, often along ethnic lines. The people in the various regions have different values, mind-sets, and worldviews, eat different foods, and speak in different ways even though the official language is the same. For your children to learn about their own country is just as important as it is for them to learn about others. They are the voters and leaders of the future. Only with knowledge and understanding can they make wise decisions.

CHAPTER Three

As They Grow

THE FOUNDATIONAL PRINCIPLES of training a child remain the same—yet more specific needs and aspects inevitably surface as your children grow older. Some difference in the type of leadership and guidance is required by parents in ministry versus that of other parents.

Calling Out the Called

There is a tendency, or even a proclivity, among some ministers to push their children toward following in their steps. Almost all ministers, including those who seem to be the most obvious practitioners of this effort to determine the future of a child, overwhelmingly deny that they have done or ever would do such a thing. No one can know ultimately what is in another person's heart. Nevertheless, the presumption is there, and the possibility exists. Parents are not the only ones guilty of pushing a child down the vocational path of his parents. Well-meaning friends, especially members of the congregation, frequently indulge in strong-armed encouragement of a spiritually sensitive child to follow his parents' steps into kingdom service.

Jesus was not hesitant about calling men to follow Him into the vineyard of kingdom service. However, no one in ministry would presume to equate himself to Jesus in the task of calling out individuals to ministry. An omnipotent and omnipresent God is capable of communicating with and leading your child. No human being can "call out the called" as well as the Commander-in-Chief Himself! A very special relationship exists between parent and child. Usually children want to please their parents more than any other human being. Ministry parents are cautioned to be careful not to project their own dreams and calling on their children. Sending a "parent-called" child to minister is like taking a child to his football game with a bat and glove.

A parent would do well to pray earnestly for God to reveal Himself to his child and to guide his steps into whatever path God has for the child. A parent can give his child opportunities to pursue interests and attain skills and observe a variety of opportunities for life's work. Most important, ministry parents should teach their children the joy of serving Christ—whatever your professional pursuit. As the hymn says, "It pays to serve Jesus; it pays every day."

Parents are required to provide the foundation principles and leadership and to guide and interact with their children throughout a lifetime. The actual call to ministry ultimately is something between God and the individual child or young adult. Creating a fertile environment in which your child can heed divine leadership in all the decisions of life is an awesome but necessary task (Deut. 6:4–9), but the call itself must come from God alone.

The fine line comes at the point of "calling out the called." Every minister has the assignment to call out laborers into the kingdom vineyards. My husband has had a wonderful ministry in calling out and equipping young people for kingdom service. In his Fayetteville pastorate, there were more than fifty who committed their lives to and began preparation for kingdom service. We met with these young people faithfully and regularly to answer their questions and help prepare them for service to the Lord. Occasionally my husband and I have felt led of the Holy Spirit to ask a particular young person to consider the claims of Christ on his life's work, but that is rare.

Observant parents will be aware when a child, knowingly at times and unwittingly at others, reveals his interests, talents, and abilities. At this time children need guidance, explanations, encouragement, and counsel. Constant interaction and conversation with your children is essential. The quantity of time is a prelude to the quality of time you spend with your children. Even loving parents, if they seldom interact with their children, cannot provide the necessary help and guidance when the interests and talents of their offspring begin to emerge. Parents ought not to expect much help from schools in this task, as their curricula are almost inevitably helplessly deficient. Consider the vast and varied array of occupations within which people pursue vocational interests and realize that middle schools and high schools put all students through essentially the same program. Only you as a parent can observe your child carefully enough to identify interests and talents that are uniquely his.

Children may begin to show particular interest or talent in certain academic subjects, music, art, sports, building and repairing things, writing, or in other areas. As they grow into young adults, these interests and talents may become more accurate and clear. They should be encouraged to pursue their dreams in whatever ways awaken their interests and gifts within the biblical boundaries of the Christian life. Again ministry parents sometimes overlook many unique opportunities they can provide for their children by virtue of their positions in the community.

Enriching the Lives of Your Children

Hobbies are important vehicles for enriching the lives of your children. If a child shows an affinity for reading, he should have plenty of books to read. If he is interested in music, find him a secondhand guitar and chord book or offer piano or voice lessons, and encourage him as he learns. If he draws well, compliment his work and provide paper, paint, pencils, and brushes. If he shows athletic ability, play ball with him, teach him how to build strength, quickness, and speed, and always attend his games and contests. Your ministry field may yield a wide range of help as you seek to encourage your child—tutors in various skills, performers who model specific talents, athletes who excel.

Our daughter Carmen has a beautiful voice. When she expressed an interest in taking voice lessons, we called a well-trained soloist in our church who had sung professionally all over the world. Immediately she worked Carmen into her already full schedule so that our daughter had the finest vocal coach available and one who had a special interest in her. Of course, we paid for her lessons, and happily so.

Ministry parents should take advantage of opportunities but not people. Never expect services or goods to be gratis. Always be prepared to pay for the service rendered or object desired. Perhaps someone along the way will insist on giving some service or bestowing a gift. When that happens, express your gratitude heartily, verbally, and in a handwritten note. In a loving church, that can mean lots of notes! What an opportunity to teach your children by example—not to think they are owed certain things because you are a ministry family but to be grateful for all the blessings God bestows. Our children have been meticulous in thanking individuals who do special things for them.

Parents must keep one thing in mind regarding athletics. Encouraging your child to compete is fine; yet you should never assume that this competition is going to be the way he will make his living and the family fortune. A very small percentage of people actually have the degree of talent required by professional competition. Many outstanding high school and college athletes will never be able to pursue their respective sports of choice professionally.

Often related to your encouragement of your children in discovering and pursuing their talents is your family's choice of sports and recreation. All families need leisure activities in their lives. Most important is the opportunity for families to be together and to maintain that cohesive bond that defines family.

A child's individualized pursuits, such as organized sports, piano recitals, spelling bees, declamation contests, or boxing matches, are a part of this bond. When I played football, for example, my mom, dad, and sister were usually present, and other relatives often came as well, making Friday night football a family activity.

Taking the Family Out the Door

Organized sports can be an enjoyable part of family leisure, but there is much more. Camping, hiking, boating, fishing, hunting, shooting, volleyball, rodeos, cycling, and walking or running the dogs are but a few of the outdoor activities in which families can engage. Depending upon where you live, cross-country or downhill skiing, snowboarding, surfing, mountain biking, or just hanging out at the beach might be your thing. Families across the country have made one or more of these activities a regular part of their lives, and many of them are not spending large amounts of money to do it.

While I was growing up in a large city, my dad and I played pool, racquetball, tennis, basketball, and football; we went bowling, boxed, built model airplanes, went to movies, watched Monday Night Football and Saturday college football together almost religiously, walked or ran the dogs, and drove an hour out of town to fish. You can do things with your children no matter where you live. The key is balancing family time with ministry responsibilities and pouring as much creativity and energy into ministry to your family as you do to serving your congregation.

At times you may want to spend a little extra money and go further afield, doing something that you do not get to do often. There is nothing wrong with that, but never forget or neglect the simple pleasures, the little things you can do on a regular basis with your children or as a family. I have lived in quite a few locales within the United States and some abroad, and in all of them families or friends could do things together without spending much money.

As a teen, I thought boredom only occurred in school classrooms, listening to monotonous sermons, sitting through uninteresting Sunday school lessons, and enduring sentimental weddings. I am still amazed when I hear people talk about being bored. I could always find some way to entertain myself, even in places I did not find interesting. Actually, even in the aforementioned "dreadful foursome," I sometimes found ways to have fun, but given that we are addressing the subject of training up a child in the way he should go, my creative "mischief" might not be the best topic of discussion here!

Increasingly children and young adults who are bored cannot find ways to entertain themselves. They find nothing to watch on TV; they have no movies or video games that they have not already watched or played until their interest is quenched; no one has a car to drive them wherever their friends are hanging out. The appetite for spectator entertainment is voracious.

The constant drive to be entertained, usually involving a television or a computer, seems to possess the average child or young adult. This view has infected adults as well as children in our country. To lecture someone on the deleterious effect of something in which you regularly engage is always more difficult than degrading pursuits of no interest to you. Ministry parents are easy prey for introducing their children to this spectator mentality. Their busy schedules often prompt the easy and cheap babysitting of television or video or computer. Although costly in time and energy, consider involving your children in appropriate ways in ministry! Make them a part of your service to Christ. When it is not suitable for them to be involved, take time to prepare directed activities suitable for them.

My granddaughters occasionally come to visit me on the seminary campus. Even though I clear my calendar of all but absolutely essential duties, I always have some "First Lady" responsibilities. How do I integrate these preschoolers into my busy life? I include them in functions they can enjoy like luncheons and dinners (at least the meal portion). I plan their activities in advance (playing with the treasures in their dress-up box, "working" at their small desks with child-friendly supplies). I have some exclusive treats with limited access—a Sunday box, which can be opened on the Lord's Day, and a Rainy Day Box to be opened only on a day when rain comes and casts a tone of dreariness over the scene. When you view your children as treasures, they sense that they are valuable. When you give them your attention in the midst of ministry demands, they not only know they are precious to you; but they also sense that they are greatly loved by God Himself.

A consistent and unrequited need to be entertained creates an intellectual, mental, and physical laziness, which inhibits your desire to engage in challenging and productive activities. This scenario, in time, results in a general lack of creativity of thought and imagination and a lowering of your personal drive to excel in every aspect of living.

Do not allow your children to fall into the lethargic haze of a video-induced stupor and apathy. Let your children and younger adults have choices regarding their activities and how they live their lives, but do not give the option of becoming a flaccid, flabby "sofa-and-soda bum."

Some may wonder whether outdoor activities are that important. The answer is yes! For families to spend time together is both valuable and crucial whatever the activity. Furthermore, when children are doing things outside, they are not sitting on their posterior anatomy dulling their minds with video games or soiling them with the garbage that emanates from video and television entertainment. Outdoors, with the leadership of parents or another knowledgeable adult, children can learn survival and wilderness skills. Boy Scouts and Girl Scouts are great, as are Royal Ambassadors, Girls in Action, Awanas, missionary education groups, and other church organizations that focus on planning outdoor activities for children and youth.

With proper adult leadership, outdoor activities, especially those in wilderness or backcountry, teach children respect for God's creation and awe for His genius—which seem to be fading as the world becomes increasingly urban and dulled by the vices of modernity. David felt this same respect and awe for the Creator and His creatures (see Ps. 8). May it never happen that those in ministry do not instill in their children a respect for the Creator and an awe for all He created.

Young men and women who revere the beauty and majesty of God's creation also revere the Creator and try to live in a way that honors the Lord and shows love and respect to their brothers and sisters who share this world. Many are Christians, but some are not. The connection, nevertheless, is indisputable. Those who truly respect creation also accept the moral responsibility of living their lives in an upstanding way, emulating Judeo-Christian standards. Consider carefully what type of outdoor activities you want to do with your family and know that in doing so you will introduce them to a more intimate relationship to the Creator and all He created.

Finding Joy Within the Walls

Since weather does not always cooperate and loading up and heading out of town is not always viable, families should also enjoy indoor recreation and leisure. There is no excuse for boredom. A trip to your local Wal-Mart or even a toy store will reveal more board games of various types than you would have time to play in a year. They range from the simple, better for younger children, to the complex and challenging, which are fun for adults of any age.

Board games bring families and friends together. Many are challenging and force players to think and be creative, and some produce humorous results, forcing players to laugh at themselves and at each other. Among our family favorites are Trivial Pursuit, Parcheesi, Uno, checkers, and dominoes.

When I was about seven, several ministers studying at a local seminary—one from the Philippines and one from Indonesia—taught me how to play chess. Although there were no chess players in my family, these friends allowed me to participate in their chess games. Chess, incidentally, is one of the best games for teaching children and young adults to think and to develop an active mind.

Find the games that are enjoyable to your family and integrate them into your lives. To be critical of what your children are doing with their peers or to prohibit them from taking part in peer activities without offering any options at home is of little value. There are games that children can play with each other as well as those in which the family as a whole can participate. A ministry home should always have options for fun not only for the family circle but for others who may come to experience its hospitality.

What You See May Become What You Do

A television itself, as an inanimate object, cannot be good or evil. Like many things, if used properly and within limitations, television can be both useful and enjoyable; yet it can also be harmful when not used with discretion.

Most Americans consider television a necessity and not a luxury item, even if they do not say so. People go into debt, put necessities on credit cards and pile up interest charges, or complain about not being able to pay bills while paying out a disproportionate portion of their hard-earned money to keep numerous satellite or cable channels coming into their homes. Inordinate amounts of money are spent on big-screen televisions, DVD and VCR players, as well as on sales or rentals of movies.

Nothing is inherently wrong with having and enjoying the best in technology and entertainment, but why would you acquire such luxury items when you are in debt or barely able to pay for true necessities unless you consider spectator entertainment a necessity as well. Children enjoy, and may even demand, television, movies, and cable; but what are you teaching them by putting yourself further into a financial hole just to have these things? Children learn some lessons that they do not fully appreciate until later in life.

However fervently a child may plead for television, cable, or movies and however often he may remind you that his friends have these modern technologies, the fact remains that they are luxury items, not necessities. Children have become successful and responsible adults despite never having had a television in their homes. They are often more innovative, imaginative, and even more physically fit than their peers who spent endless hours sitting in front of the screen.

With the difference between luxury and necessity understood, let's acknowledge the value of television. A television can be a good teaching tool for parents with children or young adults. The more varied the teaching "tool box," the more effective parents can be because certain lessons are sometimes best learned and understood, by using different methods.

Television can do much to broaden education. Visual images can bring alive faces, images, landscapes, and buildings about which children and young adults read in books. They can get glimpses of places, cultures, terrain, and animals they have never seen and may not otherwise see. To see images accompanying dialogue or narration is more fun for all.

Most video rental stores have a variety of documentary films on different subjects. These videos are a tremendous source of education. A number of catalogs specialize in documentary films if you want to begin to build up a film library to complement your books.

My parents have an audio-visual library cataloged as carefully as their books. When I was in high school, my history teacher used documentary films as a part of his curriculum. Students looked forward to his class more than others, and they paid closer attention not only to

the films but also to his lectures before and after the video presentation. Due to the variety of his teaching tools, students—even those not particularly interested in history—were less likely to become bored.

In addition to videos, the History Channel, Discovery Channel, Learning Channel, and Animal Planet have excellent educational material. Much of their programming is quite entertaining in the process. Learning does not have to be boring. My dad tells his professors that it is a sin to be boring. I do not know if being boring is a sin, but I do know that being creative and trying to make things interesting has its rewards. Not everything has to be fun, but most subjects can be made interesting.

Television is also a source of world and local news. Newspapers and news magazines have their place and value, and my parents encouraged me to read them, but they also let me watch the news regularly. Watching a half-hour or hour-long news presentation usually takes less time than reading an entire paper or magazine, and you have the active, visual component not available in print media. This medium is good for children and young adults, especially those not so inclined to read, because it is more likely to keep their attention than printed material. Watching news programs on a regular basis not only educates your children regarding what is happening in their community, country, and world; but, with your leadership, such sensory stimulation to their minds can begin to instill in them their obligation to be informed and involved citizens.

Do your best to find a news channel or program that is fair and balanced, not presenting only one side of the news. For pastors, developing an interest in news and current events within the family has an added value: Your children can help you find illustrations helpful to your preaching ministry. They can be additional eyes and ears, and what they see and hear will provide topics for conversation and maybe illustrations for you.

Before addressing the negative impacts of television, consider its value beyond education. Most people use television primarily for entertainment. Everyone needs time to relax and take his mind away from work or the problems and struggles of the day. I have a collection of my favorite Humphrey Bogart, John Wayne, Clint Eastwood, and

Charlton Heston films that I watch from time to time, and I still like to watch a good football game and Arizona Wildcats' basketball. Some, having seen the negative impact upon children and young adults who spend hours every day in front of the television, want to shun the medium completely. This overreaction would be a mistake.

The fact that some people misuse something does not make that object bad. Nor does it mean that others cannot use it wisely. The problem comes not because television is used for entertainment but rather because people allow it to take over their lives. Instead of limiting their entertainment to a sensible amount, they limit their productivity, education, and work, not to mention harming their health, because they spend so much time virtually brain-dead while being entertained and swallowing ridiculous amounts of soda, chips, and Oreos in the process.

My sister and I were basically limited to one hour of television a day. This rule was flexible and depended to some degree on what else we had to do. If we had done a lot of reading, then we might get to watch more television. The rule was flexible, not hard-and-fast, which seems logical to me.

This restriction did not include football games. These games exceeded more than an hour, but football, for my dad and me, was time spent together. We watched games and discussed strategy and plays throughout. What plays should this team run? What will they run? What mistakes are they making?

This exercise was fun for us. It stimulated our minds and sparked our emotions. More important, we spent time together doing something we enjoyed. My mom did not see much value in this entertainment, but she had the sense to know that it was good for us. Often she provided snacks and occasionally even served meals according to scheduled games.

My time allotment also did not include educational shows. Even as a child, I loved wildlife and historical documentaries and was allowed to watch as many as my schedule allowed. There were also special exceptions. When about four or five years of age, I got to stay up late with Dad and watch *Ben Hur* in its entirety. I just had to promise to pop right up out of bed early the next morning. I was up and dressed in record time.

I was allowed to enjoy television and movies, but there were always limits on how much I could watch as well as restraints on content, although the rules were relaxed some as I grew into young adulthood and showed myself responsible enough to make my own choices. What I learned then, and came to understand fully later, is that television and entertainment are enjoyable and have their place. However, they should never be your focal point.

When a child comes to this understanding and perspective, he is unlikely to allow television to take over his free time. What developed in me, probably without my parents' design or intention but as a result of their methods, was that anytime I watched more than a couple of hours of television, I felt a driving need to get outside and walk, run, play ball, or work out. Strangely, what was true in childhood and youth is still a pattern for me today, even on days when I lack the energy surge of childhood.

The issue is about keeping things in balance. I did not have that understanding when I was young, at least not that I could verbalize; but possibly this innate understanding came in my early years due to my parents' methodology and was followed by my ability to verbalize it later in life.

This assurance is important for parents, especially as they struggle through some of the more difficult issues with their children. Children and youth will learn things from your example, words, rules, and methods, even while they are arguing against you and telling you why you are wrong. Although you will not always see your impact on your child at the time, hold your ground and know that some lessons take time, and the brilliance of some methods and strategies is not revealed until the moment of truth at a much later time.

No single method or program is the "right way" for you to decide how much television your children watch or what they watch. Rather, all factors must be taken into account, as well as the personalities, attributes, tendencies, maturity, understanding, and responsibility of your children. Since parents know their children best, only they are in a position to make these decisions.

Other factors include the entertainment industry's indulgences in the portrayal of gratuitous violence, sex, and drug abuse. Hollywood "heroes" tell your children to "just say no" to drugs on the street, while glorifying in film the thugs and gangsters who move and sell drugs. They render scenes of life in the real world in terms of illicit sex yet seldom show the catastrophic consequences in the form of STDs, unwanted pregnancies, broken hearts and hurt feelings, and children without either biological parent. Amazingly, for example, the Hollywood elites who would reject a just war to free an enslaved people or who would rally to take away the right of law-abiding citizens to keep and bear arms will then make their own living off portraying violence. These inconsistencies should suggest something about the sincerity and motives of such people, whose walk certainly does not match their talk.

Depending on how much television and how many movies your children are allowed to watch, the fact that video dramas and movies do not represent reality probably needs to be explained more than once. Although filmmakers try to make their films appear as reality, the fact is that they are far from it. Even with all of the technological advances in the industry, no film can fully portray the true horrors of war and violence.

What Is Reality?

Society is increasingly obsessed with "reality TV." These programs are anything but real. A "reality" aficionado who disagrees should go to the Amazon or the jungles of Central Africa with only his survival knife and start walking. Then he will understand reality.

What does this have to do with children? Everything! It is alarming how many adults come to their understanding of reality and truth based on television and film. Continually adults and youth are reciting "historical facts or truths," which have been plagiarized so perfectly that you could identify the exact film from which they took the vignette. If adults are having difficulty making this distinction, the problem is likely worse among children and youth.

If a young person's understanding of truth and reality is distorted, then the very foundation from which he must make the important decisions in his life is already shaken. Expecting your child to make wise decisions from an unstable foundation is like giving a student on his first flight the controls of an aircraft that has gone into a spin and expecting him to bring it under control. You, as parents, must provide the foundation of truth and reality, knowing that your children will be exposed to the myths, lies, and distortions of the entertainment industry.

Revising and Distorting the Biblical Paradigm

Parents must also be aware of the conscious and deliberate efforts of those in the entertainment business to reverse the biblical and traditional roles of manhood, womanhood, and family. You see it in television shows, movies, and even commercials.

In television and in movies, you constantly see women portrayed as the breadwinners, top fighters, best soldiers, smartest scientists, and toughest cops. Meanwhile males with traditional values and beliefs just bungle along behind the superior strength and wit of their female leaders. More and more on the silver screen you are seeing men portrayed as house husbands in maternal settings. However roles may be reversed by cultural trends, you can become proactive. Teach your children biblical paradigms. Introduce them to history, noting that even history books must be carefully selected because of the trend to rewrite and revise historical records.

Research the great soldiers and generals and examine the famous military operations. Study the history of crime and police work. Study the history of science and show your children the pictures and biographies of those who invented today's technology. Introduce your children to the mothers who produced and wives who inspired these great men. Find the women who have genuinely achieved greatness without sacrificing biblical priorities and the creation order in the process. There is a deceptive power in forced conformity and mindless acceptance.

If everyone in this country held filmmakers, actors, and actresses in the proper perspective, that is, as people who merely direct and perform plays with modern technology and high budgets, then such cautions would be unnecessary. However, many adults, young people, and children equate celebrities with credentialed authorities and experts. This problem is potentially more serious with children simply because their minds and perspectives are generally more easily molded than are those of adults. They will tend to be more influenced by someone whose movies they like or by athletes whom they admire. Parents must make their children understand that just because someone is a good actor or can dunk a basketball does not mean that person has any significant knowledge outside the arena in which he makes his living and attains his fame.

The government through public education, as well as the media and the entertainment industry, will continue to present a reversing of the biblical and traditional roles of the family as both normal and proper and thus expedient. The combination of a parent's example, counsel, and explanations becomes critical. Through the example of a godly mother and father, your children see each day the model of a Christian man and woman in the home. In ministry homes this modeling becomes even more important because of your wider range of influence. You can also encourage your children to enjoy some television shows and movies; but when you see things said or done that contradict your values, then your words of instruction and explanation supplement the example of your life and solidify your child's understanding of truth and reality.

Through childhood and young adulthood I was never swayed by any of this nonsense. My father and mother modeled the biblical and traditional roles of manhood and womanhood. We watched television, news, and movies; but when something ridiculous was said, portrayed, or insinuated, my father provided ample commentary in a way that my sister and I understood.

While so-called peace activists did war reenactments on screen, I looked at my grandfather's pictures from the South Pacific in the 1940s and heard his stories about being chased into the clouds by Japanese Zeros and doing an emergency landing in his C-47 on

Australia's Great Barrier Reef. When intellectuals, media elites, and politicians tell me that most problems are caused by shortages in taxpayers' dollars in public education, I am reminded that my grandfather, with only a high school education in a rural school district, flew over a hundred combat missions in World War II, married and with my grandmother reared five children, and worked until he owned his own business, which he sold upon retirement.

The ideological bombardment continues from those who do not want your boys and girls to grow into the kind of men and women your fathers and mothers and grandfathers and grandmothers were. Television and movies will remain among the favored mediums for this destructive attack on character. Parents still must make a conscious effort to teach through example, counsel, and words.

Another option parents have is simply not to view, attend, or rent television shows or movies involving filmmakers, actors, and actresses who deliberately and actively promote an anti-American, anti-family, and anti-Christian agenda. What you do is your business, but believers ought to consider seriously whether or not they should support with their money poor role models. Ministers have an even greater impetus to consider this matter.

I love old films and the occasionally released historical films that stay closer to the actual facts. I seldom attend movies and watch television even less. There are great films that uphold traditional, and sometimes even Christian, values, or at least do not mock these values. You may want to introduce your children to older films with less polished technology.

In the Computer Age

In addition to potential philosophical, ideological, and spiritual effects, parents must also be aware of the disastrous physical and social consequences to children and young adults who spend too much time in front of their televisions. Given the number of families who have computers in their homes now, you also must include any activity on a computer—aside from study, research, or business—in this category.

Perhaps you are considering possible negative social impact. You may be thinking, *At least our children are not getting into trouble on the streets when they are watching television or playing on a computer.* True, you would rather they watch television than experiment with or sell drugs, give or receive violence, engage in promiscuity, or take part in otherwise destructive behavior. However, television and playing on the computer are not the only alternatives.

Watching television or talking or playing on a computer with people you do not know is not bad or harmful in itself. However, if what is on the television is so important to your children or young adults that they habitually rush through meals and forego meaningful conversation with those closest to them in order to get back to the screen, then they have a problem that must be confronted by parents. If they will hurry through dinner, not talking with family and friends, but will spend hours talking to those whom they do not know on a computer, there is a problem.

After we moved to North Carolina, Armour joined us while he was writing his first novel. Since I was privileged to be the typist, this temporary addition of Armour to our household made completing his task more expedient and certainly added a dimension of delight to our lives. One of the fringe benefits was the enjoyment of Armour's culinary skills as he prepared and served our evening meals. Even more wonderful than the meal itself was his insistence upon ending each meal with after-dinner tea or coffee—a relaxing finale Paige and I have continued until now. We sip our beverage and engage in relaxing conversation or shared silence.

Some people prefer or are more comfortable with fantasy as opposed to reality. The surging popularity of the films and personalities of Hollywood illustrate this, as does a weekly glance at the USA Today best seller list. Consider how seldom you see nonfiction books among the top ten, or for that matter, the top fifty. Of the few nonfiction books that do appear with any regularity, most are self-help books. What does the fact that the most frequently bought books of nonfiction are the self-help type say about this generation? People need help! Unless you want your children to grow into adults who read only fantasy, fiction, and self-help—the former two perhaps feeding the need for the latter—then you must teach them the difference between truth and fiction and between fantasy and reality while they are young.

Many people, too, find it easier and more comfortable to talk to someone they do not know on a computer than to talk face to face with someone they do know. If someone says something you do not like or asks a question that makes you uncomfortable face to face, you still must look into his eyes and answer. You can just turn a computer off, go to another chat room, or even lie and continue as if nothing were wrong. Ignoring questions and fleeing responsibility is so much easier, just as to live vicariously through the fantasized love of a character in a romance novel or a sappy movie demands less than going out and finding love in your own life. You can more easily watch Hollywood action heroes embrace danger and defy odds on the screen than to pay the price in work, sweat, or blood and traverse the valley of the shadow of death yourself. There is more to this phenomenon than what is covered here, but your being aware of what is true, real, and important will help shape the way you live your life and the way you structure family time, and that returns full circle to your own personal example—the most valuable and essential tool you have for teaching your children.

Avoiding these social pitfalls is, if anything, more important for ministry families than for others. Ministers and their children are the focus of scrutiny, and sometimes criticism and hostility, to a greater degree than others. For that reason alone, communication and the bonds of love, shared activities, encouragement, and companionship are even more important for ministry families. These building blocks of commitment, devotion, and resilience will carry you through trying and difficult times. Mental and emotional escapes to the realms of fiction and fantasy will take you nowhere but la-la land, although if you go there, you will have plenty of company.

Keeping the Temple

The detrimental physical effects of too much television, while not as serious as the potential effects on the spiritual, moral, mental, and intellectual development of children, certainly warrant parental concern. There is no nice or more palatable way to put it: Throughout this country the number of fat, effete, and physically unfit children and young adults is appalling.

Extended television viewing is not the only culprit here, but it is one. Much research evidence can be cited, but why waste space and words when there is nobody doing credible research who even claims that sitting in front of the television for long periods is physically beneficial? To sit or lie down in your waking hours on a regular basis with a deadened mind and immobile body for prolonged periods can be nothing but destructive. To sit down each day for four to six hours and stare at a single El Greco painting would be equally unhealthy, but children do not generally meditate for hours on ancient paintings. They do spend hours and hours with television, a pastime that must be addressed and controlled by parents. The medium per se is not the problem; rather the activity, or better stated, the lack thereof, makes television a mixed bag.

When people watch television and are really focused on a show or movie, they seldom move. Their bodies often slip into a more deadened state than their brains. But what do most people actually move when glued to the screen? They are reaching for chips, popcorn, cookies, or soda. If television were fattening before the sugar and hydrogenated oil-laden snacks, then you can imagine the combined effect.

One or two hours a day, as long as other tasks and obligations are done, is reasonable. Three or four hours on special occasions and all day long on New Year's Day never damaged my health or mental activity. Anything more, when considering the whole of a child's growth, development, and well-being, is suspect at best.

Television viewing, however, is not the only culprit to blame for the obesity and lack of fitness among young people. Idleness, lack of exercise, and terrible nutrition have begun to work in conjunction with sedentary video and computer-based lifestyles, causing children and young adults to be overweight and obese in epidemic proportions. Adults, of course, are not exempt from this; but while the problem needs to be addressed and corrected by adults as well, they have excuses young people do not have. This excuse does not justify their being overweight but acknowledges that they have more factors working against them than do young people. As a father's metabolism will ultimately start to slow down, he has the pressures of long hours at work in caring and providing for the family; and mothers who have borne one or more children go through tremendous change and upheaval in their bodies as well.

These factors do not affect children and young adults. There is no justification for an otherwise healthy young person to be obese and unfit. This poor condition increasingly is due to choices, by the young people and their parents, rather than to situations or external effects.

The young people of nations and families should be strong, virile, and energetic. They should exemplify national and familial pride, for they will soon become the young fathers and mothers of our grandchildren, our doctors and nurses, local and national leaders, firemen, policemen, soldiers, businessmen, ministers, and builders. What pride or promise do you feel while watching overweight youths who would be challenged to finish a mile run in under fifteen minutes and who play computer games or lie around in front of a television all day? What profit comes from this lifestyle for them or for their communities?

This judgment may sound harsh, but the problem is clearly getting worse, and it will not be solved or corrected by young people of their own volition. Neither will it be solved by schools, government, or social and psychiatric experts. The solution will come from parents if it comes at all. Ministry parents again have the opportunity to set the example.

On the Subject of Nutrition

Parents ought to take as strong an interest in their children's nutrition as they would in other aspects of their lives. Avoid processed foods and sweets. Buy fresh or frozen fruits and vegetables rather than canned or prepared meals. Use brown rice and other whole grains such as barley, millet, and whole wheat rather than white rice. Use whole-wheat pasta rather than white pasta. Use fruit for desserts rather than the sugar-filled favorites. Wild game and fish, when available, are lower in fat and cholesterol and higher in protein than the meat of domestic animals. When consuming domestic animals, focus on the leaner cuts.

Try making your own bread at home, since finding bread without sugar or partially hydrogenated oil can be difficult in some stores. It you want a good shortcut, buy a bread machine and cut down your preparation time. Also, look in stores for an excellent, all-purpose bread made from the recipe given in Ezekiel 4:9.

Prepare more meals at home, and make eating out an occasional treat rather than a common practice. Having a mother who gives her primary energies to managing her household is an advantage here. She has time for preparing food that women who work outside the home do not have. A lack of time for preparation is one of the main reasons parents choose to feed children fast food or frozen and pre-prepared meals. Again, ministry families as a rule face this challenge more than others. Additional meetings at the church are a pressure. The minister's family seems to be burdened with a "command performance" invitation to the activities of every group within the congregation. That means the temptation to have more meals on the run and the reality of more meals as the guests of others with no control over the menu.

The solution is to do what you can. Eliminate sodas, junk food, and childhood favorites, such as sugary cereals. As a child, I was angry when my mother banned sugar-based cereals and limited sodas to one per day. Looking back, however, I see her wisdom and know that she was right. Now I wish she had eliminated sodas and junk foods entirely.

Children will resent some of these changes, but one defining trait of parents should be that they know more than their children. Conversely, a defining trait of children is that they do not know as much as their parents. Parents have to make their decisions based on what they think is right and best for their children, not on what children think is best for themselves.

If parents choose to adopt a new outlook on food and eating, it must be balanced with pragmatism and realism in relation to their children's growth and increasing capacities for personal responsibility. Children should be warned; then they will know better. As a parent, you are under no obligation to keep these things in your refrigerator and pantry. When your children move into their own apartments, what they keep in their kitchens is their business. What you keep in your kitchen remains your business. If a young adult wants sweets or junk food while living in your home, then he can buy them with his money or eat them at the homes of his friends and in the school cafeteria.

This approach is both rational and reasonable, and young adults will understand when it is explained to them, whether or not they admit it. You are committed not to put harmful products into your body or theirs, whether drugs or bad food, thus taking care of the bodies that God has given you and yours to the best of your ability. I understood this as a child, even when I claimed I did not, and that understanding became even more acute as I grew through young adulthood.

Most of you probably do not keep alcohol in your home; so do not keep cookies (unless you find that rare recipe based on sound nutrition), vegetable shortening, or donuts. Alcohol kills a lot of people each year. How many do heart disease and diabetes kill? How many diseases, disorders, or injuries are exacerbated by carrying excess weight?

Avoiding the myriad of junk and fast food, while important, is only half of the equation. The other half is staying physically active. General George Patton once said, "An active mind cannot exist in an inactive body." That statement holds at least some truth. Given the innate connection between mind and body, you cannot get the maximum potential output from your mind while letting your body deteriorate due to abuse and neglect.

Active people are healthier and live longer. Most people in America at one time got adequate exercise from their work and transportation. Even riding a horse for transportation burns significantly more calories and fat than using mechanized transportation. Many people in other parts of the world still get adequate exercise in these ways, but for most in the United States those days are gone. The result is that young and old alike must get their exercise in other ways.

Thankfully many of our children and youth still have the energy and vigor to get out and get moving, but they do not appear to be in the

majority. Being a close observer of both critters and people, I notice what youth are doing and what they are not doing. I can also see what their capacities are and are not. When I see a rotund ball of twelve-year-old flesh with spindly limbs sitting in front of television and computer screens for six hours while downing a liter or two of soda and eating chips, I know that he will accomplish nothing that depends on any type of physical prowess. In most cases I know that his ability to think and reason will not advance far beyond his physical state.

Some of my high school peers once turned down a free, all-expenses-paid trip to the Middle East. Their reason? For about two months they would have to get up at 3:30 a.m. five days a week and work until noon under the Middle Eastern sun on an archaeological dig. The weekends would have been free, and they would have had a free week to travel the country at the end of the work season. They were not interested. To me it was an easy way to get a free trip and see some new places.

Things have changed. Children and, even more so, young adults should be energetic, bold, and vigorous, yet many of them are not. Parents now may find themselves in the strange and awkward position of having to get their children and youth up and moving rather than having to worry about settling them down. Because television, video and computer games, and junk food have the cumulative effect of dulling minds and degenerating bodies, parents may experience more difficulty with their young adults than with their children. Children and youth need to get up and get moving, but how to get them to do so remains an open question.

Involvement in Boy Scouts, Girl Scouts, and similar organizations is good not only for the skills learned but also because their activities get the participants moving and physically active. Encouraging youth to get involved in team or individual sports is good. If a child has no playmate, a father can play ball, run, or lift weights with him.

Your church may have a gym. If so, the minister and his family should again set the example. Plan regular recreational activities for your children. Intramural basketball and volleyball are both easy.

You can also make use of local parks or outdoor property of your church for other sports. Encourage the entire family to participate.

Once, while I was lifting weights as a youth, an older gentleman came up to me and said, "Keep it up, young man, I wish I had done what you are doing fifty years ago."

"Why is that?" I asked.

"Because it's a lot easier to stay in shape if you start when you are young," he replied.

Another good reason for young people to be exposed to older people—they have the wisdom of years and experience. That older man's wisdom and encouragement have stayed with me through the years.

Again, this dilemma puts parents in a difficult position. Do whatever you can to keep your children and youth active. As long as the activity is not something that can get them into trouble, any activity you can find to keep them active is good.

As noted previously, having a dog is a good way to get children and youth moving. Dogs need to be fed, groomed, played with, transported to the veterinarian, and taken on walks and runs. The activity is good, but there are other reasons to get your children involved with dogs or other domestic animals to whatever degree possible. As a population becomes increasingly urban, there are things that are too often overlooked.

Personally, I cannot imagine the dreariness of a world without animals. Whether it is running or hiking with my dogs or watching a leopard vanish into the African bush, animals have always been an important part of my life and a reminder of the Lord's goodness, majesty, and creative genius.

Having and caring for a dog teaches a child responsibility and provides him with a friend that is always happy to see him, accepts him just as he is, making no demands or conditions, and in the case of most dogs, protecting him if danger arises. There can be no price tag put on the debt owed to canine companions. The least we can do is to have regard for their lives and make them a part of ours.

If you do get a dog, select one that suits your lifestyle, climate, and situation. A pit bull, bred for the sole purpose of fighting, is generally not a good choice for a home with children and especially in a ministry setting. A Siberian Husky is not the best idea in Miami. You also should not get a dog unless you are willing to do the necessary work to train him so that he can go more places and do more things with your family.[11]

KISS—The Secret Weapon

Three words, if remembered and put into practice, will make the good times better and the difficult times with their storms navigable. Anyone who attempts to train a child will have both the good times and the tough times. Love, affection, and KISS are the words to remember.

As parents, show love and affection for each other. Your children will notice. They will also notice if you do not. Show love and affection for your children. They need to experience your loving affection; and when they know you love them, you can reason with them more effectively or correct them when points of contention arise. Regardless of what they may say in the heat of a moment, if they know you truly love them, they realize that you are not trying to make their lives miserable.

If a minister preaches the Word but does not show love to his wife, children, and others around him, there is a degree to which whether or not he really loves them does not matter. If children do not see love demonstrated, as 1 John 3:18 indicates that it should be, they are likely to conclude that the parent's talk is different from his walk. Any point of contention becomes much more difficult when children do not feel certain they are loved and appreciated.

In a parental relationship with children and young adults, there must be rules, order, and discipline. Here parents should learn to KISS: Keep It Simple, Stupid, a popular acronym that has worked well for parents for many generations.

The best way to be sure that any operation runs smoothly and accomplishes its purpose is to keep plans and processes as simple as possible. A process is easier to keep working if everyone understands what part he plays in the plan, and what is expected of him. A family is a unit from two to quite a few. As more people get involved, a simple plan has a much better chance of being understood and properly followed than does a complex one.

When I first started driving, my dad gave me a list of between twenty-five and thirty rules to be followed at all times. This list was a bit much, and he really needed to KISS. One was, "Do not ever, under any condition, park your car with a girl in it."

"Oh," I said, "So if we go to the movies I'll just drive by the box office slowly and tell her to jump out when we get close, then wait for me while I go park. Then, after the movie, I'll get the car and drive back by, and she can jump from the curb into the moving car!" Another rule was that I was never to drive without a shirt. Frankly, when it was a hundred degrees and I was driving down to the park to play ball, I did not see a problem in being shirtless.

Whatever your thoughts on Dad's list, thirty rules was far too many. That was not thirty rules total, just thirty for the car alone. Nevertheless, I gave him credit for creativity, because some of the rules embodied things that I had never thought of then and have never heard of since.

When you think of words and rules, think *economy*. Fewer words that are well thought out and spoken are better understood and remembered and thus have more impact than many words or long lectures off the top of your head. The same principle holds true for rules.

KISS. Too much talk or too many rules leads to confusion, frustration, and often apathy. Post the rules you need. Say what needs to be said when it needs to be said. Just think it through first, then KISS.

> Love your child unconditionally.
> Give with no strings attached.
> Be there!—everywhere, all the time.
> Never give up.

CHAPTER Four

Puberty and Young Adulthood

ALTHOUGH CHILDREN NEED to be prepared for the changes that occur in their minds and bodies when they reach puberty, there is no great mystery here. Parents know their children best, and they know better than anyone else how to relate to them. Talk to them and educate them about the changes that will come. Let them know the implications of those changes and what will be expected of them as a result. Be private but be very frank.

What is of much greater concern is what happens after puberty. Legally, your child becomes an adolescent after going through puberty. Many, if not most, Christians consider this law appropriate. The reason for this conclusion is difficult to identify.

What does the Bible say about adolescence? Nothing! The topic is neither addressed nor mentioned. Why? How could there be a void of information on a topic viewed as so important? Did God and the men whom He inspired to write the books of the Bible forget to include this subject? Were they embarrassed to discuss it or could they not find the words?

The writers of the Bible never mentioned adolescence because it did not exist. Nor is adolescence a biological fact now. Some suggest the policy exists as part of a greater program by the state to subjugate its populace. David Alan Black has written a definitive work on this subject, *The Myth of Adolescence.*[12] This ground-breaking book is recommended for parents, especially for ministry parents.

Adolescence—Mentality or Myth

Think for a moment about your own views of adolescence. Are they based on Scripture? If so, what Scriptures? Have they been thought out in a rational manner? Have the assertions and insinuations of the media, government, schools, political action groups, or lawyers shaped your opinions in any way?

Then you must ask yourself other questions. Are you, your teenager, and society better served if teenagers consider themselves to be children and thus are not accountable or responsible for their actions in the same manner as an adult and not personally responsible for improving themselves in every way, leaving responsibility for their deeds to fall on parents or society? Or are you, your teenagers, and society better served if your teenagers consider themselves responsible adults and assume that they are accountable for their actions and thus have the obligation to behave, stay out of trouble, improve themselves in every way, and pursue paths of righteousness in words and actions? If your goal is to train up your child to be a successful and righteous adult, which is the goal of most parents, then why would you want to delay that process? What true benefit is there in extending childhood until an individual reaches eighteen years of age other than providing a grace period for taking responsibility, during which your child knows he can still do many things without serious consequences that he will not be able to do ten years down the line.

From time to time adults mourn and wring their hands as they relate their sorrow at seeing their "children" forced to grow up so fast. The growing-up process in America, from a legal and often practical perspective, is just the opposite. Second, what is tragic about a child or youth growing up or maturing quickly? Why would parents and society deliberately slow a child's progress in reaching the goal set before him? Were all civilizations wrong until the late nineteenth century, when the theory of adolescence became a biological and social fact with resulting legal protection?

As Black has noted in *The Myth of Adolescence*, Paul in 1 Corinthians 13:11, acknowledges only two stages of life. "When

I was a child, I used to speak like a child, think like a child, reason like a child; when I became a man, I did away with childish things." Paul writes that he went from being a child to being a man. There is no mention of adolescence. Note also that Paul cited three differences between childhood and adulthood: speaking, thinking, and reasoning.

Is it so terrible that your teen might actually start to speak, think, and reason like an adult? But teens will still behave as children, you may argue. That argument will not necessarily stand, however, because your thinking and reasoning should undoubtedly be the primary influence in dictating their behavior. When your offspring thinks and reasons like an adult, he speaks and behaves like one. Again, are you better off, and does society benefit if you keep your teen in a stage of childish thinking and reasoning?

David Bakan writes, "The idea of adolescence as an intermediary period of life starting at puberty . . . is the product of modern times. . . . [It] developed in the latter half of the nineteenth century and the early twentieth century . . . to prolong the years of childhood."[13] He followed with three developments that made adolescence an officially recognized period in the life cycle of American society. First, compulsory education laws were passed.[14] Education was mandated by law, and parents could be punished for keeping their children out of school. They could not be punished for failing to educate them but would face legal consequences for not putting their children in a government-approved school. For thousands of years, parents educated their own children, teaching them what was necessary to survive in society. In Bible times, Hebrew and Roman parents were responsible for educating their own children. The first laws mandating school attendance came in seventeenth-century Germany.[15]

Second, child labor laws were enacted, making it illegal to employ persons under certain ages.[16] This criterion lengthened childhood since early teenagers could no longer work full-time. Because they were not allowed to work, young people became economically dependent. For thousands of years it was not this way.

Young people worked with parents or with a master tradesman as an apprentice until they could make it on their own.

Third, Bakan noted the creation of a juvenile justice system to segregate younger lawbreakers from older ones.[17] Teenagers were no longer responsible for their criminal actions, despite the fact that for thousands of years legal systems treated teenagers as adults. Because the nation's laws have turned adults into children, young people have been getting away with murder, rape, and other horrific crimes, receiving only a symbolic slap on the wrist, if that!

Lawyers and politicians seem to be among the most frequent defenders of the abrogation of teen responsibility with the coming of adolescence. Three reasons for their support are obvious and must be kept in mind when they are telling you the reasons you should not expect proper behavior and responsibility from your teens or from anyone else's youth. There is much money involved, especially in the realm of juvenile crime. Political power and control is at stake. The desire to expand power and control is natural, but no one—however respectable his profession or position—should determine what you expect of your children and teens.

The *bar mitzvah* (for young men) or *bat mitzvah* (for young women) is a significant event in Jewish society, recognizing profound changes in body and mind. This celebration has marked a turning point when young people assume responsibility for controlling their own desires, accepting accountability for mature religious actions, and assuming adult community responsibilities.[18]

Teens will behave as adults as soon or as late as they are expected to. When you theorize that teens are not capable of behaving as accountable and responsible adults and relay this message to them through words, actions, and the laws of society, they tend to behave irresponsibly like children. Thus, the myth of adolescence becomes a self-fulfilling prophecy. Tell your children that they cannot possibly be expected to behave as adults, and they will not. Why would they?

Tell them in no uncertain terms that they are expected to act and behave as adults and that they will be held responsible for their actions by you, if not by other authorities in their lives, and they are much more likely to speak, think, reason, and act as adults. As Black puts it, "Our expectations as parents are the important factors in getting our teenagers to act like responsible adults."[19]

Teaching your teens to behave as adults and demanding mature responses from them is not only the best and most logical way but also the only biblical model for transition into adulthood. Do you maintain that your children, and you, are better off by your restraining them from adult behavior until they are eighteen? Before you write off the Jews of Jesus' time as backward or ignorant, realize that they had nothing resembling the scourge of endemic teen crime that rips the fabric of modern society. Nor were they familiar with the flocks of aimless, willfully homeless teens, roaming without steady work or stability, fleeing what they cannot comprehend and protesting what they cannot understand.

Nevertheless, the idea of adolescence is here to stay. Parents must realize and understand its pitfalls so that they can help their young adults avoid the snares that come from extending childhood well into adulthood. Ministry parents again must wrestle with the ramifications of this issue and take the lead in helping their own children make the transition from childhood to young adulthood responsibly. In so doing, they are also having a wholesome influence and dynamic impact on the families in their congregation as well as an impact on society at large.

Keep it simple. Smoking pot and crack and criminal violence, premarital sex and sexually transmitted diseases, drinking alcoholic beverages and using tobacco, speaking with profanity and being disrespectful of elders and women, unrestricted frivolities at parties and during spring break trips—you have a better chance of avoiding the aftermath of heartbreak if you guide your children into maturity with an emphasis on spiritual depth and human responsibility. Your offspring can be kind, respectful, well-read, well-spoken, and they can be taught and expected to conduct themselves with dignity and honor.

The Attack of the Dangerous Ideologies

With the educational changes brought about by the creation of adolescence, the government now has much greater control over

Puberty and Young Adulthood | 89

how and what is presented as truth to children and young adults. History can be completely rewritten and taught accordingly. Traditional roles can be changed so that boys and young men are feminized from the earliest ages. Religious beliefs can be attacked freely and replaced with humanism.

Who becomes more powerful when the law prevents parents from disciplining their children? How can those same parents be arrested and prosecuted if their child or young adult commits certain crimes? What happens when young adults, although having attended state-sponsored schools, receive no real education and learn no trade? Who benefits from handouts of taxpayers' dollars? When people eat at the public trough, they usually vote for the ones who fill it and against the ones who pay for it.

You cannot change the system, but you do not have to follow like sheep those who go along with what you know is wrong. Let your teens know that you expect them to be responsible and to behave with maturity. The Lord, according to Scripture and the example of Jesus, expects the same as well.

Rather than wallowing in an extended period of fabricated childhood, your teenager must consider himself responsible for his own actions, walk with upright character, and strive to better himself spiritually, physically, and intellectually. Hold high expectations for your sons and daughters, whose rate of maturity will most often coincide with what they understand is expected of them.

Trusting Breeds Accountability

For children to enter young adulthood does not mean that they no longer need parents. Rather, some aspects of their relationship to their parents change. As a young adult shows himself to be trustworthy, honest, and deserving of responsibility, then he should be given more freedom and be allowed to make more decisions. Trust, however, is something that must be earned. Be cautious about trusting anyone merely because of who he is, what position he holds, or how old he is. He needs to show in a number of ways that he deserves your trust. In the same ways your young adults must demonstrate maturity to you.

If you show yourself to be honest, courteous, thoughtful, dependable, and are not in trouble in school or with the law without just cause, then you will earn more trust, freedom, and responsibility. Any young adult who is honest and reasonable can understand this principle. If he cannot understand it, he is in no position to earn trust or responsibility and has other problems with which you must deal.

My parents took me to meet with world leaders, to attend dinners or other functions with men of renown, and they allowed me to converse with their friends and acquaintances. My youth did not prevent them from giving me responsibilities. I was taught how to secure our home. Even when someone else was present in the house while my parents were away overnight, I had responsibilities for protecting our home and caring for my sister. My parents called daily and spoke directly to me for an accounting of how things were going. When I gave my word, I determined to carry out my father's instructions, especially when I was entrusted with responsibilities that most boys my age were not given and of which most adults thought me unworthy.

As you continue to teach, train, educate, guide, and counsel your young adults, the virtues of truth, honesty, and objectivity are paramount. Although these virtues are crucial for any parent, a minister who is lacking in any of them will probably experience more problems relating to his children than will a parent not in ministry. People, young and old, expect to see these virtues in a minister, and that expectation is justified.

Truth and honesty are demanded of all believers, but for one called to proclaim the gospel of Christ and to shepherd and comfort those under his care, they are vital. You can be a believer and still not have gained full control over your sinful nature. A minister, on the other hand, although still a sinner like the rest of us, must have a degree of control over his sin nature worthy of his position in spiritual leadership. A minister can struggle against certain temptations or with his temper or with treating a staff member in a way that he later acknowledges is wrong and sinful, but he must never lie, and he must be reliable so that even his detractors know that his words and commitments are binding.

How does this matter affect children in the minister's home? No one knows parents—whether in ministry or not—any better than the children of their household. No one is watching any more closely than these impressionable young people. Matching your walk with your talk is a goal that will be measured daily by your children.

Some sins, although not acceptable before God or man, are understandable because all believers are fallen and sinful creatures. The believer must acknowledge his sins before God, and sometimes to an offended party, then try to do better next time. Honesty and truth, however, are not flexible options for a minister, who has greater responsibility because of his leadership role (see 2 Tim. 4:1–5).

Objectivity, likewise, is a critical virtue in the character of a minister. People may look to him for help in resolving problems with one another. He must answer their questions and explain the meaning and relevance of Scripture for their lives. He must show love, compassion, and acceptance to all without partiality. These obligations demand objectivity, and most people inherently expect this even-handedness in a minister. Even the hardest of men, the boldest sinners, the most vicious criminals, and the most selfish narcissists will sometimes seek out or listen to a minister when they need help.

With these being the expectations of individuals and of society regarding ministers, naturally these expectations also become those of the minister's sons and daughters. In fact, due to the constant proximity and interweaving of lives, which is the nature of family relationships, sons and daughters can sometimes be more demanding in their expectations than the general public and church members.

Therefore, a minister must embody truth, honesty, and objectivity in his actions and dealings at home. His calling demands these virtues. If you have upheld them in your preaching, teaching, and counsel and fail to live by them at home in your relationships with your spouse and/or sons and daughters, those closest to you are sure to notice your inconsistencies and might even label such actions as hypocrisy. Once this happens, your relationship with the young adults in your home, as well as your leadership goals, will have been undermined and compromised.

The Priority of Family

One of the most common complaints from the sons and daughters of ministers is that ministers are so busy with the work of the church and the problems and challenges of its members that they neglect the needs of their own sons and daughters, and sometimes those of their wives as well. These needs are usually spiritual, emotional, and relational—foundational in scope.

Physical needs are more readily apparent, as would be their neglect, to all looking in from the outside. If a minister's sons and daughters lacked adequate food, clothing, or medical care, this inadequacy would be easily noticed by all, and he might quickly be called to give an account. Physical needs are also much easier to meet than are emotional and spiritual needs. They essentially require only money and the willingness to spend it, something most parents—ministers or not—readily and willingly provide.

Tending to your child's spiritual and emotional needs—whatever his age—on the other hand, takes time, energy, and often a long-suffering and determined will. Tending to their relational needs is your responsibility. Your continuous interaction with each son and daughter as a distinct individual with unique needs, desires, strengths, and weaknesses will best manifest itself as you relate to, counsel, and lead in a way accommodating the different needs of each. Such commitment requires much time, thought, patience, and creative initiative. All of these obligations are more difficult and time-consuming than writing checks and in some ways more demanding than your financial resources; your children need you to give of yourself physically, spiritually, mentally, and emotionally.

I was privileged to know personally and to grow spiritually under the ministry of a man who cemented his legacy as one of the greatest preachers to take the pulpit. He was one of the most popular, beloved, and influential pastors in the history of Christendom; and, by anyone's standards, he was one of the most successful.

Having known him and associated with him over a period of twenty-five years, I can affirm that his reputation in these matters is deserved, that the world and the Church are better for his having lived and ministered, and that his love, compassion, and desire to serve his fellow man was genuine and at the core of his heart.

Tragically, his single, complete, and outstanding failure was in his family. He often remarked that he was "married" to the church. The failure at home haunted and saddened this godly man to the day he drew his last breath and, though unrealized by many, took its toll on his ministry and his heart.

The family is the foundation not only of a society and nation but also of the community and the church. In the family circle, values are taught and character is formed from the earliest stages of life; and there love, acceptance, and forgiveness should be found even when it can be found nowhere else. These virtues of family are crucial to children and young adults as they embark on the early steps of their lifelong journey and spiritual struggle in pursuit of righteousness.

If the family, and in particular the head of the home—the husband and father—is not there to fulfill this need, then who or what will be? History has shown that even when chaos, violence, injustice, economic woes, wars, natural disasters, and ideological assaults on Christian values rage like wild fire in high winds, love, compassion, gentleness, and righteousness can survive so long as the bond of family remains. Conversely, when the family begins to fragment and disintegrate, even the benefits of long-standing peace, prosperity, and security are not sufficient to maintain moral order and hold together the fabric of a society. The decadence, violence, and social woes such as crime, divorce, drug abuse, and children living without one or both parents—mostly at taxpayers' expense—have skyrocketed during the years in which America has become wealthier and more powerful and when its people have become more prosperous than their grandfathers and great grandfathers could have imagined. This perceived progress has come in the years when education is not only available but mandated by government for all.

The family is the one institution that is indispensable. Under communist, Islamist, or Fascist regimes in which Christian worship and assembly have been outlawed and Christians have been hunted, killed, and imprisoned, Christian families still survived.

They continued to read the Scriptures, pray, worship, and live and walk in the ways of the Lord Jesus Christ. Love, compassion, forgiveness, and righteousness therefore have survived amid the fires and chaos of evil. A minister must put his own family before every other obligation and responsibility in his life except his personal commitment to God (1 Tim. 5:8).

You cannot train a child without love, counsel, teaching, and time. You cannot love your sons and daughters with a full understanding of your obligation before God as a parent and not determine to put forth every effort to train them to walk in the ways of the Lord. A minister cannot forsake his family to put in more time for his church or to better the kingdom of Christ just as he cannot practice hatred so as to better understand love.

Inconsistencies, perceived or real, between what a parent preaches and teaches and how he actually lives will frustrate relationships with his sons and daughters as quickly as anything. Children and young adults are keen observers, often more so than older adults and especially on matters that relate to their own lives.

House Rules

Even as your children enter their teen years, they still must live in your home. Parents are entitled to and must have rules for their home and for those living in it. With truth, honesty, objectivity, and the wisdom bestowed upon them by the Lord and Scripture, parents must lay down those rules. A good dose of common sense also seems appropriate in these matters.

As a parent, in your house you make your rules. This principle is both reasonable and right. Remember the KISS principle, though. Clearly think through the goals and objectives you plan to accomplish with these rules, discuss them with your spouse, and then lay down as few rules as possible. There is no benefit to making things any more complex than they have to be.

Consider any subject or task you like; prepare to teach this task to your teen. You have two possible plans. One is a three-step program followed by a brief summary or explanation of what is to be done and accomplished. The other is a twenty-one step process.

By which method is your child going to grasp your teaching and attain efficiency in keeping your rules most quickly, and which method has the best chance of long-term success with the lowest probability of human error? Of course, it is the three-step program. The adoption of fewer rules does not automatically suggest oversimplification.

God gave Moses Ten Commandments to take down to the Israelites (Exod. 20:1–17). Jesus gave eight Beatitudes in the Sermon on the Mount, summarizing the essential principles of righteousness that invoke the blessings of God (Matt. 5:1–11). Jesus gave the rich young ruler, who explained that he had always kept the commandments of God but wanted to know what else he lacked in order to gain eternal life, only one thing to do (Matt. 19:21). Why only one command? Because Jesus knew the man's heart. Even though he was a good man, his first allegiance was to his own wealth and prosperity, not to pleasing God. Jesus gave only one command because there was only one pertinent issue—the rich young ruler's first allegiance (Matt. 19:22). Money was not the issue, and neither were the other commandments of God. Jesus only needed to point out that one thing was more important to the young ruler than his relationship with God. Jesus could have said much more, but He was not one to waste words. Another example of an economy of rules is found in Exodus 20:12: "Honor you father and mother." It is simple yet thorough. God could have extended the list: Show love to your parents. Do not talk back to them. Do not criticize them or speak ill of them. Be there to help and assist them. Provide for them as they grow old. Speak to them with reverence.

The list is just getting started, and already there are six new commandments. Fortunately God encapsulated all needed. Honor is a principle that was ingrained in Hebrew children from their earliest years and one that needs to be likewise ingrained in ours. They knew what honor was and all that it entailed. Honor encompasses all that is in the previous six ersatz (that is, fictitious) commandments and then much more. As the Hebrews fully understood the concept of honor, God had only to give the command, "Honor your father and your mother."

Keep your rules simple in content and few in number, and everyone will benefit. When words and principles are well thought out, you really can say much with few words. When parents interact with their sons and daughters on a regular basis and remain aware of what is going on in their lives, they will find ample opportunity to make the finer points and deal with the details.

Dogmatic Monologue vs. Respectful Dialogue

When you lay down your rules, explain yourself and be open to respectful dialogue. You are a family, not a marine recon unit. Explanation and dialogue are a part of the educational process. You do not want your young adults to do what is right only because you said to do it. You want them to do what is right and good because, understanding the difference between right and wrong, they prefer to do what is right and honorable in the eyes of God. When your young adult is striving to do what is right and good because of his own convictions, you have made the greatest achievement in parenting. All you can ask of any person, young or old, is that he try to do what is right.

In addition to its educational value, parents should be open to respectful dialogue because young adults, as a result of the culturally accepted and legally supported policy of adolescence, find themselves in a difficult and often confusing position. They should have the capacity of thinking and behaving as adults, yet they are not challenged with the responsibilities or blessed with the privileges of an adult.

If teens were as inherently irresponsible and incapable of adult reasoning as the policy of adolescence would have you to believe, then the rate of crime, accidents, and utter chaos among teens would be so astronomical as to make the current situation seem like social utopia. Young adults are capable of thinking, reasoning, and behaving with maturity. To tell them directly, or indirectly, that they are not capable of behaving as adults and then to demand that they be responsible and not get into trouble is confusing, aside from being ridiculous and self-contradicting.

For example, many proponents of abortion say that abortion is not a desirable thing so they want it to be rare and infrequent; yet they also want it to be legal and widely available. Both your children and you can abide by the laws of the country without adopting its bankrupt moral code or hedonistic philosophy of life.

By remaining open to dialogue and allowing young adults to make as many decisions for themselves as they prove trustworthy to do, you facilitate their maturing into responsible adults. No alcohol in the home, no drugs, no disrespectful or profane language, everyone comes to the table for dinner, everyone to the living room for Bible study, only the allotted amount of entertainment television, never showing disrespect towards a guest, cleaning up what you mess up, getting the trash out on Monday and Friday, no shooting guns in the house (I once blew a sizable hole in one of the interior doors because the large and uninteresting book I chose as a backstop for my target was not as resilient as I thought. Although my parents never knew, since I had the door fixed and repainted before they returned home, I must agree that the no-shooting-guns-in-the-house rule was reasonable). All of these are examples of good and reasonable rules that are solely the business of the parent.

In regard to activities outside the home—what sports your off-spring play, what hobbies or recreation they choose, the choice of friends with whom they associate, what they study and read, what type of jobs they do, what pets they want, what trips they take, and what clothes they wear—they should be given as much choice and leeway as they have proven themselves ready for. Only by making choices, having success, surviving mistakes, and learning from them does a young person grow in maturity and understanding.

Drawing the Lines

Although freedom of decision and expression for teens both within and outside the home is important, definite lines are to be drawn by parents regarding what teens do away from home. Séances and long parties are out of the question, as should be any venues or events that promote alcohol and drug use, sex, and rebellion against moral order and structure.

Although these issues involve activities outside your home, there are reasons why parents have both the right and the obligation to overrule. If anything goes wrong, you will be paying the medical bills and increase in insurance. The police will be coming to your door to ask you questions and possibly press charges against you. You have a right to insist, for the sake of your testimony and convictions, that there are activities in which no one living in your house is going to participate.

The line between what is acceptable and what is not is sometimes clear and bold and at other times fine and more difficult to distinguish. As for the finer lines, there is sometimes not an easy answer. Parents, knowing the dispositions and capabilities of their young adults, must make the judgments based on their own thoughts, wisdom, and prayers.

In my own teen years, the fact that my dad explained to me the connections between demonstrating responsibility and honesty and having more freedom to make my own decisions was a motivating factor. I wanted to do what was right rather than what was wrong, but being rewarded for honesty and reliability provided further encouragement. Teach when opportunities allow, admonish when necessary, and always reward and encourage when things are done well.

How to Do Education

By federal law, young adults must be in school up to a certain age, differing to some degree state by state. Unless you are a minister serving on the international mission field, the issues at hand do not appear to be any different for parents in ministry than for parents who are not. The choices come down to public school, private school, or homeschooling.

The rating of public schools among most evangelicals is not high. One young minister testified that he did not see any problem with public schools, citing as evidence that he got saved while attending public school. First of all, he did not get saved as a result of the public school curriculum. Second, people have been saved in concentration camps and in prisons, which does not mean they are good places to be.

The initial factors that must be considered by parents are finances, time, and resources. If you do not have the money to pay for private school tuition, then that option is out. If at least one parent does not make the commitment of time and resources—chiefly knowledge, education, and teaching and reading material, then homeschooling is not viable. Some may not have an option beyond public school education.

If this is the case, you must prepare to make the best of it. If you have taught your young adults the precepts and principles of Scripture at home as children, then they will be entering the philosophical "lion's den" with a good foundation, and that is crucial. Talk to your young adults regularly about what they are studying and being taught in school, then study the same subjects yourself as much as possible so that you can either affirm or correct what they have been told in the classroom. Make it very clear to them that they are not to take their moral values or spiritual and philosophical beliefs from what they are taught in the classroom.

If you or some of your children have been fortunate enough to have had a good teacher with solid Judeo-Christian values in a public school, you are blessed indeed. There are some good ones out there, and I have an aunt who is one of them. However, teachers do not always control what material they use in a classroom, and they certainly cannot control school policies.

Schools refusing to teach abstinence until marriage, classes that have students practice putting condoms on bananas, that serve chocolate condoms as snacks, that teach homosexuality as an alternative lifestyle rather than as a deviation, that introduce gross revisions of history with the intention of either defaming our forefathers and other outstanding Americans or skewing their words and ignoring context in order to attack the traditional values that made America great, that teach relative rather than absolute truth (which leads to the violence that has plagued schools), and that build a general hostility toward Judeo-Christian principles are but a few of the reasons why public school education has failed and in so doing has driven parents to look for alternatives.

Despite the constant clamor of the educational establishment to be given more funding, a lack of money is not the problem. More money is being spent now on education and per student than ever

before in history; yet we have more school violence and more poorly educated students today. A hundred and fifty years ago the average teen may not have known as much about math or sciences, but he knew what he needed to know to make a living and to function in society as a law-abiding citizen who did not have to rely on government handouts. Furthermore, many of them knew more of foreign language, culture, history, philosophy, literature, and the English language than do students today. Why is the state of public education getting worse as increasing amounts of money flow into its coffers?

If you must send your sons and daughters to public school, be vigilant and communicate with them daily. Maintain an ongoing dialogue regarding what they are being taught and shown. Correct what must be corrected, backing up points with reason and documentation, something public school educators often cannot do, and teach them important lessons that the schools omit. Finally, due to the recent events that illustrate the problem clearly enough, get your young adults into boxing or some other martial arts or defense program. Physical skills are at a disadvantage against firearms, but some knowledge of defensive skills is better than none. This last point is not a spiritual mandate, just a thought based on current events and the state of public education.

If you have the option of private school or homeschool, such a course is well worth your consideration, even if it means some sacrifice. To expand upon the academic distinction of public school, consider these points from Robert H. Bork in his book *Slouching Toward Gomorrah*. Between the turn of the century and World War I, an exam was given that all high school students planning to attend college were expected to pass. Neither Bork nor most of the educated people with whom he discussed the exam could answer most of its questions.[20] That likely means that I, as well as the great majority of high school and college students today, would fare even worse.

The *National History Standards*, funded by the National Endowment for the Humanities, are intended as guidance to teachers, curriculum planners, and textbook publishers. As is to be expected, contributors from the West are trivialized or ignored in American history, while those among Africans and Indians are magnified. Men who played important roles in our history are left out, and organizations and events that reflected poorly upon America are magnified.[21]

The *Standard* makes no mention of the Constitution of the United States, yet McCarthy and McCarthyism are mentioned nineteen times, the Ku Klux Klan seventeen times, and Harriet Tubman, who helped rescue slaves through the Underground Railroad, six times. Henry Clay and Ulysses S. Grant, on the other hand, are mentioned only once, while Daniel Webster, Robert E. Lee, Alexander Graham Bell, Thomas Edison, Albert Einstein, and Jonas Salk are not mentioned at all. George Washington appears fleetingly but is never identified as our first president. The founding of the Sierra Club and the National Organization for Women are considered noteworthy, while the first meeting of the US Congress is not.[22]

A new version of the history *Standards* appeared in April 1995. According to Bork, it is less political and not as biased against America, yet some bias remains. Students are to learn about the religious beliefs of American Indians and Africans but are to be given nothing about Christianity. This obvious injustice, though to be expected, is amazing, considering the worldwide impact and influence of Christianity in contrast with the religions given preference by the *Standards*, to say nothing of a comparative analysis of theologies. In the new *Standards* students must also analyze feminism, described as "compelling in its analysis of women's problems and the solutions offered," and fifth and sixth graders must be able to explain why the National Organization of Women was formed.[23]

These examples make very clear two aspects of American public education that should be of concern in view of the dollars being poured into the system. The modern education is academically inferior to that available to students a hundred years ago and to that which many parents are able to give in their homes. There is a decided bias against Christianity and against Judeo-Christian values. This fact is further illustrated by recent efforts of some public schools to ban prayer, the Ten Commandments, Christian clubs and organizations, and ban of the phrase "under God" from the nation's Pledge of Allegiance in the Ninth Circuit Court of Appeals.

Who Protects the Children?

The safety of students is also an issue. While private schools are certainly not immune from violence, most of the violence and murder on the rise in schools nationally has been in public schools. There has been the usual effort to blame accessibility to firearms. However, school violence was virtually nonexistent in years past when firearms were more readily available and their usage less regulated than now.

The attacks of September 11, 2001, have awakened some Americans to other potential terrorist targets. Schools are one of these targets—public schools being the most likely to be hit simply because they are generally bigger, offering the opportunity to inflict more casualties with a single blast or a shooting spree. Clearly from some of the captured video tapes, terrorists have been training to infiltrate buildings and kill people. These targets could be business offices, government buildings, airports, or schools.

However, you need not be alarmists, nor should you be engulfed with panic or necessarily change your lifestyle. My family has not changed ours, either because of thugs on the street or because of terrorism, and we are not going to. We still do everything that we did before September 11, 2001, and frankly, are not worried about much. Yes, we are alert and have food and water and provisions for a week at a time, but that precaution was on the scene long before September 11. Ice storms and hurricanes have sent us to the emergency box a few times, but terrorism never has. Do not live in fear—except, of course, a fear of the Lord, which should prompt you to seek His face more determinedly.

The point to be understood has come down to two questions. One, can you give your children and young adults a better education than the public school system either via private school or by homeschool? Two, can you provide a more secure learning environment than the public school system? If you answer yes to one of these questions, then you have some things to think about. If you answer yes to both of them, then you would be hard-pressed to come up with a good reason to send your sons and daughters to a public school. The principle is a simple one. If you can provide something that is better for your sons and daughters than that which someone else can provide, whether in education or anything else, then why entrust someone else with the task?

As for private schools, some are better than others. Most are better than public schools in maintaining discipline and teaching the academic curriculum. The fact that you can choose one that upholds the philosophical and spiritual principles in which you believe is an advantage, as is the fact that parents, at least in some private schools, may have more influence upon matters involving their children and youth. In public schools they essentially have none.

For example, by attending a private school, I was able to travel extensively with my parents so long as arrangements were made with each teacher to have class work completed by the time I returned. In public schools, this option would not have been allowed. Parents of private school students also often have the opportunity for an ongoing and productive dialogue with teachers and administrators, which seems absent in most public schools, despite the fact that parents pay the salaries of these teachers.

Students educated at home continue to score at higher levels on tests than students in public schools, and they have distinguished themselves with their academic achievements. Aside from the benefits of a superior education, homeschool is marked by the lack of wasted time. When I look back on my junior high and high school years, prominent is the massive waste of time. One thing in which our schools have achieved distinction is their uncanny ability continually to excel in noncreative ways of wasting increasing amounts of time.

Never did a week pass when I was not aware that I could have completed all of my work in a quarter of the time I had to spend in class and on homework. Too many teachers had lectures, or what passed for them, which were long on words and short on substantive content. If someone is merely regurgitating the words from a textbook that I am going to read anyway, why am I wasting my time, hours out of my week, listening to him? I could simply read the chapter, the book, or his notes, and be ready for the test.

The single activity that accounted for the most wasted time, however, was the continual assigning of busywork to pass class time. Answering questions at the end of a chapter, when the student simply goes back through the chapter, finds the answers, and copies them down is one example. The most ridiculous and wasteful aspect of this method came after engaging in busywork for an hour in class; then the teacher would assign more busywork to be done at home in the evening.

Sometimes the homework assignments were legitimate, but why not use class time for work that is relevant and legitimate? Either give a lecture that is informative and pertinent or give an assignment that actually has educational value, making the time spent in class profitable. Time alone is not equivalent to work, as many educators seem to think.

When I protested this practice of wasting class time and then assigning homework as the bell rang to signal the period's end, I was usually told that this was preparing me for the "real world." Clearly they thought that being a young adult precluded thought and reason. I got to school at 7:30 or 8:00 a.m. Classes lasted until 3:00 or 3:30 p.m. Then I had athletic practice for the school teams, from which I did not get home until 7:00 or 8:00 p.m. Then, on most nights I had a minimum of two hours of homework and sometimes four or five hours. I may have been a bit slower than some students, but the work still had to be done.

That was an eleven or twelve hour day before I even started my homework. So on a light day I was putting in thirteen or fourteen hours on school, and often more. What percentage of adults in the "real world" put in an average of fourteen to sixteen hours, five days a week, on their jobs? I know a few who do because they want to or because they have chosen to think that it gives them the best chance to reach their lofty goals. Most people I know put in eight or nine hours and then go home and do what they want to do. So, which "real world" were those teachers getting me ready for?

There is nothing wrong with people working long hours. Those who choose to do so make the choice either because they want to or have put themselves in a situation in which they have to. In the case of the latter, I am not only referring to those who have, by bad luck or bad judgment, put themselves in a financial hole and therefore must work more hours or more jobs. There are many whose lifestyle or occupation infrequently requires more time spent on the job. Ministers often find extended demands and longer work days. That is fine. However, these are choices that young adults should make for themselves once they get out of school and start being paid for their work. You can steal my money, my car, or my possessions and I will get by, but if you steal my time you are stealing part of my life.

Perhaps the greatest virtue of homeschool is that it is not based on the premise that time equals work accomplished or lessons learned. There need be no one-hour class periods with bells ringing in between. Success is measured solely by accomplishments and proof of knowledge and learning, not by time spent. If you can accomplish something in three or four hours, why stretch it into eight?

Homeschooling allows more time for travel and family activities than does conventional schooling, and parents do not have to force children and young adults to sit under the authority of someone who may hold different spiritual and philosophical values than they have projected for their family goals, which can be a serious and confusing problem to young adults. I have known parents who taught their young adults that homosexuality was wrong and then had to explain to them why they were under the authority of an openly homosexual teacher in a public school.

As for academics, homeschooling is one way to ensure that your young adults get an education and not merely a daily trip to school. The challenge here is that parents must be on top of things academically. Do your homework and be willing to work in conjunction with other parents who are homeschooling their children. Hold yourselves to higher standards than those of public schools. If the government and the education establishment can ever show that homeschool students regularly score lower on testing than do public school students, they will quickly have homeschooling shut down by law.

You want your young adults to be educated and equipped for the journey ahead of them. This fact alone should motivate you to put all of your mind, heart, and soul into supervising their education. Be innovative and creative and make sure that your youth have the opportunity to socialize with their peers and with older adults as well. Any education should be varied and well-rounded. Some private schools have begun to allow homeschool youth to participate in their athletic programs. If your son or daughter wants to compete, check possibilities in your area.

There are different views on the matter of education even among Christians, and each of these three options have both fervent supporters and ardent opponents. It is neither our desire nor objective to instruct parents in the matter or to be critical of their respectively chosen paths. Our objective is to raise and define the relevant issues as we understand them and then, as in all matters, to prompt thought and dialogue among the readers.

Missionary Kids

Parents who serve as missionaries in an international setting have special challenges. The practices and policies of various denominations and sending groups vary, but the primary issue is the same for all: Who decides how children are to be educated? Some would say that it is the sending board's choice. That alone offers many options—the administration at headquarters or the regional supervisor or the mission-sending agency's governing board. A few might suggest that the child should make the call. Hopefully most would opt for parents to make this decision, considering options available and the needs of each child. The latter would certainly be closer to the biblical paradigm, which invests care of the child to parents, who then have the prerogative to enlist help from others as needed.

Some missionaries have been forced, as a matter of the sending board's policy, to send their children and young adults to boarding schools where they study and live most of the year away from their parents. The reason for this policy, to give it the best twist, would be the belief that local schools may not provide an adequate education to prepare students for stateside universities. Some board personnel seem to have prejudicial opposition to missionaries who want to do homeschooling. Unfortunately, the reasoning often associated with this position suggests that such a commitment would demand an inordinate amount of the mother's time, thus keeping her from "meaningful ministries."

Such policy, at best, is misguided and lacking in cogent reasoning. At worst it is hypocritical and defies principles of Scripture. How can you train a child in the way he should go if you are rarely with him? Given the fact that young adults are considered children and must, to some degree, be kept dependent through their high school years, how can you continue to meet their physical, spiritual, and emotional needs, spend time with them, counsel them, and teach them the important lessons of life if you spend most of your time away from them and leave their education and spiritual growth in the hands of someone else who may or may not share your values?

Evangelical Christians have been outspoken in their belief in the importance of family. Southern Baptists added an article on the family to their confessional statement by mandate of their Convention in annual session. Making the family important seems to imply that family members love, serve, and support one another. At the very least parents would be expected to have an active relationship with their children and young adults, observing them, listening to them, teaching them, counseling them, and participating in activities with them on a regular basis (see Deut. 6:1–12). If parents are not doing these things, then what are the purposes and obligations of a parent?

Is a parent obligated only to provide food, clothing, and shelter? No one can study Scripture seriously and come away with this view; yet if you do not take an active and regular part in the lives of your children and young adults, then you may be providing little more than these necessities.

"Hear, my son, your father's instruction and do not forsake your mother's teaching" (Prov. 1:8) seems to extend far beyond the three physical necessities. "Train up a child in the way he should go"

(Prov. 22:6). Anyone who knows anything about training any kind of critter—four-legged or two—knows that this verse implies much more than these necessities and acknowledges the undergirding of love in a myriad of ways. Common sense can be nearly as helpful here as Scripture.

Training is a process that takes time, patience, repetition, observations, and much interaction, regardless of what or who you are training. Training up a child requires time, patience, and a lot of work. Unless you are there to observe the child on a regular basis, you cannot know which things need to be praised and commended and which lessons need more work and reinforcement. This discipleship cannot be accomplished without interaction, and that means being together.

Aside from the requisites of teaching, trust must be built through associations, shared experience, and communication. For parents and children to have these things to the degree necessary is challenging, to say the least, if they live in different places. Most parents want their children and young adults to confide in them and to feel comfortable in coming to them with their problems and questions. That happens when a strong bond of trust is built over years of an active child-parent relationship, which can, and under the circumstances, should continue to grow through the young adult years. Taking children or young adults away from their parents' home and putting them under the care, influence, and rule of someone else can make a child vulnerable to losing the foundations necessary for this type of relationship and in so doing runs contrary to tenets believers hold and profess regarding family.

Some have agreed that the boarding schools are better for the children because they are westernized and offer a more familiar environment in which the child is more comfortable. The fact is that children often adjust more quickly to a new environment than do parents. Languages are learned more quickly and easily by one who is young, and children often learn languages faster than their parents. Furthermore, children adapt quickly. They do not have twenty or thirty years of an established pattern, culture, job, and circle of friends to leave behind. Children are pretty good at living wherever they are. As long as their basic needs are met, they can always find activities and friends with whom they can enjoy fellowship and fun.

Contrary to what is often assumed, the children and young adults of missionaries usually do not ache longingly for their home in the United States. The country where their parents serve and where they have grown up is the one they consider home. It has been far more common to hear of children and young adults who were born or grew up on the mission field having trouble adjusting to life in the United States than to hear of their having difficulty coping with life abroad. Believers should be more conscious of being helpful and supportive of missionaries' children and young adults when they return to the United States and have to settle into a new way of living in what to them may seem to be a foreign culture. Life on the mission field with its problems and challenges seems to be best addressed by families who find their strength in one another.

Missionary parents who face a problem with their sending boards on how to educate their children have the right and, for the sake of their children, the obligation to take a stand and if necessary fight for whatever God has placed in their hearts concerning the education of the children God has entrusted to their care. No sending agency or denomination or any other organization has the right to tell parents where their children should live and go to school, let alone to mandate their exodus from the parental home. There are often sacrifices that those called to missions must make. The unity of the family, together with the right to supervise the education of their own children, however, is not one of them.

Even differences of educational standards in local schools can be compensated with supplementary homeschooling. There will be minor difficulties between doing education abroad, whatever your method, versus in the United States. Although there are different challenges, the same basic principles apply. The bottom line is that parents must prayerfully and carefully consider all options and make their own decisions concerning the venue and methodology for the education of their own children.

CHAPTER Five

Gender:
Is It an Issue?

IN CONSIDERING THE CHALLENGES of training children and leading young adults, a question unique to modern times must be answered. In an increasingly gender-neutral culture, should you rear girls and boys differently? You better! This answer is not a popular, politically correct one. To explore the question fully would constitute a book, but any treatise on parenting would be incomplete without some discussion of an issue that has so pointedly attacked the foundations of the Judeo-Christian faith.

According to Scripture, the creation order began with God's creation of the man and woman—both in His image but each with a different role to play in the divine economy.[24] The model for marriage in Ephesians 5 does not denote a difference in the value or spiritual status of men and women, but it does clearly set forth a difference in roles. Common sense and science have verified that there are biological differences between men and women. God, knowing better than any human being the intricacies, needs, and capacities of His own creation, has thus assigned to men and women different, but complementary, roles. The roles are clear, despite the desperate spins of those who, although detesting this model, still wish to live under the umbrella of obedience to Christ (Eph. 5:22–23).

Christ is not merely a symbolic head of the church with whom men and women negotiate the parts of Scripture they want to embrace or deny. You do not live and adapt your way of life as co-heads or co-leaders of the church. Christ is the head of the church and, therefore, over all. You either live by His commands and precepts to the best of your understanding and ability, or you are not following Him.

In a ministry family, the husband must be the head of the wife and of the home. He is obligated to provide, protect, see to the well-being of his wife, children, and even his animals. In this responsibility, of course, the animals may be much easier to please! When a decision must be made and there is no consensus between husband and wife, then the husband must have the final word. He would do well to consider carefully the input from other family members, especially his wife who is one with him and created to be his helper.

A wife must be subject to her husband (Eph. 5:22) and must respect him (v. 33). A husband is the head of the home (v. 23) and is to love his wife just as Christ loved the church and gave Himself for her (v. 25). Consider the ramifications of these instructions on how parents are to train a son or daughter.

For a man to be the head of his home, he must be knowledgeable, wise, and resourceful. To provide, he must be reliable, efficient, and energetic. To protect, he must seek to maintain physical strength to the best of his ability. To lead spiritually, he must be fully committed to Christ, to the study of Scripture, and to living by the precepts found therein. He must be a servant to both his family and others. He must know how to love and show his love. His love must be active—felt by his wife, children, and others around him—not passive so that those around him are left to wonder where they stand in his affections. He must be able to forgive just as God does (Ps. 103:12).

When you understand this requirement for godly manhood, you begin to realize the enormous and challenging task before you if the Lord has blessed you with a son. You should also realize the pitfalls and consequences awaiting you if you allow your sons to be feminized by modern theory and the twisted feminist ideology being taught in schools and universities and being promoted by the media and entertainment industry.

The roles assigned to men by Scripture require masculinity, that is, taking manhood seriously. This mandate does not suggest that men should, or can, with the blessings of God, be abusive or insensitive toward their wives and children. To the contrary, they must be loving, gentle, understanding, and forgiving, while at the same time providing counsel, wisdom, education, guidance, the necessities of life, and a shield of protection and security. This challenge will usually require the utmost of a man's masculine virtue.

Fathers and Sons

My father spent years teaching me by word and example to love, serve, give, and forgive. To teach me to protect, defend, to be courageous and aggressive, to compete in athletics, and to survive and provide without the resources of urban civilization cost him immeasurable bumps and bruises, a broken hand, ankle injuries that never completely healed, muscle cramps in the middle of the night, a lot of sweat and some blood, and more than his share of trips to the emergency room.

A father who is not the head of his home cannot teach his sons to assume the responsibility of being heads of their households when that time comes. An effete or effeminate father cannot teach his sons to be tough, courageous, and aggressive when aggression is needed. Either he will raise effete or effeminate sons, or they will be strong and aggressive but beyond his control and perhaps beyond the control of anyone else except the enforcers of law. An inseparable component of teaching boys strength, toughness, and aggression is helping them determine the proper time and place for their use of these components. Boys and young men must know when to love and when to hate, when to heal and when to kill, when to be silent and when to speak, when to mourn and when to dance, when to embrace and when not to, and when to pursue war and when to make peace (Eccles. 3:2–8).

None of this is easy, and the burden on the shoulders of a father is tremendous. Such a burden is not bad or unfortunate. A son is a great blessing, and many sons are a greater blessing; but to whom much is given, much is required.

Those who disagree will undoubtedly point to men who had little or no interaction with their fathers yet turned out to be good

and strong men. Men can rise above the most challenging circumstances, but many more bear tragic scars of life because of the
absence of the influence of a loving and strong father. Pointing out
exceptions only proves the rule.

When boys and young men have grown up and done well without a father, you often find other men in their lives who made up
for what was lost. Older brothers, grandfathers, teachers, coaches,
police officers, or merely a concerned neighbor may have "taken up
the slack" at times. In no way is the father's necessary influence in
the lives of these men meant to minimize the invaluable contributions of the mothers, who, without the help of a father, reared their
boys and young men to be noble and successful. When something
must be done and no one else is going to do it, all credit and praise
is due to those who do. Many mothers, with sacrificial and unconditional love, devotion, dedication, and timeless effort have made a
difference, against all odds, in the lives of the boys and young men
that God has put into their lives. For this unconditional loving
commitment to a formidable task, they are to be commended and
given utmost respect.

The intent is not to trivialize or discredit the contributions of
women who have had to rear children and young adults alone. On
the contrary, they are to be admired and respected as having lived
by love and given their best regardless of the result. Nevertheless,
the best way to train children and young adults and the only way
mandated by Scripture, is for a loving and nurturing wife and
mother committed to her children to work with a strong, gentle
husband who is equally committed to his wife and children and
who accepts the assignment of being the head, physically and spiritually, of that home.

Fathers and Daughters

The role of a father is critical not only for the development of
boys and young men. Whenever women find themselves in trouble or in difficult situations of their own making—whether in
relationships, lifestyle, or any other realm—almost always the
father was not there. Even when present, the father sometimes

fails to show adequate attention, affection, and leadership to his daughters.

The impact of such negligence cannot be overstated. The degree to which this connection prevails is astonishing. The connection is painfully obvious in the cases of girls who had little contact or interaction with fathers who did not even live with them. The number of women suffering the consequences of bad decisions—even when they have come from families which, on the surface, seemed to be the embodiment of the archetypal Christian family—has been both amazing and telling. These are families who seem to have everything going right for them—well-dressed, well-spoken, polite, caring, spiritually sensitive, and respected in church and community. Most people, tending not to observe much below the surface of things, cannot imagine that anything within these families could be far from perfect, let alone wrong. Certainly this scenario increases its tragic impact in ministry homes where the fallout not only affects the minister's family but the families of the congregation as well. Families can be like the ocean. What you see on the surface reveals little of what lies and moves below.

Things go wrong in families who seem to have it right more often because of a lack of understanding than from deliberate neglect on the part of the father regarding the needs of his daughter. Girls and young women have an innate need and desire for the attention and affection of a strong and loving man in their lives. Until the time they decide to marry, this obligation falls upon the father's shoulders. If a daughter does not get this attention and affection at home, she may seek it elsewhere. Fathers, in addition to training up their sons to be strong, loving, and protective men, must also spend time with their daughters and show them the attention and affection they need and desire.

The role of a wife in Christian marriage is set forth in Scripture with equal clarity. Together with the other powerful forces attempting to feminize men and masculinize women within our culture, there are many who wish to spin the precepts of Scripture until they have subjected the Word of God to their own notions of how things should be.

Nevertheless, in Ephesians 5, wives are admonished to be subject to their own husbands in everything, as unto the Lord, and they are to respect their husbands—two separate commands. Being subject to her husband requires that a wife choose to be submissive, faithful, loyal, and respectful.

On many occasions women who, while obedient, faithful, and loyal in their crucial commitments, speak or act disrespectfully toward their husbands. Sometimes this lack of respect manifests itself in what they say or do. Other times what they say about their husbands to others or their behavior in casual conversations with others while away from their husbands reveals their disrespect. These things include answering questions not asked and discussing private matters, which their husbands would not have approved being aired in public conversation.

A Mother's Influence

The biblical admonition affirms that it is just as important for a wife to respect her husband as to submit to him and remain faithful and loyal to him. A wife and mother must teach these principles, by word and example, to her daughters as preparation for their future happiness in marriage. The wife of a minister, rightly or wrongly and whether she wants to be or not, will become a role model, at least to some degree, for the families of her husband's congregation.

Wives are admonished to be submissive to their own husbands and to conduct themselves with a chaste and respectful attitude (1 Pet. 3:3–4). Peter does not suggest that wives should not enhance their appearance, but rather he emphasizes that outer beauty should not be their only, or even their foremost, concern. Physical beauty is a wonderful thing; but when unfortified with an inner beauty composed of love, gentleness, faithfulness, compassion, and the grace of a gentle and quiet spirit, beauty limited to the outer shell can sour and even turn ugly. When you see a woman blessed with incredible physical beauty and yet lacking the qualities of character that form inner beauty and cultivate, sustain, and exemplify the "gentle and quiet spirit, which is precious in the sight of the God," you need not wonder what a life of close confidence or companionship with her might look like a few years down the line.

The gentle and quiet spirit that is precious in the sight of the Lord is precious in the sight of many men as well. Such observations tend to anger feminists. Most fathers want their daughters to marry a loving man who is gentle, who lives with wisdom and discretion, and who will protect his wife with his life. A man with this character will usually have no interest in a marital commitment to the woman who wants to be just as drunk and loud as the boys, who thinks that she can do and say everything they can, and who attempts to prove above all else what she calls her "independence," meaning that she will do and say whatever she wants, whenever she wants, and as loud as she wants, with no one telling her what to do or not do. Women who behave in this way often end up with the weakest and most effeminate men as husbands. Certain behaviors that are tolerated, and even expected, on the part of men are not taken so lightly when embraced by women.

A minister's wife must consider the fact that her daughter's behavior, which can and should be influenced by her own life and wisdom, will have much to do with the quality of the man to whom her daughter gives herself in marriage. That which is precious in the sight of God is noteworthy in the eyes of many good men. Solomon put forth this insight, perhaps with a bit more color (see Prov. 9:13; 11:22).

The oracle of King Lemuel in Proverbs 31 reveals a godly mother's description of an "excellent wife" whose "worth is far above jewels." Verses 10–31 should be exemplified by and taught by all mothers to their daughters.[25] Although the tenets of Proverbs 31:10–31 are considered radical and even irrelevant in the modern era, ministry wives certainly should know that timeless principles never change. Each generation must simply find timely ways to manifest those timeless principles.

You can fully understand much in Scripture; but if you start to alter or ignore even those passages in which the points are simple and clear, then there are no limits to the kinds of behavior in which you can engage and to the experience-driven beliefs you can hold, while still claiming to be a follower of Christ. If you can change some parts of Scripture, there is no logical reason why you cannot change all. Jesus simply did not offer such flexibility of commitment. God did not give His Word in Scripture to facilitate human debate. He gave mandates to be followed just because He said so.

The excellent wife found in Proverbs 31 is trustworthy and thus honest and loyal. She is kindhearted, wanting to do good for her family (vv. 11–22). She performs the necessary tasks of keeping the house with a positive and cheerful attitude (v. 13). She does whatever she has to do, with what means she has, to procure and prepare food for all those in her household (vv. 14–15).

According to the feministic spin, the Proverbs wife and mother is a precursor of the modern "working" (that is, employed) woman (v. 16). OK, so she bought a field and planted grapes on it. Is this a career in real estate or agriculture? There are people who have bought fields and planted crops for a hobby to pursue when vacationing from the obligations of their careers. Such fabrication is not merely a theological stretch but more likely theological yoga. Those who make this argument have completely divorced the verse from the context of verses before and after, something interpreters who seek an accurate interpretation of Scripture with honesty and objectivity cannot do.

The woman described by King Lemuel's mother clearly gives plenty of time and attention to her husband; gathers and prepares food for him, her children, and her maidens; makes clothes for herself and her family; keeps the house; spends the necessary time with her children; and gives time and bounty to the poor. When, amid all these obligations, does an eight-hour work day five days a week, a one-hour commute time, and a one-hour grooming and preparation period for the day-away-from-home fit into this equation? It cannot. A professional woman does not belong to her family for usually a minimum of fifty hours a week. Somebody is going to lose much of her time and attention, and rarely, if ever, will it be her employer, clients, or customers. Her husband and children inevitably are the losers.

The entirety of this passage clearly suggests that the woman bought the field and planted the vineyard with money allotted to her by her husband or by profits earned making and selling linen garments and belts through her home-based family industry or from her personal inheritance or dowry (v. 24). This innovation and productivity is not only permissible according to Scripture but is to be commended and encouraged. Women can do many profitable things that do not control their lives or take time from their families amid the tasks inherent in maintaining a household and caring for their families. Making clothes, doing arts and crafts, baking pies, selling real estate part-time, keeping a vegetable garden, and many other endeavors can be interwoven with family responsibilities with flexibility and creativity.

All women who plan to be wives and mothers would do well to learn some skills whereby they can bring extra income, food, clothing, or other necessities to their families. As with the woman in Proverbs 31, however, these endeavors must be secondary to the obligations of home, husband, and children. Clearly, Proverbs 31 teaches that a woman's commitment to home and family should and does require most of her time. Planting vineyards and producing clothing were pursued secondarily when other tasks were done.

This principle inspired me to establish the Magnolia Hill Cottage Industries on the campus of Southeastern Baptist Theological Seminary to provide a venue through which mothers who wished to remain in their homes could prepare products for sale and thereby earn extra income. They have no overhead; they control their own schedules; they remain at the heart of home and family; they add to the family income during the austere days in which their husbands complete schooling and professional preparation.

Sending your children to day care while you are at work, to a setting in which you have no idea what they are being taught or what might happen to them because you are not there, may not be the best way to fulfill your maternal obligations. Leaving your children with a babysitter all day does not provide maximum mothering, regardless of how well you know that babysitter. Ministry moms must take note that filling your days and evenings with the work of the church, volunteering for every task and making yourself available to the beck and call of everyone, is as challenging as employment when it comes to managing a home and family.

The evidence of the pitfalls, stress, and harm done to children as a result of long-term day care and parental neglect in the home is clearly there. To present and delve into the relevant research on this modern phenomenon would be a book in itself. Although some research claims that children suffer no negative effects from long-term day care and from having less time with their parents, the overwhelming evidence—even from secular psychologists and general surveys—presents another story.

When thinking through this matter,

- First, use your common sense. How did families function in cultures throughout the world for thousands of years and in our culture until the 1960s? Did these cultures have more juvenile crime than this generation or was it substantially less? Were the divorce rates higher or lower? Did they have more children and young adults on drugs— legal and illegal—or fewer?

- Second, the idea of women going to work while their children are put in day care or tended by feminized stay-at-home fathers is now a significant aspect of the liberal-feminist agenda. They are seeking to create a reversal of traditional male and female roles through numerous emerging "scientific studies," which "show" that such reversals have no consequences. Of course, there are also "scientific studies" that show no relationship between smoking and cancer. The case has been well made that any premise can be proven through the manipulation of statistical data.

- Third, you must ponder the obvious correlation between the rise of juvenile crime, crime among women, the number of children and youth on legal drugs with negative side effects, and the rise in divorce with the exit of mothers from the home and into the workplace. You could say that there is no connection, only mere coincidence, but actions and facts are more revealing than words.

Returning to the virtuous wife, hard work does make a woman stronger and tougher (Prov. 31:17). Much excellent research has revealed that lifting weights is very beneficial to a woman's health for a number of reasons. A good workout will build some muscle, tone, and maintain it. Cardiovascular work four days a week with treadmill, aerobics, or whatever your preference is also important. Gird yourself with strength and live longer and healthier. A wife can and should be proud of her work and her family, and she will work as long as she must to accomplish her tasks and goals (v. 18).

No Christian woman who is serious about her faith can ignore those in need, even outside the family, when it is within her power to help them (v. 20). Again ministry moms have an excellent opportunity to weave together family and church efforts to help those in need. By involving your children, you use ministry time to build family values. You will not fear nature's fury because you will have done your part to be sure that those in your household are prepared (v. 21). Many commentators see meaning beyond clothing your children to include a mother's commitment to lead her children to spiritual protection and salvation in Christ (v. 21). This efficient and hard-working woman adorns herself beautifully (v. 22).

Given the context, you must assume this woman's husband is known and respected in his community, in part at least because of the character and grace of his wife (v. 23). When you encounter a married woman who has no grace or discretion, the lacking in her often returns to haunt her husband.

This woman has tremendous strength of character, spirit, and will, which are all properly channeled (v. 25). Dignity appears to be a virtue nearing extinction in our culture. Increasing numbers of women are loud and even profane in speech, lack discretion in behavior and dress, and carry in their manner no semblance of feminine grace or charm. However, the virtuous wife can smile at the future because she knows that her work has been done well and that she walks closely with the Lord. She undoubtedly has the inner peace that passes understanding and reveals itself in a cheerful countenance and a manner that exudes optimism and lovingkindness.

Some would tend to think of men when considering wisdom, but a woman of wisdom is to be desired and cherished (v. 26). Depending upon a woman devoid of wisdom for anything of significance can be costly. She will be unlikely to provide any help. Conversely, a wise woman will be a source of considerable support and valuable counsel to her husband, children, and all who call upon her. A truly wise woman is kind, and she teaches this kindness to her children and others through her lifestyle and her words.

In verse 27 is found the fourth mention of "household," and the bulk of the passage is filled with references to the work that must be done in the house. Clearly the chief role assigned to wives by mandate of Scripture is the care and maintenance of the home and the task of caring for their children. Although all wives cannot be forced into these priorities, those who consider themselves to be anything more than nominal Christians certainly should consider boundaries so clearly identified. Those who do not like its precepts and are unwilling to abide by them perhaps should be honest enough to acknowledge openly a source of authority other than Scripture. Although there are obscure and difficult-to-interpret passages in Scripture, Proverbs 31, Ephesians 5, and 1 Peter 3 are not among them. The words, their meaning, and the commands therein are quite clear. Any woman should refrain from placing her faith in, or giving her allegiance to, God if she finds His precepts repulsive.

The point is not to push anyone away from the love and saving grace of Jesus Christ. Certainly for ministry parents, the emphasis is rather upon the importance and sanctity of Scripture and the necessity to be consistent in living what you teach and being governed by what you embrace as truth. All Scripture is inspired by God; it is not merely a road map for optional excursions on the journey of life. Rather, it is to be studied, followed, and obeyed without debate. Ministry parents will find their greatest agony with their own children if they teach truths they themselves reject in their own lifestyle.

Considering what is known of the virtuous wife from the previous verses, you would think the words concerning idleness are superfluous (v. 27). Perhaps King Lemuel included them merely for emphasis. Scripture has nothing good to say regarding an idle and lazy wife. Nor do I. In fact, there are few things more burdensome or troubling for a man or child to endure than life with a lazy woman.

"The proof," it has been said, "is in the pudding." The children of the virtuous wife and mother, "Rise up and bless her; her husband also, and he praises her" (v. 28). A virtuous woman in the tradition of King Lemuel's oracle does not have to prove anything to anyone. All those who have dwelt with her know her. They have been the beneficiaries of her kindness and compassion and have observed her virtues and tremendous worth. They will be pleased to lift her up and to care for her as she journeys toward the twilight of her life. Indeed, "Her worth is far above jewels."

The essence of true and lasting beauty is found in verse 30. There is nothing wrong with physical beauty and personal charm. They are blessings from God and are lovely to behold in a woman. The manner in which beauty and charm are carried and used can be wrong or noble.

Women can remain beautiful and carry themselves with grace and dignity into their golden years, and many do; but the years take a toll on all. It is the truth of life and beauty. Everyone suffers the effects of the aging process. I look pretty bad at thirty-four, but in twenty years it will be a lot worse.

To admire and enjoy physical beauty is fine, but you should not let it become an obsession, as is the strong tendency in our culture. Take care of the body that God gave you and do all that you can by natural means to enhance your beauty. Beyond that, however, it should never be your driving passion.

As King Lemuel indicates, the true and lasting beauty of a woman is engendered from within—her heart, her spirit, her attitude, her demeanor, and her character. She begins with fearing the Lord, and she continues with a willingness to walk in His ways and to abide by His commands. Her actions are bathed in a spirit of love, gentleness, kindness, and compassion. This composite is the quintessence of true loveliness and beauty in a woman, and only this beauty is immune to the ravages of time, years, and disuse.

These obligations are for every God-fearing woman to fulfill in her home and teach to her daughters. She must also transmit these principles to her sons, as did King Lemuel's mother (Prov. 31:1–2) so that when the time comes, they, too, will know what qualities to seek in a woman.

The Strength of Fathers

Fathers must challenge their sons to be men of truth, honor, love, and vigilance. They must teach them a strong work ethic, as well as some skills for making a living. Even if they choose to pursue a different work than did their fathers before them, or one that does not incorporate the skills he teaches them, still these lessons will be good for a young man to have as a resource for the furture. To possess such skills is even more critical if the son chooses to go into ministry. Unfortunately (and an indictment of the callous and ungodly behavior of many Christians), occasionally churches have used the fact that a pastor with a family for whom he must provide has few or no other job skills as a method of coercing him to act against his convictions—even when the point of disagreement involves no violation of Scripture or breach of integrity on his part.

Fathers must also teach their sons to be protectors of their wives, children, and of others who cannot protect themselves. A man should protect his family at all costs, but it is advisable to know the laws where you live and in the places you spend time as much as is possible. Being a protector means not only being able and willing to protect but also knowing when and when not to act. Again ministry fathers grapple even more with these issues since they are often called upon to mediate volatile situations when civil authorities fear to do so and thus refuse.

Fathers must teach their sons to be gentle and to treat women with honor and respect. As in all things, a father should do so first by example and then with words. To the best of their abilities, fathers must teach their sons how to relate properly to women and to understand their needs, desires, and mind-set. In this matter, mothers can also be of great help.

Mothers, too, must teach their daughters how to relate to and understand men—their needs, desires, and ways of thinking. As with the converse, the fathers should help as well. Mothers must exemplify and teach the principles of Ephesians 5, 1 Peter 3, and Proverbs 31 to their daughters. They should teach them how to care for the home and for their children, how to cook, how to shop efficiently, and how to manage the household. They should be taught skills they can use to earn extra income or to save money at home, such as making clothes, gardening, typing, or computer skills.

An Emerging Gender Issue

In addition to being protectors of family and loved ones, men are also the protectors of the nation. This assertion will undoubtedly anger certain people. According to the April 8, 2003, edition of *USA Today*, there are currently 210,177 women in the United States military, composing about 15 percent of its armed forces. However, men are still the protectors of our nation.

This statement is not meant in any way to be hurtful or disrespectful of those women serving, or who have served, in the armed forces. All women who have served faithfully and given their best to the task assigned them are to be commended and respected for their commitment and work. As the civilian beneficiaries of a strong and dedicated military, the nation thanks all soldiers who serve and have served, making sacrifices on its behalf.

The issue has been pushed upon society from within as well as from the highest echelons of government. The debate does not arise as a challenge to a system or way of life that always has been or even one that has a long history. The situation is quite the opposite. In the long, bloody history of warfare, the idea of allowing women into the military, let alone combat, is a very new one. The genesis of the American servicewomen came with the establishment of the Army and Navy Marine Corps in 1901 and 1908. Decisions to place women into or near combat came decades later.

To go into much detail on this matter would be beyond the scope of this book, but anyone who wants to give serious study to the matter can find ample research and writing on the issue. Brian Mitchell lays the facts out without the sugar coating of political correctness, which seems so prominent in a postmodern era.[26] For the brutality and horrors of war are neither sweet nor politically correct.

The broad question remains: In an increasingly gender-neutral culture, should you raise boys and girls differently? By way of illustration, you can focus on an issue real to the new millennium. If women are placed in combat roles, men will still do the fighting, killing, and dying. Even marginal enemies cannot be defeated by only launching missiles and dropping bombs. If women are placed in front-line combat against a capable enemy, our men will suffer even higher casualties as they risk their lives and compromise their missions to protect the women; and the women, when captured, will suffer horrible torture, as the Israelis learned in 1948.

To change this quite natural and noble response on the part of men, a nation and society would have to completely change the way it rears children. Only success in reversing the training of boys and young men can nullify this impulse for them to put themselves at further risk in a combat situation in order to protect women.

Is this the kind of society in which you want to live with your children and grandchildren? I don't think so. Ministry parents then must give themselves carefully to moving counterculturally with their own children. God-given role distinctions must be honored and guarded in interaction among siblings in your home and with their friends. Social issues quickly become theological issues as you understand God's far-reaching purposes in the creation order. With the onslaught of a unisex culture, ministry homes may well prove one of the last bastions training youth to pursue the genuine biblical paradigm for manhood and womanhood.[27] In an increasingly gender-neutral culture, should you raise boys and girls differently? Yes, not just to fight our nation's wars but also to pursue the biblical mandate with which we as believers have been charged. Especially is this mandate true for those in kingdom leadership.

Of course, women must sometimes fight to defend themselves, their children, and loved ones. Pioneer women in our nation shouldered a rifle or shotgun to defend their homes or wagons against marauding Indians or bandits. Sometimes they were alone with their children, and at other times the attackers outnumbered the defending men to such an extent that all potential shooters were needed. Modern-day cases will also arise when women must take up arms to defend themselves, and they should be applauded and saluted. Teach your young women who are able how to defend themselves with and without weapons. Defensive skills are better had and never needed than to be needed even once but unavailable. For a woman to defend herself and her children when her back is to the wall is noble, but to seek or desire the right to pursue combat is lunacy. You might consider how many men with front-line combat experience would hope that their daughters someday could train for such combat and be among the first sent to the battlefield in the case of hostilities.

Steven Goldberg, chairman of the department of sociology at City College, City University of New York, has provided some of the clearest and most honest research on the inherent differences between the sexes in his book *Why Men Rule*. His observations provide further confirmation that parents should rear their boys and girls differently.

The argument in Goldberg's book centers upon the universality of patriarchy, which he defines as, "The presence in every society, past and present, on which we have any evidence . . . of male attainment and male dominance."[28]

Goldberg illustrates that the uniqueness of male and female begins with the physiological differences in the sexes, not because of mere socialization. Socialization, to the contrary, is determined because of what is understood and acknowledged (by most) to be differences in men and women. An understanding of these differences prompts most parents to teach their boys that they cannot hit girls, to help their mothers or any other women who are trying to carry a heavy load, and to learn skills that will enable them to provide for and protect their families. Those in ministry families have a much higher mandate because they know that beyond physiology and sociology is theology and God's immutable creation order.

Understanding physiological realities and limitations should be further encouragement for parents to refrain from pushing their daughters to be fighters or bread winners or to focus on the career ladder and abandon thoughts of family. Because most understand innately what all anthropological evidence suggests, that is, that all societies have been and must be based upon the family, the importance of motherhood looms ahead and challenges parents to teach their daughters qualities that will make them attentive and caring wives and mothers.

No masculine quality is superior to any feminine quality. These distinctive characteristics of manhood and womanhood should not be classified as superior or inferior. They simply are what they are. Your boys are boys; your girls are girls. You always love them equally but sometimes treat them differently. Masculine qualities are not superior to feminine qualities, only different. In the same way, the role assigned by Scripture to men is not better or more prestigious than the role assigned to women, only different.

Ministry parents must be aware of the failure, or inability, even among committed Christians, to understand the interconnectedness of ideas, actions, cultural shifts, and what may seem to be the most minor and insignificant shifts away from the precepts and commands of Scripture as this movement affects the overall health, stability and goodness of society at large, the quality of life for their children and grandchildren, and the effectiveness, or lack thereof, of Christians to impact a world that burns with hatred, evil, and all forms of immorality. When ministry parents ultimately stand at the judgment seat of Christ, first and foremost, they want to place their own children at His feet as crowns.

The interconnectedness of ideas, actions, cultural shifts, and seemingly small deviations from Scripture must be considered in how the future will be formed and shaped and in what will become the reality of all institutions and society, including the family and the church. Otherwise committed Christian men, including ministers, may take the directive of Ephesians 5, which places the husband as head of the home, as a license to behave as a dictator who makes all decisions but fails to consider the needs of his dependents. He may fail to hear his wife's counsel; he may refuse to listen to her with an open mind and heart; and he may be derelict in treating her with gentleness, lovingkindness, and respect. He may fail to spend sufficient time with his children, to show them adequate affection, or to give priority to being a part of their lives in every way. To those who question him, he may respond with some retort regarding his God-appointed position as head of the home and of the church.

Ministerial Obligations

What of the minister's obligation to love his wife as Christ loved the church and gave Himself for her? The kind of love that Christ had for the church demands much more than a statement, especially from the man who is God's anointed shepherd to lead His people. This love must be lived out; it must be accompanied by sacrifice when necessary; and it demands devotion, gentleness, forgiveness, and lovingkindness. And no one stands any more responsible before God to emulate this love than the minister.

These obligations are further stated in 1 Peter 3. To live with your wife in an understanding way and to show her honor as a fellow heir of the grace of life is challenging indeed, especially when the caveat suggests that to ignore this responsibility means your prayers will be hindered or, more literally, "chopped off." That would be quite a blow for a minister husband! If the minister is also a father, more questions evolve. How would the daughter of such a father fare as the years passed? How would his son treat women based on what he had observed at home? Especially for ministers, what model would be set by such a husband and father for the men in his congregation? What would be the long-term result for enriching or wrecking church families? What would be the impression and reactions of non-Christians who visited the church or interacted with its members?

The integrity of a minister reaches outside the family circle. Can he support political leaders who blatantly violate biblical principles in their own lives and fight to eliminate any vestige of Christian principle from laws, schools, currency, or even from the nation's pledge of allegiance? (see Prov. 17:15). Ministry kids, as well as members of your congregation are continually watching for consistency and integrity in the lives of their leaders.

On the other hand, ministry parents are just as responsible to model acceptance and love for the individuals in contrast to rejection and hate for the wrong they espouse and do—that is, loving the sinner while hating his sin. Your kids must learn the heart of redemption and forgiveness. Forgiveness is an act that emanates from the heart, and you must be willing to forgive someone for a wrongdoing. You can and should say, "I forgive you, but I will not support the wrong you are trying to do." Nowhere are these lessons better learned than in a ministry home, and no setting provides a better channel for lessons in redemption and restoration to flow throughout the congregation.

Some ministry parents have great gifts in the marketplace and unusual capitalistic instincts. Amazingly, these gifts are used in diametrically different ways. One pastor will harness these gifts and pour them into extending the outreach of his congregation. John Morgan, pastor of Sagemont Baptist Church in Houston, Texas, is such a man. His entrepreneurial skills have produced one of the most vibrant churches and multifaceted ministries on God's earth. The church spends no money on advertising its programs and pours that money into community ministries—disaster response, crisis support, physical relief.

On the other hand, other pastors with such gifts devote a significant time to building a lucrative business on the side to increase their own net worth. Unfortunately, this time is not only taken from the church but also from time this pastor could be devoting to his family. Bi-vocational pastors are not the target here; rather the attention goes to pastors with full-time salaries who exploit ministry time and demands with side ventures for their own gain. Their children are in the box seats, observing these moves carefully and probably embracing the ethical system behind the choices of their parents. Capitalism in itself is not wrong—even for preachers. However, a preacher carries greater responsibility to be scrupulously honest and forthright in how he spends his time and energy on the field and in his own home. What will it profit a minister to gain money and possessions and lose his own children to God? Ministry parents must stand against those things that are clearly and strictly forbidden by Scripture.

Even the practice of usury or collecting interest must be carefully considered before the minister is a participant. My husband and I love making gifts of cash as well as things, but we do not make loans to family or friends. By painful experience we have learned it brings only grief, and by Scripture we are forewarned of its potential harm. What positive effect could a practice forbidden in Scripture possibly have on society and upon individuals? When engaging in that which is forbidden in Scripture, what is a Christian father teaching his sons and other young men in his church who might look up to him?

Christians, especially those in ministry, must be aware of this interconnectedness of things. What may seem to be the most minor deviations from Scripture and harmless adoptions of new cultural roles can, and do, have serious consequences and repercussions for the individuals, families, and the society of generations that will follow. The tendency is never to return to right—that comes only at great cost, if indeed your own way is the inevitable result, and that means hitting bottom sooner than later.

Perhaps you in ministry homes can bring change for the better to your world if you live your lives according to Scripture and resist compromise on your convictions even in your family life. Maybe you cannot. But some must try.

You ought not to follow Christ for the purpose of bringing about change in government, institutions, societies, or even your own family. You obey Him and walk in His ways simply because it is right, and because He has commanded you to do so. You honor and praise Him because He is your Creator and Lord and the giver of every good gift. You do not have to give an account for the actions of nations, governments, and institutions, but you are accountable for your own personal actions and for what you do with the gifts, blessings, and opportunities bestowed upon you by the Lord. Children are the most precious gifts any ministry parent can receive. Although parents are not accountable to God for all the actions of their children—whether in childhood or in adulthood—they are accountable for whether or not they have done their best to train their children up according to the precepts of Scripture, regardless of whether those precepts of Scripture blend easily with the trends, preferences, and ideas of modern culture.

The Gender Question in the Church

All who understand that there are differences between boys and girls that emanate from creation order find logical progression to the fact that those differences come into play in church order, as well as in the home. God, through Scripture, has clearly mandated male leadership in the home, as the metaphor based upon the home and relationships within the home unveils the Lord Himself and His relationship to His church.

No logic would presume that God would mandate a model and design for His church that is different or in opposition to what He mandated for the family. In fact, the model He used for His relationship to His beloved bride, the church, is beautifully illustrated in the husband's sacrificial love of and service to his wife. The solitude of your own quiet place is the perfect setting to lay these questions before the Lord in prayer, to study and contemplate the Scripture with an open heart and mind, and to think through these issues. God's Word has conclusions for you, but you may be surprised at how clearly the setting of a ministry home with its inner personal relationships can bring the Scripture to a living model.

In the church, just as in the family, there must be strong male leadership—not only at the top but at every other level as well. Of course, women have important roles and pivotal assignments in the church. Women have Sunday school classes, Bible study groups, missions activity groups, and other edifying organizations. Woman-to-woman ministries are strongly mandated by the apostle Paul (Titus 2:3-5), and they have much to offer to the women and girls in their churches and communities.

To teach one model at home and a different one in the church makes no sense. Therefore, ministers who determine to be heads of their homes will carry this biblical pattern of male leadership into the church. Ministry parents again cannot function effectively in their own homes using a standard in contradistinction to what they put in place in the church. That the training boys and young men receive from their parents at home prepares them for their responsibilities in their own homes and that these principles be solidified and reinforced in the church is both desirable and necessary.

The importance of having strong male leadership in place in the church as well as in the home is the training structure for rearing up strong leadership in young men of integrity who are committed to walking in the ways of Jesus Christ. If a church accepts overall feminine leadership, its membership will not likely include a significant number of strong men of determination, commitment, moral courage, and strength of purpose.

There is little likelihood that a man who is truly the head of his home will be comfortable or enthusiastic about sitting under the spiritual leadership of a woman. There are exceptions to every rule. You may find a strong man eagerly sitting at the feet of a woman who teaches him and leads him. However, unless the number of exceptions is enough to become greater than the number that constitute the rule, then exceptions only further prove and establish the rule.

Strong men who are truly the heads of their homes will usually select a church led by a man of integrity and strength, and the presence, help, and leadership of these men is greatly needed. Fred Luter in New Orleans, LA, is one pastor who complemented his leadership in his family by calling out men to lead in the church. As a result, his congregation continues to reach more men than the average congregation. In the process, Pastor Luter's church has gained national attention as a church of strong families, and his own family is the strongest among them!

As boys get older, and particularly as they reach puberty and move into young manhood, things change. Their thoughts, desires, needs, questions, attitudes, demeanor, and behavior start to change; and strong male leadership becomes vital. They need a pastor who is a man of integrity, principle, and strength to whom they can look, and how much more does that need to be true if the pastor happens also to be their father. A pastor cannot do everything or be in all places at all times. The men under his leadership should have the same virtue and strength and take the lead in the lives of the young men in their families and in the church. These men will be counselors, teachers, organizers, and leaders for the boys and young men who take part in the various church classes, seminars, and activities. How much more effective they will be if they have seen exemplary fatherhood in their pastor's home! Yet again being all you ought to be at home enhances a man's ministry as well.

When a woman is the primary teacher or counselor for young men in the church, they inherently know that she has never been and will never be where they will be. Men and women have different experiences and react to the same thing in different ways. They think differently; they often tend to like or dislike different things; their desires are different; their fears are different; their reactions to their desires or fears are often different. They may, and even should, feel that different things are expected of them as they mature, and some of these differences are most decidedly gender-based!

The same is true with girls and young women. They need to have godly and committed women as their teachers, counselors, and leaders. Aside from the obvious difference in the sexes, occasionally young women will need to ask questions or seek counsel on matters best discussed without the presence of a man. Committed Christian women are needed to prepare young women for their roles in home and society.

Chapter Six

TRANSITIONS: PASSING THROUGH

DURING TRANSITION FROM CHILDHOOD to young adulthood, parents dare not let family activities stop just because sons and daughters are growing older, maturing, and developing new interests—not to mention becoming busier with extracurricular activities. Their offspring will begin to be more independent, which is both good and natural. If an otherwise healthy young adult does not begin to claim his independence and move toward maturity, something is wrong.

Siblings—Unite or Divide

Interaction with parents and family never ceases to be important for teens. As young adults continue to mature, they need access to the counsel and wisdom of parents; they need to see examples, assuming they are good, of how their parents handle situations, challenges, and difficulties, which they will soon encounter in their own lives. Brothers and sisters can develop and maintain a bond of love and empathy that will remain for the rest of their lives.

In many families siblings do not remain close after leaving home, and a close relationship is not essential for success or contentment. Nevertheless, those siblings who do remain close and who look out for and support one another throughout their lives are better for having maintained that bond than are their counterparts who have forsaken it. When giving general consideration to the precepts of Scripture and to the nature of unconditional love, any other choice than to remain close and connected would seem counterproductive to the task of continuing the generations through family legacy. Sometimes the issue of fellowship among siblings will be decided by the disinterest of one.

As for family activities, some will remain constant and others will change as young adults, or parents, develop new interests. For my father and me, building model airplanes, throwing the football and playing basketball have faded with the passing of time. Lengthy discussions of history, philosophy, and religion remain a regular occurrence; and hunting, seeking new restaurants and coffeehouses, and returning to enjoy old favorites continue as barriers of time and geography are overcome. I know several families who, though sons and daughters are grown and gone from home, still get together for a camping trip to the same place they have gone for twenty or thirty years.

The point is that parents must maintain this interaction with their sons and daughters even through the years of young adulthood. The bond of shared activities and conversation keeps open the doors of communication between parents and teens. More importantly, this bond helps to build and maintain comfort and trust.

If teens are not comfortable with a parent or someone else, they will generally be hesitant to be open with questions, problems, struggles, and desires. When they do not trust someone, the chance of any serious engagement or frank discussion approaches nil. This much I remember clearly from my own teen years. When certain adults came to me with unsolicited advice, admonishment or reprimand, or an appeal to share my heart and mind with them, I would ignore whatever counsel they had. Whether or not I talked to them, I made sure that any words were without substance or meaning.

This response is to be expected. If you do not trust a person, why should you talk seriously to him or heed his words? Teens have genuine reasons for not trusting someone. Whether those reasons are legitimate is a moot point. Trust must be earned; and assuming that the teenager in question is reasonable and does not have deeper problems, the obligation for earning trust lies with the parent or other adult.

Regular interaction with young adults in simple conversation and through activities they enjoy establishes a comfort within the relationship. They understand that you care about them, enjoy their company, have some of the same interests, and are not "out to get them" or to make their lives miserable. This understanding knocks down walls and lays the foundation of trust. With more time spent together, more shared experience, as well as frequent, genuine, and open conversation, trust finds fertile ground to grow.

Most parents want their sons and daughters to talk openly, freely, and honestly with them. However, such openness will not usually happen without trust. Some would argue that they can get the truth out of their sons or daughters through pressure or punishment. Although certainly true, the trust factor then becomes rather a dim hope.

When a parent can get truth from a son or daughter only through pressure, duress, or manipulation, there is already something wrong in that relationship. Moreover, whatever may be accomplished by such means is merely a temporary measure, a sort of duct tape home repair job. As that youth matures, becomes more independent, and eventually goes out on his own, meaningful interaction and communication will lessen and in all likelihood eventually be shut off completely.

Doing activities and spending time together are not the only pertinent issues. A young adult also must genuinely feel loved; he must believe he is treated with fairness and respect. The spending of time together with parents and their willingness to participate in the activities favored by their sons and daughters are ways of showing their love to their offspring and breaking down barriers that may have come between them.

The thought process of a young man is both conscious and subconscious. Juxtaposed, that process—whether to the father, mother, minister, youth pastor, uncle, or whoever gives him time—will be something like this:

- This guy is OK. He likes the same things I like.
- Wow! She is pretty cool. What other mother or lady would take me to the Demolition Derby or buy me three burgers while we watched the Sugar Bowl on the big screen?
- If he likes the same things I like, then he must be like me in some other ways. Maybe he is just like me, only older. If he is like me, then he will understand me. He will know where I'm coming from. He has not asked for anything from me. He has not tried to manipulate me or to talk me into or out of anything. He is having fun, too. He seems real. He's a Christian, but he likes to have fun, too.
- Maybe Mom really does understand some things about guys even though she's a woman.

You do not have to be able to deliver a grand speech or lecture or to quote long passages of Scripture. Just spend the time. I am not naively suggesting that you magically solve all of a young man's problems by taking him out a few times. However, you will open doors that allow you to become a confidant to him and a positive influence in his life.

Interestingly, I was also open to leadership and counsel from women. I had the desire and felt the need for strong male leadership. In addition to my mother, however, there were other women who won my full respect, and I responded to them with equal respect and openness. The few women who tried an "in-your-face" attitude, which they thought would appeal to my masculinity, were both humorous and pathetic to me. They instantly lost all credibility, and I tuned them out as quickly and easily as I turn off the television. The women who won my trust and respect did so as women. They complimented me when they thought credit was due. Somehow they knew how to give me counsel or warnings in ways that were neither intrusive nor forward, yet in which their points were quite clear. There is an art to this type of counsel and few women ever master it. One lady who has been special to me hunts, fishes, and rides horses. Still this wife and mother is a lady in everything she does, an exceptional one at that. She has never tried to be anything else.

Both mothers and fathers, and other godly men and women, can win the trust and respect of young men and play a valuable role of leadership in their lives. They bring to the table different activities and perspectives, but the core attributes and virtues by which they win trust and respect are the same. Such an investment again increases its dividends in a ministry home. The lessons you learn in meeting the needs of your own children equip you to impact the lives of young people in your congregation. For many of them, you become a surrogate parent.

Young women might be a bit more complex than young men, at least from the perspective of a man. Nevertheless, the same basic principles apply. A young woman will likely understand when someone is genuinely interested in her and cares for her in contrast to someone—whether a parent, a youth minister, or anyone else—who is showing interest merely because of a sense of obligation.

Mothers will usually find it easier to spend time or to find common interests with their daughters just as fathers tend to do with their sons. Even so, a young woman will need the time and attention of both parents. Fathers may have to work a little harder, just as mine did with my sister. He did not have to work harder because of a lack of desire or commitment on his part but rather because the thoughts, needs, desires, and preferred activities of young women were foreign to him, just as they probably are to most men.

With me things were wonderfully simple. If he did not want to go anywhere or was not sure what I wanted to do, he could go out in the yard with the football or simply attack, and we would wrestle until we wore ourselves down. With my sister, he had some learning to do; he had to spend some time in study and observation. Being an astute student of life, he quickly learned that anything involving the mall was good. He learned her favorite shops and restaurants and took her to the movies she wanted to see. He made sure that he spent sufficient time with her, aside from time the family spent together, so that she had ample opportunity to talk to him about whatever was on her mind. I still have no idea what was discussed on such day trips because my dad kept those things between my sister and him. It was their time. Certainly he did not do everything right, for I doubt that anyone has, but my sister could never have doubted his love or his commitment to her since his efforts and actions backed up his words.

When a young woman has a mother who spends time with her, whom she fully trusts and respects and with whom she is comfortable talking, the chance of her going to someone else, whose counsel or advice might not be so conducive to her well-being, is significantly less. A genuine closeness between a mother and daughter makes that daughter less susceptible to peer pressure that would send her down the wrong path.

When a father is committed to being the man in his daughter's life until the day she marries, there is little chance that she will look elsewhere for male attention and affection until the appropriate time and the right kind of man arrives. Her father is her provider, protector, counselor, and spiritual leader, and he is also the man who takes her out for a nice dinner and a movie, who takes her shopping and buys her a dress for a special occasion, and who shares in her hobbies or favorite activities.

A daughter who is treated this way by her father is not likely to give herself to men whose only interest is her body and whose commitment is only for the moment. She is secure in the love and attention of her father, safe under the shield of his protection, and she can bask under the glow of his adoration, as well she should. Moreover, having learned from his example what love really is and how it manifests itself, she will understand what love is not. When a man comes to her claiming love without showing all the attributes and commitments of her father, she will know that either his love is not true or he does not understand what love is and what it entails. Whichever may be the case, he will not be the man she chooses to allow into her heart.

There will always be exceptions—women whose fathers have done everything right and yet who still made terrible choices that scar their lives in their pursuit of love, affection, and attention from another man. There are other cases in which the mother and father apparently do everything right, yet a daughter still goes astray. Many fathers who give the appearance of being very active and affectionate at home were, in fact, largely unavailable to their daughters except to drive them to church on Sunday.

Surface appearances can be extremely deceptive. Ministry parents are especially vulnerable here. After all, they are expected to have "church clothes" and "holy faces" all the time. Easily a façade can wipe out an alertness that enables youth to "test the spirits" on a regular basis. Also, this situation does not rest completely upon the shoulders of parents; sons and daughters have their own minds and are ruled by their own wills, and they ultimately determine the final result of this living equation. Notwithstanding this aspect of the relationship, when parents are genuine, active, and involved with their young adults and win their respect and complete trust, despite mistakes along the road, which all parents make, for a son to forsake the path of his father or a daughter to fold to the pressure of her peers or settle for the promises of a man who exhibits anything less than the virtues of her father, becomes highly unlikely.

Where? What? With Whom?

Parents must know where their young men and women are going, with whom they are going, and what they will be doing. Parents have a right, and indeed an obligation, to be aware of these details, and this requirement can be easily and logically explained to their young adults. Such an explanation for a young adult would go something like this, in your own variation.

Because of my obligation before God as recorded in Scripture, I am obligated to do everything I can to look out for your well-being. If I fail in that, I answer to God. According to the laws of our state and nation, I have further obligations. If you are involved in something that violates those laws, or even if you are not involved but happen to be present, uniformed men with shiny badges and big guns are going to come to my door and start asking questions. I do not wish to be standing there without answers.

This perfectly reasonable, logical, and understandable explanation is adequate. If my father had said some variation of it to me as a teen, I would conclude that he had good reasons for asking the questions he was asking. I would not want to be on the wrong side of God, a policeman, or a gun; so why should my father feel any differently?

This explanation is different from saying, "Do it because I said to. My house, my rules. I don't have to explain myself to you," or some variation of that. Teens are not stupid, nor should you assume they are belligerent. They can be quite rational and understanding when given the opportunity. As long as they are trying to cooperate and do what is right and are showing no inclination for getting involved with things in which they should not be involved, parents should try to be as patient and flexible as possible. If they have trusted you and have shown themselves to be trustworthy, dependable, and honest, you can logically conclude that they should be given a chance. Just as bad behavior must be punished, so should good behavior and righteousness should be rewarded.

When Do the Lights Go Out?

One subject almost certain to come up in any home with teenagers concerns curfews. We have neither a personal divine revelation nor a desire to dictate to any father and mother when their teens should be at home or in bed each night, but we offer a few observations on the matter, which ultimately must be settled among the members of each household.

Some degree of awkwardness will usually exist between parents and teens, especially in their later high school years, because young adults have the minds and bodies of adults but not yet the privileges, freedoms, responsibilities, and accountability of adults.

Even though the laws seem to hold your child to less responsibility, that does not mean your sons and daughters cannot conduct themselves more responsibly than most of their peers. They can, and it is to your and their advantage, and to the advantage of society, if they do. Especially is this principle true in ministry homes. It is worth an investment of your time, energy, and creativity to motivate your teens to step up to the plate and set new and higher patterns than their peers rather than merely following the herd.

However you resolve this issue with your teenagers, think and pray through anything you want to put in concrete concerning their boundaries. You are at a critical point in preparing your teens to move from parent-control to self-control, and you want to do everything within your power to demonstrate the God-control you ultimately wish to see in their lives.

You may have good reasons for not wanting your son or daughter to be out late in certain places. You may not want them out late at all, but do not use ridiculous statements or clichés to justify your reasons. Young people think and reason. They notice inconsistencies, hypocrisy, and ignorance. You are foolish not to expect them to react negatively to thoughtless reasoning.

Be ready to back up with fact and reason whatever decisions you make. Your condescension may not violate Scripture, but things are likely to be easier and more peaceful if you treat your teens with respect and invest time in helping them understand the big picture from which you are working. Authority is unquestionably yours, according both to Scripture and the law, but as you consider a matter, explain your rules and decisions, reason with your teenagers, and treat them respectfully in the process.

For example, consider this thought, which might come from a responsible teen:

If I have shown myself to be honest, dependable, and responsible, why should I be restricted, especially on weekends? I have not gotten into trouble. I am not violating civic laws or parental rules. Why am I not trusted? Why do you give me a curfew to keep me from doing something that I say I would not do and that you say you do not think I would do? Is there anything I could do to prove myself to you?

That paraphrase of thoughts from the past, from many conversations and more eavesdropping than I would ever admit to is not meant as a suggestion to turn all of your teenagers loose from dusk till dawn. It is my effort to help you understand what your teens may be thinking.

A number of cities in the United States now have as law a curfew on all people under a certain age. If you live in one of these cities, the government has actually made your life easier. If a curfew is the law, abide by it, and that should make the process of explaining the rules to your teenagers much easier.

When there is no municipally mandated curfew, I offer this suggestion. For a young man (or a young woman) to be trusted to the degree that he has proven himself trustworthy seems logical and right. If he has shown himself to be lacking in any of these virtues, then that should be considered. Personally, my trust of anyone, young or old, comes as that individual proves himself to be worthy of my trust.

Young adults, like anyone else, do need a certain amount of sleep each night. Since ministry families often seem to be a place for burning the candle at both ends, adequate rest for anyone in the household is a challenge. Actually, ministry children would fare much better physically, as well as intellectually and spiritually, if parents would set some boundaries early in life on scheduling activities (and most of these seem to fall in the category of church activities) to assure not only proper rest but also balance in all activities that make a profitable lifestyle. The sleep requirement will vary according to the individual.

The crux of the matter is that there are legitimate points to be made with regard to caution and prudence, and there are salient points to be made concerning the privileges, rights, and obligations of responsible young adults. How you come to terms with these issues in your family is up to you. Just try to be sure that all factors are taken into account with reason, objectivity, and, as always, with an awareness of the obligations of Scripture.

The Custom of Dating

Dating is another issue sometimes related to curfews. The Bible contains no model for dating, nor are there any allusions to the practice. Marriages were usually arranged by the young lady's father or, in his absence, by the oldest male relative, who would take the lead in working out the details of the contract. Romance, at least as viewed in the West, had little to do with the arrangement. Even though the feelings of a son or daughter were probably in most cases considered, and obviously love entered the equation before betrothal and marriage in at least some cases, these were not the driving factors or chief considerations.

When the Jews were a pastoral nomadic people, the primary goals of arranged marriages were to maintain the social continuity of the tribal group, to keep the divinely appointed divisions of the land within the tribes as their respective inheritance, and to ensure that children were brought up to be a credit to the group as a whole.[29] Even as the Jews became more settled, these objectives remained in the minds of those seeking the arrangements, although other factors came into play.

Solomon clearly arranged marriages for political reasons, which, according to Scripture, came with some grave consequences. When the Jews began to return to Palestine from exile, a desire to settle quickly, gain social acceptability and status, and acquire title to land prompted many to marry into the Moabite, Ammonite, and Samaritan families already established in the land, a practice not without consequences according to Ezra 9 and Nehemiah 13.[30]

Once a marriage was arranged, a betrothal ensued. A betrothal was more binding than are engagements in modern society. People can back out of engagements, and often do, with no legal consequences and without any violation of scriptural precepts. A betrothal could be broken only by a legal transaction, which was essentially a divorce and only legal when adultery had been committed.[31] A man who was betrothed could be exempted from military service (Deut. 20:7). If a woman who was betrothed was raped by another man, she could not become that man's wife, as would have normally been the case, for she already belonged to her husband-to-be. The rape was considered not only a crime against the woman but also against her father and her betrothed husband.

Many young men did not marry when they could legally do so because of the necessary financial requirements for accepting the responsibilities of marriage. In addition to getting enough money to establish their households, they often had to pay a dowry to the bride's father. In some societies today a young man still must pay a dowry to the father of his bride.

Dating and engagement are not betrothal. An arranged marriage is completely different from the way modern couples pursue marital union today. There is no question but that parents, and even extended families, were an integral part in the decision-making leading to choosing a marriage partner. This custom does not generally bode well in a postmodern society that elevates individual choice and experience over Scripture. Yet as we in ministry homes seek our own answers, we do so knowing the burden of influence and example resting upon our shoulders.

Our parents were very much a part of confirming the choice of me and my husband to link our lives in marriage and in determining the timing of that union. I cannot imagine making the second most important decision of my life (after my conversion) without input from those who had shown me unconditional love, who had poured upon me sacrificial service, and who had modeled godly marriage and Christian commitment before me through the years.

No doubt ministry parents struggle under this burden of wanting to be included in the lives of their adult children, with the opportunity to share personal wisdom and godly counsel and know it will be received and considered even when their children move into adulthood. Their testimony and reputation in ministry is under constant scrutiny as parishioners look to see how the "experts" handle their own household.

Honoring and respecting parents, if it means anything, means a deference to them, listening carefully and only rarely and with great caution ever dismissing their counsel. Over the years in the counseling room, I have seen conflict on this important decision between parents and children—even in ministry homes. I have several observations:

- Who is right and who is wrong is not the issue.
- Even if a wrong decision is made, God is still on His throne; and He specializes in restoration and renewal.
- Honoring parents is the only commandment with a promise, and defiance moves far from honoring.
- Giving God time to work is the hardest but safest strategy when godly parents and children find themselves at an impasse.
- Loving someone unconditionally comes at a high cost; investing in a life—whatever the sacrifices—must be a gift released and not an obligation purchased.

Ministry parents are sometimes faced with an excruciating choice: (1) To accept and affirm any choice their child makes lest they be embarrassed by the child's defiance or rejected by his anger, or (2) To offer their counsel as God directs in gentleness and love, without compromise, allowing the child to go his way and make his choice, and then to embrace and undergird the child with unconditional love despite his rejection of parental counsel. The second choice has much more risk because any ministry parent who is perceived a failure because he is rejected by his child will suffer criticism and in some cases lose his ability to lead and to influence others effectively.

But again, those in ministry are first and foremost parents, and to lose a staff position and thus your livelihood would be nothing compared to losing a child. Never should ministry parents put their ministry—however noble—above their responsibility to shepherd their children through troubled waters. Never should they couch biblical admonitions or family guidelines or personal behavior as important because of how they will look before the congregation. Children and young adults must be taught to do what is right because of their own commitment to go God's way. Their love for parents and their desire to please them should rather be an encouragement along the way.

What young people can and should do is to apply the same biblical principles for all aspects of life to their relationships with members of the opposite sex. How difficult is that? Scripture absolutely forbids adultery or fornication. Scripture prohibits even considering marriage to an unbeliever. Scripture clearly affirms that you must love people and treat them with gentleness and lovingkindness, and certainly you should look for a mate who does the same. Above all you must love the Lord your God and walk in His ways and do His will, and you would want a mate to do the same. In standing under Scripture and observing common sense, you would do well to end a relationship immediately unless the person you are dating has these qualities or changes of his own volition.

Beyond these basic factors and principles are others not necessarily directly linked to Scripture but still worthy of consideration. For example, if a young man takes a young woman out for the evening, he should treat her as he would want his sister or his daughter to be treated.

Allow me a personal thought directed more toward younger readers. With no theological expertise or spiritual revelation, here is my counsel: Do not get into dating during your high school years. Kick back, hang out with your friends—male and female—and have a great time. Life is so much bigger and better than high school. You will have plenty of time and opportunity to get to know members of the opposite sex, and you will be able to do it under much more relaxed and enjoyable circumstances.

No, this is not what I did in high school. Although it was never an obsession with me, I did date some. I succeeded in wasting time and money, which could have been better spent and enjoyed elsewhere.

You may think, "Well, it is easy for him to say. He tried it, but now he tells us not to. That's kind of hypocritical." Although your point is well taken, I think it incorrect. There are three ways that qualify a person to give good counsel and advice. One is to possess much knowledge, wisdom, and understanding. I do not qualify there. Another is to have lived an exemplary and Christlike life that can be a beacon for all around you. I'm out on that one, too. Third, you can go out and make mistakes and then look back and see where you went wrong and why and what you could and should have done to avoid those missteps. You can also see how you could have made better use of time, energy, resources, talents and opportunities. In this way I qualify.

Although nothing to brag about, to be sure. My only point is that because I made the mistakes or misjudgments, you do not have to. You can if you want to, but you do not have to.

Are you wondering if I would do it differently if I could turn back the hands of time, knowing what I know now? Absolutely! I do not lose any sleep over it, but I wish someone I trusted and looked up to would have told me then what I am telling you now. "Hey, don't bother with the dating thing. It's frivolous and pointless at this time and place. Have a good time for now and take care of your studies so you can get out of high school as soon as possible." Yes, a few people said such things to me, but I needed to hear it from someone I respected, trusted, and to whom I could relate.

In addition to the physical temptations, you also must contend with the logistics of dating. Your parents and the parents of whomever you are dating will have a significant role. All of their rules and requirements must be understood and met. I am not suggesting that their establishment of boundaries is wrong or that they are trying to make your life difficult. They are doing what they are supposed to be doing—that is, fulfilling the responsibilities required of them by God. Their task is an extremely challenging one, as you will learn when you have your own kids. Should you have certain rights and privileges as a young adult? If you behave yourself, yes; but you must also recognize the seriousness of parental obligations and the burden that comes with making difficult decisions. Every kid should take this factor into account when he starts to get angry or frustrated with his parents.

Young adults also lack certain freedoms that older adults have. In high school your schedule and the way you use your time is pretty much set for you. Even when not in class, you still have to do your homework. Again, this demand is not the whim of your parents; it is the authority of the classroom.

Whether you go to college or enter the marketplace after high school, you will have much greater freedom in forming your personal schedule. You can decide which classes to take, how many to take, and when you want to take them. You can decide what kind of job to pursue and, to some degree, what hours you work. You will also have greater freedom in how you use your spare time; and if you are not living at home or in institutional housing, you do not have to answer to curfews. High school, although ostensibly designed to prepare you for the "real world," actually has little in common with it. Life, thankfully, is much more interesting, diverse, and fun.

Furthermore, you will not be getting married in high school. What, for a Christian, is the point of dating if not eventually to find a mate for life? Though I have no statistics to offer on the matter, I can say that most of the married people I know, especially those recently married, did not even meet each other in high school. You would therefore have to question the wisdom and practicality of trying to pursue a serious dating relationship in high school.

Since I am not naïve enough to think that because I advised you not to date, most of you will not do it, I want to offer a few tips to you. First, try not to take dating too seriously, keeping in mind that you have many years ahead of you. Dating is that social process in which one person attempts to gain the attention, favor, preference, and commitment of another person of the opposite sex and in so doing enhances those features, characteristics, and attributes that he believes the other person will find desirable and camouflages those that he believes may not be deemed attractive to the one he wants to impress.

In almost every dating relationship, the chief characteristics have been enhancement and camouflage. The degree of this deception varies according to the couple and spans from the trivial and minor to matters that are serious and major. Therefore, if you are going to date, find somebody you can "hang with."

Forget about enhancement and camouflage and be who you are. If that is not good enough for the person in whom you are interested, then let him go. Of course, anytime your date or anyone else can point out a flaw in you and give you solid reasons as to why you should make a change in some facet of your life, you would be wise to listen and consider their words. However, I am referring to people who change or alter their behavior solely for the purpose of gaining the favor of another.

If you quit doing things that you have always enjoyed just to make yourself more appealing to another person, there will probably come a time down the road when you will long to do those things again. Your spouse may then wonder why the sudden changes. Do not change who you are. Be open and honest. If someone will not accept you as you are, then why would you want to live with her for the rest of your life?

Many repeat the mantra "opposites attract." If it works for you, that is fine. Personally, I have always thought it a bad idea. I like the outdoors; she likes the mall. I like to go camping, and she hates hotels that do not offer room service and a beauty salon. I love animals and have a dog and two cats living in my home. She does not like animals, especially in the house. I like sports, historical movies, and news channels. She hates sports, could care less about current events, and watches only soap operas and romantic dramas. I like to read, and she thinks books are a waste of time and space. Yes, this relationship is going to be fun and harmonious! I am not saying that two people who are opposites cannot live together happily, only that it is a lot more fun to have someone with similar interests so that you can enjoy your favorite things with them.

Find someone you can "hang with" and be who you are. Do not try to make things happen. Many times people try to force something to work that clearly is not working. If two people are struggling and not getting along well before being married, what do you think is going to happen when they actually start living together every day?

Do not enhance and camouflage. Be as honest and open about your negative character traits as you are about your positive ones. Answer questions honestly and ask a lot of questions, especially those kinds of questions that tend to make people nervous. Those are questions for which you must get answers. Do not be afraid that your questions or statements of principle, conviction, and belief will turn your date off or scare him away. If a person backs away because of your convictions or beliefs or because one of your questions puts too much pressure on him, then there is no reason why you should want to be with that person anyway.

The person you marry should be your best friend. If you will think of your dating life and your choice of a mate as a search for the best friend with whom you want to live the rest of your life and reject the shallow criteria so common among those avidly pursuing at random members of the opposite sex, you may see these things in a different way.

Although there is no biblical model for dating, there are biblical standards for how you are to live. What your sons and daughters need to know is that these standards apply to their dating relationships as to any other aspect of their lives. Not only do the standards reveal the way in which they should conduct themselves with members of the opposite sex, but also they present a pattern for those qualities of character they should seek in a person with whom they wish to spend the rest of their lives.

The Sound of Music

A subject that seems to be a frequent source of controversy between parents and teens and one that received a tremendous amount of attention when I was a teen is music, especially rock-and-roll and its derivatives. What music you should listen to or not listen to in your own home is your choice.

Music has been blamed in recent years for many things that it did not and could not do. A song itself or even the musician who writes and performs a piece of music cannot force anyone to do anything. He could possibly influence someone to do something that he might not otherwise do, but that begs another question. Why are so many young people open to the influence of those who are morally derelict and whose sole abilities and contributions to the world are playing instruments, writing songs, and, in some cases, singing, and who, had they lived in any culture other than modern Western society, would have been paupers, beggars, or exiles?

Forget the music for a moment. How could a young person look at disgusting specimens of humanity like Marilyn Manson and pop-star Michael Jackson and be interested in what they have to say about anything? These individuals have no virtue; they are not pleasing to the eye; and they have not done anything to distinguish themselves other than, as some would argue, through music; yet some young people are open to the influence of them and others like them. Why?

Something is wrong in the hearts, minds, and perspectives of these gullible young people, and it has nothing to do with their choice of music. Their embracing of music in which the lyrics and message are vile and debased is merely a symptom of a greater sickness. The music is not the sickness or even the cause of that sickness. To attack music as the source of the problem is like trying to cure malaria with aspirin or to fix a broken leg with painkillers. The fever is only a symptom of the malaria virus, not the cause of it. For a cure, you must take the medication that attacks the virus itself. Painkillers will make the broken leg feel better, but they will not set the bone. If you are going to be able to help a young person who is listening to a vile and unwholesome message and idolizing the musicians who produce it, you have to be able to recognize the difference between symptoms and causes, just as a doctor must know the difference between diagnosis and treatment for his patient.

Every society and culture has had the perverted and degenerate within its population. The United States is no different and has its share of the deranged. What is different in the United States and other "progressive and enlightened" nations is the enthronement of these degenerate personalities to preferential social status and to a platform from which they can spew forth their twisted views.

Most often modern Western societies give credence to the perspectives and opinions of celebrities—whether actors, musicians, or athletes. In the minds of many, celebrity status has become equivalent to credentials of authority and knowledge. Most celebrities have no credentials, and few ever attain credibility outside their respective professional pursuits. Actors, actresses, musicians, entertainers, and athletes appear on major news programs and are asked questions about economics, taxes, domestic policy, foreign policy, war, peace, poverty, religion, and other issues, although most often they do not have the training or experience from which to speak on these issues.

The problem of equating celebrity position with credentialed authority is not one that can be blamed on young people. Consider a simple, pragmatic approach. An actor pretends to be someone else and gets paid for doing so. If you have a question about movies, acting, or getting a job in Hollywood, ask him. If he takes a ten-year sabbatical in Hokkaido to study snow monkeys and produces a body of credible research, ask him about snow monkeys. Why would you ask this man, whose résumé consists of high school graduation, movie roles, and even a study of the snow monkeys, how the president and congress of the United States can improve the economy and enhance the education of American children? Why would you ask him to explain the implications of the separation of church and state? People, young or old, give these celebrity figures credibility by attaching to their opinions and views the same, or greater, credence on a given matter than they would give to someone who is actually qualified by education and experience to speak about the subject.

You as a ministry parent may not do this, but society often does. Because of your position of influence and leadership, you must not only be aware of how this phenomenon affects your children, but you must also find ways to break the hold of this evil influence on your children and the children of your church.

For over four thousand years the people in every other society in the world have viewed musicians merely as people who play instruments and sing songs. They listened to them, sang with them, danced to their music, and threw a few coins into the harp or box, but never did they push them into the echelon of the wealthiest people in the world. Never were they sought for political insight or elevated to be role models by the masses. Many musicians have earnings that dwarf those of a captain in the US Army, or of a general for that matter, just as they would dwarf those of the average successful businessman or even the secretary of state.

The influence of musicians on young people has manifested itself in drug and alcohol abuse, increases in sexual promiscuity and its diseases, increases in suicide, murder, violence, and open rebellion against society and traditional values—all of which have been detrimental both to individuals and society. No causal force in music nor any ability of musicians alone could generate such upheaval and change. However, a sick society is like a virus quietly attacking the vital organs and inner workings of its being while causing numerous outwardly visible symptoms. The massive surges in crime, violence, abortion, divorce, drug use, pregnancies out of wedlock, and the degeneration and perversion of many in the music business and the subsequent glorification and rise in status of some of the worst role models cannot be dismissed as coincidence. The American family began to self-destruct; many began to abandon the traditional and religious values by which people have lived since the founding of our nation; determined efforts began in earnest to remove every vestige of God and the Judeo-Christian foundation from the nation's laws, schools, money, and conscience.

What is happening in music and the susceptibility of many youth to its influence is merely one of the symptoms of the greater sickness. As with a virus or some other illness in the human body, you can treat symptoms; but ultimately you must diagnose and attack the virus or the bacteria that causes the symptoms if health is to be restored.

The fact that many have turned their backs upon God and upon the principles and precepts of His Word, and that many, if not most, in governing and ruling bodies have done the same is the ultimate cause behind the symptoms. This tragedy is not the fault of those committed Christians who strive to live their lives according to the Word and who have stood with courage for the causes of truth, righteousness, and justice. Nevertheless, if you are concerned about the music in your teenager's life, you would do well to understand and keep in mind that you are dealing with a symptom and not a cause.

Other symptoms of the virus within our culture are contributing factors to the negative inclinations of our youth. We undoubtedly live in the most medicated society in the history of the world. The fact that some drugs are legal does not make them all good— at least, not their unrestrained use.

One of the more common complaints parents make about rock-and-roll is the widespread use of drugs by its musicians and the resulting influence upon teenagers to do the same. You can understand why some young people might see signs of hypocrisy. Advertisements for legal drugs for almost every illness, or perceived illness, bombard them on television and radio. Emphasis is heavy on cure with very little attention given to possible side effects, such as diarrhea, nausea, vomiting, fever, digestive trouble, headache, heart irregularities, and blurred vision—some of which often sound worse than the ailment they are supposedly going to cure.

Older adults, if anything, are more involved in the legal drug craze of the culture than are young people. The one glaring exception to this is the alarming number of young people who have been put on drugs to treat ADD and other disorders, which for the preceding four thousand years and until very recently either did not exist or were somehow dealt with and overcome by natural means. Physicians and the pharmaceutical industry, with the support or passive consent of parents, are peddling drugs to children and young adults for a substantial and sustained profit. Most of these drugs have negative side effects; some admit to being unable to cure a condition but only to treat or control. Even the existence or the degree of need with some of these disorders to be treated is questionable at best. What some parents describe as ADD sounds more like a normal, energetic youngster who is completely bored with school.

Ministry parents, perhaps more than other parents, seem to feel the pressure to produce placid and docile children. The issue is further complicated by the environment in which they find their families—a myriad of church activities, more invitations to homes of others, and more command performances at events in the community. Add to these factors higher expectations for children in ministry homes just because their fathers are considered public figures or community leaders. Ministry parents must find the courage to insist that their offspring be allowed a relatively normal childhood—while finding the creativity and ingenuity to entertain their children and rein their illusive attention into acceptable behavior when the occasion demands.

I met this challenge with creative preparation appropriate to the age level of our children. I was the "bag mama," giving a great deal of time and energy to preparing a special bag for each of our children whether we were embarking on a local outing or an international trip. Each bag included an inventory of snacks (not messy but a variety of food and beverages), hygienic necessities (Kleenex, Wet Ones, handsanitizers, etc.), reading material, games or self-entertaining toys. The bags became famous, and I often prepared them for other children as they prepared for special trips.

The bottom line for me as a mother was the conviction that I needed to train myself to have realistic expectations of my children. My own persistent preparation was prerequisite to their pleasing performance.

Another inconsistency is found in adults who, facing problems brought on by an unhealthy lifestyle, seek and use prescription drugs rather than change their habits and lifestyle. In the mind of a kid, how does this response make such adults any better than those on the street who destroy themselves with illegal drugs? Even to turn to drugs as a quick fix for legitimate illness can cause confusion to young people who are watching. I observed a minister with a common cold select four different cold medicines. A warning was printed on each of them noting that they should not be taken in conjunction with any other medicine. He ingested three of the four simultaneously. Young people notice inconsistencies.

I am not saying that all drugs are bad. Nor do I wish to demean those in the pharmaceutical industry whose research and work has saved and improved the lives of millions. Prescription drugs are sometimes the best, and at times the only, option; but parents need to rethink how they approach the use of drugs in their own lives.

The prevalence and promotion of sexual promiscuity in rock-and-roll is another common complaint. The point here is not to argue whether what rock stars or politicians or any public figure would do in his private life is his business and not that of the public. Rather, young people are taught from childhood to respect these people as role models and as the embodiment of success, honor, and service to their country. Overlooking the transgressions of public officials or other "respectable adults," while condemning the same actions in rockers and pop stars, might draw skepticism from young people. Any moral high ground from which to attack the sins of public figures has been lost. The same can be noted for ministers who engage in immoral behavior; except that in their cases the situation is more reprehensible since they have violated not only moral law but the covenant of their calling as well. "If you cannot trust the preacher, whom can you trust?" No child is any more devastated than one whose ministry parent is guilty of immorality.

Christian parents sometimes allow their children and youth to listen only to Christian music, and many others encourage this restriction, insisting in extreme cases that secular music is "of the devil" and from a more moderate perspective, unwholesome. In addition to the music itself, parents often cite the artist's lifestyle.

Parents who take this position need to be aware of what is happening in the world of Christian music. The conduct of some of the most prominent contemporary Christian music (CCM) artists in recent years has been both inexcusable and disgusting for what you would expect from people in positions of Christian leadership and influence. Some of the best known and most popular have had public extramarital affairs, and several divorced their spouses afterward. Print news keeps well abreast of the lives or careers of CCM artists. One female artist commented that after several years of Christian counseling she had concluded that her divorce was God's will. She, of course, cited no Scripture.[32]

If you ever have conflicts with your teenagers over music, I would strongly recommend that you defend your position carefully. Parents who make comments that have not been well thought out and are inaccurate will ultimately hurt themselves, their efforts, and sometimes their relationships with their sons and daughters.

The ability to produce music is one of the most lovely and blessed of the gifts that God has given, and all can find pleasure in some form of its diverse strands. You may not enjoy all forms of music, and you may not approve of all musicians or of the content of their music. However, you can be open to the right of musicians to compose, play, and sing their music the way they want to and to the right of others to listen to the music.

Even valid points about certain music are lost when parents are critical of everything they do not like and when they cannot provide justified and reasonable explanations for their criticism. I would not expect any parent to like all music, but your criticism should be reserved for those cases in which the content of the music clearly warrants your intervention. Even when your criticism is just, do not react and erupt or take what is known as the "ready, fire, aim" approach. Be sure of your aim before you fire. Make sure you have thought through your points thoroughly before you lay them out to your teenager. If you have approached him in conversation rather than by a knee-jerk, emotional reaction that degenerates into argument, then he will be analyzing everything you say and probably looking for weaknesses or soft points in your reasoning. Your chances are far better that he will listen to your reasoned response than to an emotional or angry outburst. If a teenager decides to do what is right of his own volition, having thoughtfully considered the matter himself, you have accomplished something much greater than what you could accomplish only by command.

In my home, as I recall, rock-and-roll, blues, or anything resembling them—hard and fast or slow and easy—was forbidden. Furthermore, when I started to drive, I was told never to listen to it in my car, even when alone. It was on the long list of car rules mentioned previously.

As a teenager, I did not think that this restriction was fair or right because there was no distinction made between the various artists and bands and the different kinds of songs. Nevertheless, Dad paid the bills and it was his home; but to tell me not to listen to it in my car or not to remain anywhere where it was being played, I found to be quite unreasonable. I knew that some songs depicted activities and actions in which I should not be involved; but I never understood the insinuations or assertions that if I heard something enough times in a song, I would do it or that if I listened to the music of the world long enough, it would drive me away from my relationship with Jesus Christ. I do not think it unreasonable to suggest that young adults should be allowed to make some decisions of their own concerning the music to which they listen.

If your son decides that suicide, murder, or some other terrible act is something that he should do, then what is already wrong with him goes far beyond his preferences in music. Among other problems, he has lost perspective and has abandoned even his most basic sense of what is right and wrong. Moreover, almost certainly you as a parent have failed in your obligations. The preference for bad music would be merely a noticeable symptom of the deeper sickness. The fact that the vile and depraved musician is putting out his music is not the problem. The problem to be addressed by parents is that your teenager might find the music and message of a clearly depressed or demented individual to be appealing and worthy of his consideration.

I am not suggesting that all music is fine or even that all music has good within it. There is music that is bad in every way, including lyrics that are vile and antagonistic toward the values held by Christians. I do not believe that anyone, especially Christians, should be listening to or supporting the artists who produce such music.

Although I enjoy many kinds of music, I have a line drawn. I will not listen to or buy anything that crosses that line. If music is openly and decidedly satanic, which some of it is, then I will not buy it or keep it in my home, even if it might appeal to me musically. If the artist or the music is decidedly anti-Christian, and I am aware of it, then I will not have it in my home. If an artist uses his platform and influence as an entertainer to pummel or oppose Christian values or to do or say things hurtful to American military men and women and their families, then I will have nothing to do with him. I have no interest in any music performed by effeminate men, masculine women, or individuals of whose gender I am unsure. If a band or an artist generally attempts to sow discord in society, such as starting or encouraging riots, violence, or lewd behavior at their concerts, I will not support them.

When I was free to listen to whatever, I became more selective in my listening and quit listening to some music I had listened to in the past. There are a couple of dynamics that could have been at work here and that could be present in the lives of your teenagers. One is the "forbidden fruit" syndrome. When you ban something completely and turn it into a major issue out of context and proportion in relation to the potential it has in and of itself to do damage, you may actually make the item more appealing to those from whom you are trying to keep it.

The other dynamic is the culmination of resentment, anger, and frustration over what is seen to be an unjustified intrusion upon privacy and personal choice and one that lacks adequate grounds and reasoning. The fact that all rock-and-roll was forbidden and that the only reason given aside from those already mentioned was the constantly repeated motto that "all rock-and-roll carries with it an open commitment to illicit sex, drugs, and open rebellion" was frustrating.

There was also no distinction or allowance made for the difference between singing a song about something bad that happened as opposed to singing a song in order to encourage or promote bad behavior. Normally, when a rock-and-roll or country and western artist sings a song about a love gone bad or cheating spouse, they are not writing or singing from the perspective that they are glad that it happened or that they hope it happens again any more than Marty Robbins sang songs about gunfights in the old West in hopes of promoting more gunfights among his fans. There is a difference. If a teenager is regularly listening to music that deliberately promotes wickedness and bad behavior, you have grounds for seriously addressing the issue with him. If, on the other hand, he is listening to songs in which the writers and musicians are singing about the various turns of their lives, good and bad, yet not actively encouraging the bad, then perhaps a bit more lenience is in order.

I know as a teen that some of the music to which I listened was in direct and deliberate conflict with Christian principles. Had I been approached with more reason and less dogma, I think I would have come to some of my decisions more quickly instead of after I left home. No one wants to be constantly hounded about something, especially when those doing the hounding are heavy on preconceived dogma and light on reason. Had I been confronted regarding music with pervasive foul language, satanic overtones, or lyrics clearly advocating wicked behavior, I would have understood. Even if I argued at first, I think I would have conceded the point in the end. To point out those things that are obviously in conflict with what I say is a legitimate point, while blindly attacking or criticizing everything I listen to is not helpful.

Classical music has proven itself timeless. Its great composers are worthy of utmost respect, and teenagers should learn to respect and appreciate their contributions whether they enjoy the music or not. The same is true of jazz, a distinctly American art. What passes for jazz today is another matter, but the old jazz greats like Duke Ellington, Louis Armstrong, Miles Davis, John Coltrane, Ben Webster, Thelonious Monk, and many others of their era have made truly remarkable and timeless contributions to the world of music. In addition to the talent and versatility of its artists and the quality of the music, Americans should appreciate jazz because it is a part of our heritage.

The great blues artists, too, deserve recognition and an appreciation for their contributions. Respect for this genre of music deepens when you learn more about the environment and the times from which it sprang. There are some in rock-and-roll who also deserve credit and recognition for their talents and contributions, and the same is true of many country and western artists.

Endorsing the lifestyle or personal views of artists without careful scrutiny is always dangerous. Mozart's personal life was a perpetual disaster, and he could hardly be considered a good role model, yet what he accomplished musically was phenomenal. The same has been true of artists in other types of music.

The music to which you listen and what you allow or do not allow in your house is your business. Try to appreciate music for what it is and be cautious about making more of it than is legitimate. There is no virtue in fighting a battle that does not have to be fought; but if you do have to confront your sons and daughters over music, make sure that your facts are in order and that your points are well thought out.

There are times when parents must lay down the law, so to speak, and say "Do this," or "No, you cannot do that." There is nothing wrong with doing that when it needs to be done. With music as with other issues, however, you accomplish something greater with a young adult if you can reason with him, educate him, and get him to come to the right decision by his own thought and of his own volition.

The effect your ideas and beliefs have on your children is an interesting challenge in parenting and teaching. Almost inevitably children tend to magnify what parents emulate or teach, which points to my surprise in Armour's memory of limited musical genre in our home.

I remember a greater variety of music in our home than does Armour but concur that there was no rock on any level. Paige and I learned to enjoy jazz during our days in New Orleans and even spent happy hours in Preservation Hall listening to live performances; Paige imparted to both of our children a love for country and western, although that genre didn't really take with me. Classical and easy listening still remain our overall favorites, along with orchestration of great hymns and gospel music. Now music is piped throughout our house and is more instrumental in genre because we are usually studying and writing—but still quite varied in style.

Here are some lessons I learned from Armour:

- *Introduce your children to a variety of music from infancy. Weave it throughout life.*
- *As a parent responsible to God for what is heard and seen in your home, set your standards and don't back down anywhere on your property—house or cars or vacation properties—when you are paying the bills.*

- *Be respectful of your children and young adults. They deserve reasoned answers for your decisions just as you would give to parishioners who ask a question of you. Study the Scripture so that you can give biblical responses. Although the Bible does not discuss various genres of music, it does contain clear principles for how to live in a pagan world while maintaining a Christ-honoring lifestyle. Even if your reasoning demands research and study, you will find it worth the effort. Give your kids as many choices as possible, and don't limit choices to your own preferences.*

In conclusion, your goal as a parent is not to clone yourself in your child, but you do have a responsibility to disciple your children in the way of the Lord. You are to make His ways winsome to them; you are to teach them the virtues of music that honors Christ with patience and diligence. Music can honor Christ without mentioning His name or dishonor Him while mentioning His name. I concur with Armour that you do no service to your children and young adults if you do not bring them to make their own decisions, and that is better done sooner than later. I cannot help but believe that if you are spending time and energy and money to introduce your children to a wide spectrum of music that is appropriate for a Christian, you will produce in your offspring listening habits that will not hurt his example in the kingdom of Christ or even tarnish your testimony as a Christ-honoring parent. As has already been discussed, however, such training takes time—not just a few quality hours but a quantity of hours invested in lifestyle teaching. The ultimate challenge for ministry parents remains a commitment of your full energies, best creativity, and long hours to the training of your children and rearing them "unto the Lord."

CHAPTER Seven

Problems Unique to Ministers and PKs

SOME CHALLENGES AND PROBLEMS are unique to parents in ministry and their children. This chapter will suggest how to deal with them in a better way and will prompt thought and dialogue among readers for finding their own unique solutions.

The most common complaint from the sons and daughters of ministers, or preacher's kids (PKs) as they are more commonly known, is the time issue, "Dad spent so much time at church that he didn't have any time to spend with me." Or, "Dad was hardly ever home when I was awake. He was always at the church, making visits, or traveling to preach somewhere."

Some have said it a bit differently. "Why is that church more important than our family? . . . . He preaches about family, talks to everyone about how important it is, but he doesn't spend much time with us. . . . The only things we do with Dad are church activities. He never takes us to do fun stuff unless it has to do with church. Other people are around, never just us. . . . I feel more like a member of Dad's congregation than like his daughter."

Personally, I cannot relate to these complaints in the same way that many PKs can because, as active and busy as my father was, he never had a problem in making time for our family. My experience would seem to prove that this problem can be overcome, for there would be few ministers who have more commitments and obligations than my father. In addition to being an associate pastor at what was then the largest church in the Southern Baptist Convention, he was also a college president, a writer, and an itinerant preacher and Bible teacher in demand around the country and the world during my youth.

Dad knew that only four things mattered to me, aside from spiritual matters—football, fishing, hunting, and shooting. He was faithful to take me hunting each year and to take me fishing or shooting quite a bit more. He planned his schedule around football season so as not to miss any of my games. Sometimes he had to cancel something, which he would try to reschedule, in order not to miss a game; but he was always there, and he had something positive to say about my performance, even after my worst games. He also managed to attend most of my other athletic contests even though I had told him not to bother. I played the other sports to fight the never-ending boredom of school. Although it was not that important to me that he attend anything other than the football games, still he did.

Furthermore, he took the time to be with my sister and participated in other family activities unrelated to sports. He took the time to talk to us individually on a regular basis about spiritual issues and other aspects of our lives. I did not always agree with him and still do not on some things, but I could never have thought that I was neglected or that he was unavailable to me or the family in any way.

As his obligations and commitments began to increase during my teen years, he came to my sister and me and told us how much time he would be gone and asked if we would be OK with that. I always said yes. I have never felt neglected. He had always spent time with me doing things that I liked to do, and I had no reason to believe that was going to change. I also believed that what he was doing was good and right, and I knew that he had a passion and conviction for his work.

I did not give this conversation concerning his schedule much thought at the time; but as I look back, I have realized the significance of his coming to my sister and me and offering to cut back on his commitments if my sister and I felt that we were not getting enough time with him. First, to involve us in his decision-making process let us know that he was thinking about us. Second, he would make changes in his schedule if we needed or wanted him to. We knew that our opinions and feelings were important considerations for him. All ministers who find themselves increasingly busy may want to think about involving their children in assigning priorities and managing schedules.

The Bane of Neglect

Testimonies of those PKs who have felt neglected, at least to some degree, by their fathers comes both from those who are older and from those still living at home. This problem, if not solved, can have serious consequences.

No one with an open and honest mind-set can read the totality of Scripture and not be aware of a father's obligation to spend an abundance of quality time with his sons and daughters. How could you possibly "train up a child in the way he should go" (Prov. 22:6) if virtually all you do is feed your child, put him to bed at night, and take him to church? Try training a dog by only filling his chow bowl, tucking him into his blankets with a biscuit each night, and taking him to church to show him off each Sunday. If that was all that you did, instead of a family pet you would have chaos and terror on four legs! The same is true of children and young adults. "Fido" certainly deserves his time, but your children and young adults will require much more time.

The word "provide" in 1 Timothy 5:8 is not limited to the provision of physical necessities. The context and the whole of Scripture affirm that much more is required. Not only is there the command to "train up a child in the way he should go" but also the mandate to "observe the commandment of your father and do not forsake the teaching of your mother; bind them continually on your heart; tie them around your neck . . ." (Prov. 6:20–22).

This kind of teaching and training cannot be accomplished by sermons and Sunday school lessons alone. Rather, a commitment is required for teaching and training from parents and for learning and understanding on the part of children and young adults. This challenging accomplishment comes over time in academic institutions but much more from the daily example and many hours, year after year, of discussion and shared experiences between parents and their offspring. There are no shortcuts. If there had been any, surely Solomon would have figured them out and added a chapter to Proverbs.

There is no substitute for actual time spent together. The time you spend with your children brings action to your stated love for them. Seeing genuine love in action tears down their guard and leaves their hearts and minds open to your instruction and to the example you set with your own life. Their hearts and minds will not always be receptive or cooperative; but the bond of shared experience opens lines of communication and builds trust and a kind of respect that would not otherwise be there. Time spent in church and doing church activities does not count for much here. Time spent doing things that they want to do, not things they have to do, sets the foundations for openness, responsiveness, and trust. Why would your son or daughter be inclined to trust, respect, or listen to someone who preaches about the importance of family, love, understanding, compassion, and the importance of looking out for the needs and well-being of others, yet never finds time in his schedule for them.

Many kids actually see this inconsistency as hypocrisy. They will probably not suspect malice on the part of an insensitive parent, and most may not think it to be deliberate. They are even unlikely to suspect or ascribe apathy to a neglectful parent. Nevertheless, a hypocrite acts in a manner inconsistent with his words. The fact that wrong actions were taken due to bad judgment and not bad intentions seldom improves the status of the perpetrator. Although judgment about a person and his actions is seldom fair or just, the point is not what is right but what is reality.

Hypocrisy, whether it is real or merely perceived, makes the already challenging task of parenting even more difficult. A perception of apathy is a more serious matter. If a child or teenager thinks his father is a hypocrite because he preaches about the importance of family but neglects his own wife and children; yet after the matter is brought to his attention, he apologizes, admits his mistake and promises to do better in the future, his children would probably accept his apology and give him a chance to regain their trust. They would understand that everyone makes mistakes, even Dad. So why not give him another chance?

If, on the other hand, a child or young adult's perception is that his father simply does not care about him, then his heart and attitude harden; and he will be less open to any explanation or counsel. The long-term effects of this conclusion can be much more devastating than perceived hypocrisy. If a child thinks that his father's actions are inconsistent with his words but that his father does care about him, then he gives him the benefit of the doubt. Once he establishes in his mind that his father does not care, he will close his mind and heart to his father.

Of course, the vast majority of ministers who have neglected their sons and daughters care deeply for them. This neglect is more the result of bad judgment or a lack of understanding of the situation than apathy or bad intentions. However, what they know, what they think, or what the truth actually is does not matter. All that matters is what is understood and perceived by their sons and daughters. Right or wrong, the perceptions of their children are the realities with which these fathers must deal.

A minister must know where he stands with his sons and daughters. How does he acquire this knowledge if he does not already know? The best method is just to ask.

There are three reasons why ministers cannot afford to neglect their sons and daughters and why they must know where they stand in their relationship with their kids. They are accountable to God for fulfilling their obligations as fathers to the best of their abilities. Several PKs have told me that their fathers, when trying to explain why they had not spent more time with them, said that they were so busy with the Lord's work or with trying to evangelize the lost that they had not had as much time at home as they would have liked. This is a huge mistake.

- Your foremost obligation is to the Lord, who has made your obligations clear through Scripture; and most important is to provide for your family, to love and care for your wife, and to love and train your children. If you come up with anything different, it had better be because God has spoken to you outside of Scripture in the way He spoke to Abraham when He told him to sacrifice Isaac, and then you had better be certain of the source of your instruction. When a man loves, cares for, and spends time with his family, he is doing the work of the Lord.

- Think about the message you are sending to your child or teen when you tell him you spend little time with him because of the demands of the work of the Lord or of the church. How will this message be received? Is it likely that such an explanation would endear the work of the Lord or the church to his heart? It would seem more probable to have the opposite effect.

Some PKs have harbored bitter hostility toward the church—often by inferring such an explanation in their own minds. Some admit to such feelings; others betray their hostility in voices, eyes, and body language.

Furthermore, you cannot avoid the possibility that the presence of an inadequate or neglectful father in the life of a child or teen will figure into the child's understanding of his Heavenly Father in a negative way. The universality or inevitability of the connection between a child's experience with his earthly father and his mental image of his Heavenly Father is not automatic, but it is reasonable to believe that the possibility exists.

A minister has an obligation before God to love and care for his wife and children, and that includes, but is not limited to, spending adequate time with them. Further, he has an obligation to present to them, as well as any man can, the image, nature and loving ways of the Heavenly Father. This process, in turn, will be a major factor in determining the child's understanding and disposition toward God, the church, and eventually his own family and others who cross his path. These are serious obligations with eternal ramifications, and they rest upon the shoulders of a father. The work of the Lord cannot be an excuse for failing to fulfill paternal responsibilities to your own children, who in themselves are the work of the Lord.

- A minister must know where he stands with his sons and daughters because he is responsible, inasmuch as it depends upon his leadership in the home, for the spiritual growth and general well-being of his children. This obligation before God is also an obligation to your children. Some PKs who believe that their fathers neglected them in every way except for the provision of physical necessities and amenities, through their own commitment and by the grace of God have matured spiritually and lived stable and exemplary lives. Sadly, however, others, having had the same experience, have lived lives that fluctuated between circus and tragedy and will carry the resulting emotional scars to their graves.

All parents bear the immense responsibility of preparing their children for the trials and challenges that come with life. They must also prepare them for the blessings and opportunities. They are not responsible for every action taken by their children, for that child has his own mind and, ultimately, will be accountable for his own actions; but parents are responsible for fulfilling the obligations that God has given to them. If they fail, they not only find themselves in the unenviable position of having to give an account before God but also of facing the pain, embarrassment, and lifelong regret and sorrow resulting from seeing and experiencing firsthand the sorrow and suffering of your own flesh and blood.

From those who have had to travel this road come words of regret beneath a pain-ridden stare that combines the emotions of helplessness, hurt, and despair in a way that is at once terrible and unforgettable. There is no pain so unbearable or so enduring as to witness the suffering of those you love most, unless it is the pain born of the realization that you did not exhaust your capabilities to prevent their suffering.

Living in a Goldfish Bowl

A minister bears this obligation; yet his burden is heavier. Unavoidably for a time, if not a lifetime, the image and understanding his sons and daughters hold of Jesus Christ and His church will be influenced to some degree by his example and his treatment of them.

A minister must know where he stands with his sons and daughters, if for no other reason, because some of his church members will know. Regardless of how good an actor the minister may be and how discreet or convincing an actress his wife is, some in the church will know the truth. In some churches nearly all are aware, sometimes painfully, of the pastor's situation at home.

When a pastor's relationship with his family is good and his sons and daughters are responsible and well-behaved, the congregation's awareness helps him and them. They sense and see the pastor's influence for Christ consistent with the message of his teaching and preaching, which establishes him as a man of God with integrity, and a leader worthy of being followed. He builds trust and respect and brings legitimacy to his counsel and power to his exhortations. People can be moved and inspired by a minister's words, but the power in his words will fade if not fortified by the consistency of his actions.

There will be repercussions when a minister fails in his obligations as a father. The question is what consequences will there be, to what degree will they be made manifest, and what degree of severity will the resulting damage bring?

A minister cannot fail in his *obligations* as a father and still be within the will of the Lord. He cannot fail to fulfill his responsibilities as a father and be blameless in his standing before his congregation. There is no assertion that his children will not be guilty of bad behavior at some point or that they will not ultimately fail in their responsibilities to God and to their fellow man—only that the minister must not fail in fulfilling his obligations to God and to his children.

Ongoing Rebellion

Children have their own minds and wills, and they become adults who will make their own decisions, choose their own beliefs, and select their own paths. Although unlikely, a minister can fulfill those obligations given to him by God through Scripture and still be unable to quell willful rebellion in the hearts of sons or daughters who have chosen to turn their backs on the ways and laws of their Creator. Almighty God certainly knows when a father has done all that he can do, and most people will understand as well.

A minister has to be a good father and cannot neglect spending time with his sons and daughters. His own standing before God is at stake as is the personal and spiritual growth and maturity of his children. Finally, his effectiveness and perceived legitimacy as a minister, to some degree, will be contingent upon his commitment and efforts as a father.

An Illusive Identity

I often ask PKs: "What is the hardest part of growing up in a ministry family?" One with whom I talked recently said, "PKs are the only people who can lose where they're from."

This PK's father had been pastor of a large church in Tampa, Florida, for a number of years. He spent his childhood and young adult years in Tampa. Before he graduated from high school, his father was accused of embezzling a large sum of money. The allegations came from one of the church's most influential members, and other prominent members went along.

No one, even those who in private said that they thought the allegations were groundless, would stand with the pastor against those accusers, church members who made the largest financial contributions. The allegations were proven to be false. Everyone, including those who brought the accusations, knew and admitted it. The evidence not only proved that the pastor had done nothing wrong but also that he had done nothing unethical or even questionable. This PK's father was forced to resign from the church, which hurt his family financially and emotionally. Furthermore, an investigation into the matter revealed that the ringleader of the accusations against the pastor was himself guilty of immoral acts within the church and in his personal life.

This PK expounded upon what it means to "lose where you are from."

> People ask me where I'm from, and I really don't know what to say. I grew up in Tampa and spent more time there than anywhere else, but I don't want to tell them I'm from Tampa. I have no ties there anymore, and I don't ever want to go back.
>
> It would have helped a lot if adults in the church would have checked on me once in awhile, to sit down and talk and ask how I was doing. My mom and dad were great parents to me, but it would have been nice not to feel so alone; to know that there were other people in church besides my family who cared about me and would be there for support if I needed it. No one ever did that.

There is much in the testimony of this PK for ministers and laypeople alike. The potential to "lose where you are from" may not be unique to PKs, but the argument could be made that they stand a greater risk of such a loss than do most of their peers. The totality of their loss and the way in which that loss unfolds are difficult to parallel.

Military children and teenagers can certainly be moved around a lot, as can the families of some civilian citizens whose companies transfer them with regularity. To be transferred for a different duty, the same duty in another location, or to a new job is very different from being forced to move while simultaneously losing the support and friendship of an entire church. To lose a job and a church family and to feel betrayed, let down, or rejected by a group of people among whom you had felt loved, accepted, and supported and with whom you share common faith, belief, and life principles is much more devastating. In essence, you lose what you previously thought to be your extended family.

You often hear church members and leaders refer to themselves as the "church family," and fellow believers are called brothers and sisters. References are also made to spiritual fathers and mothers.

What makes families special and indispensable? No matter what any particular family member may do or say, no matter how crazy he may seem, how arrogant he may be, how thoughtless he is, how ugly he is, how annoying he is, or how eccentric he is, he is still family. Whether linked by blood, marriage, or adoption—all are family. As such, each is entitled to all familial rights and privileges.

When a member of the family needs help, you help him. If he is in trouble or in a mess of his own making, you do everything within your power to help him, even if you fight it out with him once the trouble has passed. He is always welcome in your home, even though he may empty your refrigerator and annoy you by talking during the football game. The bonds of families compel you to do things and to tolerate actions that otherwise you would not.

Obviously there are limits. If your nephew is shooting heroin and refuses to stop or get help, you are not going to hand him a couple of hundred dollar bills. Within proper limitations, however, families look out for one another, accept each person as he is, and do not forsake one of their own. Your brother and you might fight one day like a pair of bobcats with one tree between them; but if someone else lays a finger on him the next morning, you will come down on that intruder with everything you have. You may rarely see or talk to some family members. Some you may not care to see; yet if they call and it is within your power to help, then you do so without a second thought.

Most families operate this way, or at least they used to. Family members fuss, they fight, they annoy each other, even talk badly about each other, and sometimes avoid each other; yet when all is said and done, they stand together. They have their scuffles and disagreements in good times; but when the bad times come, they set aside their differences and extend a hand to walk through difficulties together. None of us talks about the nature of the family in these terms, yet we know, and take comfort in the fact that this familial solidarity is in place.

Now you understand why losing a "church family" would be so devastating. People expect the possibility of losing a job or of being laid off or transferred. They do not expect to lose the companionship, love, and support of their families. To think of the message going to rejected fellow believers looking in from the outside is chilling. Who would want to be adopted by a family who might love you for five years and then kick you out and tell you not to come back?

Such behavior is counter to the principles of Scripture and to the ways of Jesus Christ. Church members need to be more aware of the needs that many PKs have, and they need to be sensitive to their struggles. A PK may want to be where he is, or he may not want to be there. One thing is certain: He does not have a choice. He goes where his father goes.

Church members must understand that a minister's sons and daughters are each unique personalities with their own respective minds, thoughts, needs, desires, and dreams. They may agree with their father, or they may not. They may think like him in many ways, or they may hold ideas very different from his. They may like his sermons, or they may not. Their relationship with him may be congenial and smooth, or it may hit some bumps in the road.

An Extension of the Minister?

The one thing that church members should never do is to assume that a minister's son or daughter is an extension of the minister. First, consider the PK in Tampa. His suffering was more the result of indirect action and passivity than a result of direct actions taken against him. The "church family" assumed he was an extension of his father. He suffered because no one made a significant effort to distinguish him and his siblings from his father; so what happened to his father engulfed the entire family. They suffered not only from seeing their father hurt by false accusations, but also from the inevitable fallout on them personally because no effort was made on the part of the church members to separate them from the matter at hand. No efforts were made to support them and care for them, despite the knowledge that they were going through a difficult time.

Sometimes the presumption of an extension from father to children is made directly and acted upon deliberately. I know PKs who have been on the receiving end of such treatment, and I have been there myself. Lay people and those in ministerial positions have said some unkind things to me simply because they did not like my father or were angered over something he did. Others would not say as much but were very cold and distant in their attitudes toward me. Since my school was connected to my church, I also had teachers and coaches who not only said unkind things but also took unjust actions against me based on their contempt for my father.

Some may wonder how I could possibly be aware of and understand such actions. Young people can observe behavior and listen to things said and see the connection between such behavior and comments and the way a given individual treats them. Surprisingly, a number of these people did not leave me anything to question or contemplate or figure out. Somewhat to their credit, they said to me exactly what was on their minds.

"You think you're special because of who your daddy is. . . . Your daddy may be something in that church over there, but he's nothing here. . . . If you think we're going to put things on a silver platter for you because of your dad, you've got another thing coming," just to note a few memorable phrases from the past. What would you have deduced had you been in my place?

For the record, I never asked for or expected anything because of who my father was. Actually it was quite the opposite. Like many PKs, I tried to downplay my connection to my father. I love him and respect him, but I wanted to be known as Armour, not as "Paige's boy" or "the preacher's boy."

The result was that I did extra homework, made visits to the principal's office, did extra running and push-ups, and got hit with boards because some adults with obvious emotional and attitude problems either did not like my father or resented his position. My view of Christians in general took a downturn because some of the same guys who walked around the platform with contorted faces (the "holy" expression) and said long prayers were unkind to me because they did not like my father. I am amazed that people still ask why some PKs have a bad attitude or why they do not want to go into the ministry like their fathers. I need to interject that most church members, teachers, and coaches did not do these things. Further, I never harbored any bad feelings or resentment when I was criticized or got into trouble for the things I actually did wrong, and I readily admit to being a prankster and not always exemplary in my behavior.

Nevertheless, like the PK from Tampa, I know from experience what it is like to see your father accused and attacked by those who are supposedly his friends and "church family." To see such injustice coming from his enemies or from those who were openly opposed to him ideologically and philosophically was not pleasant, but I understood and expected it. For the attack to come from those in our own church who claimed to love and support him and to be his "church family" was much more hurtful. For children and young adults, actions like these are very confusing because much of what they have been taught about the nature of a church family, how they are to behave, and how they are to treat one another is reversed before their eyes. All of these nice, godly people are doing things that are not so nice and godly. There was little difference in the sense of betrayal and rejection felt from those who instigated things and those who took no part but remained silent. There were many who expressed love and respect for my father and knew that he had not done anything wrong. They assured me of their prayers but never took a stand or defended him.

To tell someone you are praying for him but that you are not going to take any action to help him or his loved ones when they are being treated unjustly is neither impressive nor comforting. None of those who wanted to force my father out of his job ever accused him of any moral, ethical, or legal violation, or of any violation of Scripture; yet he was forced to leave. No one in his right mind wants to be in a conflict; but when a man who has done nothing wrong is falsely accused and attacked, you had better get into the fight and take a stand in his defense. As stated in the quote attributed to Edmund Burke, "It is necessary only for the good man to do nothing for evil to triumph."

Most of the support and protection PKs need in this situation must come from the church family. Ministers are limited as to what they can do. However, they are not without options. For one thing, ministers, when being considered for a church or when accepting a call can make it clear to church leaders and members that his children are not answering the call. He can let them know that he expects his children to be treated like other children and teens in the church are treated. Then he should be sure that he does not put them before the church in ways uncomfortable to them.

For example, the minister, and church members as well, sometimes place more pressure upon ministers' sons and daughters to take leadership roles in youth groups, or they pressure them to be exemplary role models for other teens. Sometimes ministers pressure their children to get up in front of the congregation and recite Scripture, sing, or take a lead role in a Christmas play. If a child or a teenager wants to do these things, then it is fine. If he does not want to, then it is a foolish mistake to try to force or pressure him to do so. You will build resentment within him that may not soon be forgotten. To single him out before the church, and place more focus and attention upon him, whether intentional or not, is exactly what you should avoid.

Finally, a minister, through his leadership role, can educate his congregation as to its role in helping and supporting the children of ministers on staff. He can do this in a variety of ways—from the pulpit, through teaching, or through individual interaction. If a son or daughter is having a particular problem and a minister thinks that one or a few of his church members might be able to help in a way that he cannot, he can simply go to an individual, explain the situation, and ask for his help. Not only might this action be the best thing for the child or teenager, but it will also be good for the minister. Besides getting the help he needs, he will be demonstrating to church members that he is not one who claims to know everything or to have all the answers, and he shows those in his congregation that he has respect for their wisdom, counsel, and knowledge. When a mutual trust and respect is built between a pastor and his congregation, working through the difficult times that may come later is made easier.

No one should lose his church family because that family rejects him or fails to love, embrace, and support him. To leave the family of his own volition and for his own reasons is his business; but no one should have to leave or be inclined to leave merely because the family has failed in those functions to which it has been called.

Expecting More May Get Less

Another complaint from many PKs is that they feel like more is expected, and sometimes demanded, of them than would be expected from their peers. Sometimes parents are the source of these expectations; other times it is church members; often it is both. How common this problem may be is not really the issue. Rather what brings the situation to the forefront is the significant number of PKs who obviously bear the burden of these expectations. The perceptions of PKs are more significant for our discussion than is the risk that the problem has been overstated. If a teenager feels like too much pressure is being put on him, then he responds to that feeling. His assessment of the situation may be inaccurate, but he responds to his assessment and reacts to his feelings. The actual truth of the matter becomes secondary.

After you have thought things through, you may decide to sit down and give that PK a thorough explanation as to why you believe his assessment is wrong, but even then you are addressing his feelings and, in essence, acknowledging the importance of his point of view. The opposite of this approach would be to tell the PK that he is right and that his way will prevail. Both of the latter approaches have been tried, and we do not recommend either. In the short-term each produces a result similar to that of dumping lighter fluid on a fire. That fire may stay contained for a while as it burns within the PK, or it may manifest itself quickly and spread to others around him. Neither situation is good, and neither is likely to resolve the problem. The long-term result may not be disastrous, but it also may not be what a parent would want.

How a teen ultimately will respond to such an attitude and to pressure put upon him depends upon his character, convictions, and the degree to which he has matured spiritually. Some can look back and see that they were not treated fairly, while leaving that injustice in the past and getting on with their lives, harboring no ill feelings years afterward; and for others the experience may have an effect on decisions they make later with regard to spiritual matters. People—PKs and others—turn away from the church and from

Christ over things that were insignificant relative to the full scope of life.

A Root of Bitterness

You do not want to leave your child, or anyone else, with a bitter memory of his experience in church if you can help it. There are enough forces working against the church from the outside. There is no virtue in adding to the problems from within.

When you taste a bitter food or drink—one extremely disagreeable to your taste buds, you want no more of it. Bitter tastes are not easily forgotten. What is true of food and drink is also true of human experience. You remember the bad experiences, often more vividly than the good ones. Interestingly, when some of the most successful professional athletes are asked about their most memorable moments, they immediately begin to recount the worst or most embarrassing moments or games of their careers. Despite tremendous successes, they sometimes remember pain more readily than gain.

You will remember the bitter experiences. If a PK has a hurtful experience in church and if it is continuous or if its effects continue to burn within him, the chances of his wanting nothing to do with church once he moves away and can make his own decisions increases significantly. This situation is one in which you can win a battle and lose the war. You can totally disagree with a teenager's thoughts and feelings, and you can force him to do whatever you want him to do, but at what cost? It reminds me of a minister who decided to take the harsher, "in-your-face" approach to his teenage son. Disdaining explanations, he said, "When you turn eighteen, you can do whatever you want to, but until then you do everything I say, however I say to do it, when I say to do it." His son never forgot the words. Be careful what you suggest to a young man or woman, for they might take you up on your offer.

If a minister demands more from his sons and daughters in regard to their obligations and responsibilities as young adults, he is doing something that is good for them, for the church, and for society. This

expectation is unrelated to the church or to his role as the leader of the church. He is not saying,

> I want you to think through your words and actions before you speak or act. You are responsible for your own actions; I want you to conduct yourselves with honor and dignity; I want you to treat older people with respect and gentleness; I expect you to obey the law, to respect people and their property, and to respect the authorities in your life; I expect you to be truthful, and other such things *because* I am a minister and you are my children.

Rather, the minister father says these things because these are the obligations and responsibilities of an adult and because he wants his teenagers to live in a way that honors God and is beneficial to society and to others.

These requirements have nothing to do with the fact that this parent is a minister. They are things that all parents should require of their teenagers, and a minister is no exception. Expectations and requirements that are out of line are those that arise only because a child or youth happens to be the son or daughter of a minister.

Expectations

The pressure of greater expectations can come in different ways. It can be direct and deliberate, or it can be direct or indirect but inadvertent. If a minister tells his son that he needs to take a more active role in the leadership and influence of his peers because they will look to him more, knowing that he is the pastor's son, this approach would be direct and deliberate. If a youth director or Sunday school teacher singles out the pastor's son more often than others to answer questions or to take the lead in various projects or activities but does not realize what he is doing, then his actions would be direct but inadvertent. If nothing specific has been asked or demanded of him, yet a pastor's son feels pressure due to comments from people in the church or due to what he has heard attributed to people in the church, this pressure is indirect and inadvertent. For example, if it were to get back to the pastor's son that several church members were overheard saying that they were sure he was going to be a preacher of the Word just like his father, then he may feel pressure to be something that he does not want to be. If his father were to tell his mother that he feels within his heart that God is raising their son up to be a preacher or a missionary who would do great things for the kingdom of God, that son might feel pressure to go in a direction in which God is not moving him. This pressure, too, is indirect and inadvertent.

Even though these three types of pressure differ in nature and come in different ways, they are felt by a PK, while not always the same, at least in a similar way. The accuracy of a PK's perception is not the primary issue here. As you work through problems like these, you will have the opportunity at some point to explain to your child why you think he is mistaken. First, a minister must be sure that none of that pressure, perceived or otherwise, is coming from him as a parent. He must do everything he can to keep his son or daughter from feeling that pressure from other sources.

Some of this pressure, of course, will be beyond a minister's control. But he can see that none of it comes from sources he does control. As a minister is certainly capable of exerting pressure in all three of the aforementioned ways, he probably should think very carefully through his words, actions, and the ways in which he relates to his children.

The easiest mode of pressure for him to avoid is that which is deliberate and direct. For a minister to pressure a son or daughter in this way is simply wrong, foolish, and inexcusable. The repercussions and consequences such pressure can bring are serious and varied, and despite what some wish to think, without grounds in Scripture.

Some ministers have pressed their sons to follow their own steps into the ministry. They may have even told their sons that it was expected of them by God. More often it has been done by slightly more subtle methods, for there are many ways in which you can encourage someone to do something without actually telling him to do it.

For example, a minister can make sure that most of the conversation and family activities are centered around biblical subjects and around the church. He can make sure that everything he teaches his son about how to make his way in the world revolves around the way he conducts himself and accomplishes things in ministry, and he can be sure that he does not teach his son or make him learn other skills by which he could make a living as an adult, which, by the way, is a foolish thing to do even if his son does plan to enter the ministry. The minister can explain to his son that there are other ways to make a living but that all of those ways, in the end, are selfish, and are centered only upon personal gain. Only in the ministry is one truly doing things for other people and for God. He could even point out a few perks. If you get into a good church situation, pastoring is easier than selling real estate, and it certainly beats working in the hot sun or freezing in the snow at ten below. All of these arguments have been used by parents in ministry, according to PKs I have interviewed.

You can deliberately and directly prep a young man to enter ministry without specifically telling him that he should. The pressure for a PK to follow in his father's footsteps usually comes in this way, though in varying degrees, rather than his being told specifically that he has been called by God to enter the ministry. Both, however, are equally foolish and wrong. I do not doubt that most, if not all, ministers who have pressured their sons in this way think that they are doing a good thing. Unfortunately, this confidence does not keep them from being wrong. Some ministers may employ the same pressure yet do so infrequently and without conscious intent. Although still nonproductive, their pressure would fall into the category of direct but inadvertent, which certainly is not as egregious an error as would be deliberate pressure.

Only God can call a person into the ministry. Responding to that call is between an individual and God. It is not the business of the young man's father, mother, minister, or an interested layperson. If a young person comes to you for counsel on the matter, then you should counsel him to the best of your wisdom and knowledge. Until that time, stay out of it—parent or not. My father always told me that "the most miserable people in the world are Daddy-called preachers."

This type of pressure is not limited to young men. One minister's daughter shared with me her frustration over a strained relationship with her father. She has been working on her own in the entertainment business. Nothing she does is in conflict with the principles of Scripture. When she talks with her father about current projects, his next question is inevitably, "What are you doing for God?" Then follows a lecture and hand-wringing talk about how his child is working in an industry of sin, when there are many positions she could fill in churches, in missions, or in Christian programs of one kind or another.

First, a father is not responsible for dictating to his adult daughter what kind of work she should do. He had seventeen years to give lectures and to say yes to this and no to that. That time is now gone. Furthermore, he is not really making sense from a spiritual perspective. If the entertainment industry embraces and promotes wickedness and sin, which much of it does, one of the best things you can do is to create entertainment that is wholesome in content and sound in quality, which is exactly what this daughter is trying to do. No one is going to make the entertainment business go away, and most would not want to. Some films and music are good, and you can strive to make it better for those who want to avoid the smut.

A minister has the obligation of teaching, encouraging, and in some cases, enforcing behavior that conforms to the precepts and principles of Scripture. However, he should avoid pressing a son or daughter toward any action or behavior, noble though it may be, beyond calling for his offspring to be obedient to Scripture. Does he teach his son not to lie, cheat, steal, fornicate, murder, do drugs, and engage in other sinful and destructive acts? Yes. He teaches these virtues and calls for compliance to the divine mandate, as should all fathers.

The Scripture commands honoring the Sabbath and keeping that day holy, which is described as refraining from work on that day and corporately gathering to worship God. I find no commandments for young people to go to car washes, choir practice, church camps, weekend youth seminars, or other youth activities. As for handing out tracts, sharing the gospel is good; and believers are commanded to be ready and willing to share their faith. However, the last person you want to be sharing the gospel is someone who is angry and does not want to be there. "You're either going out there and share the gospel tonight, or you're going to lose your car for a month!" Such threats have been made, and any type of force or coercion on such matters does not set a good stage from which to share the love and grace of Jesus Christ.

I am not against the other activities mentioned, but I am against pastors making their sons and daughters participate in these activities when they do not want to. I have nothing against American traditions and culture. I was born to them, and I participate in them; but when it comes down to stating what is right and wrong, what is good and not good, and what is required and prohibited by God, I want my standard to be Scripture—nothing more and nothing less.

Believers are admonished not to forsake assembling together (Heb. 10:25). This reference to corporate worship is an obvious parallel with "Remember the Sabbath day, to keep it holy." Just as the Israelites worshipped in the temple and tabernacle, so should believers in the churches. They do so on Sunday—the first day of the week—in honor of the Lord's resurrection instead of Saturday as did the Israelites.

"As you see the day drawing near" presumably refers to the coming of Christ. Of course, none of us has any idea when Christ will return. It could be tomorrow or next week, or it could be in thousands of years (Mark 13:32). "More" is probably an admonition for greater intensity of commitment and faithfulness to the discipline of corporate worship—not so much how many gatherings but how devoted you are to the body of believers with which you align yourself. Believers now, and a thousand years from now, should make the Lord's Day an interlude for physical rest and spiritual renewal as well as corporate worship.

The debate is not over the value of additional church services and extracurricular church activities. Most gatherings of believers are good and those who desire to participate should do so. The question for ministry parents centers around what extracurricular activities are mandated by Scripture directly or indirectly. Should ministry parents force their teens to attend all activities and services sponsored by the church? Are all believers obligated to appear at church every time the doors are open?

Perhaps many ministers want their sons and daughters to be present for most or all church activities because it is embarrassing to them if they are not there. Yet no one should expect more of PKs than of other children and teenagers in the church. A minister should not be embarrassed or troubled because his sons and daughters do not take part in every service or activity, and church members have no right and no Scriptural grounds to expect this from them.

Most ministry parents expect their children and young adults to participate in the heart of corporate worship. As Southern Baptists, our tradition has included morning and evening participatory corporate worship (Ps. 100:1–5), in which the church family gathers as a testimony of their devotion to Christ, as a lighthouse for those who have not accepted Christ, and as a nurturing time for the edification of believers. Sunday school has been the classroom for biblical instruction for believers, and church training on Sunday evening was the time for more practical outworking of your faith. Evening worship is often set apart because of its greater spontaneity (Ps. 134:1–3). A midweek service was a time for fellowship—often around a meal—and prayer. From my childhood, my parents, who were humble laypeople and not in vocational kingdom ministry, determined that corporate worship and the fellowship within our church family would be at the heart of our family activities (Ps. 116:12–14, 18–19). That commitment to the Bride of Christ remains in the lifestyle of my parents and of my siblings and me today.

Are there ever exceptions to passing this joy in being a part of the church and worship from generation to generation? There are adults who reject the lifestyle of their parents. In ministry homes, some say that their parents gave all their time to the work of the church to their neglect, and they resent the church and its ministries and thus want no part of it. Others say that they don't find any spiritual nurture in the modern church—only busyness and hypocrisy— and, therefore, they worship more effectively on their own.

As a ministry mom, I respond to these "churchless PKs" in this way. Many in ministry make "head" mistakes in going about their divine assignments, even while their hearts are dedicated to a high and holy calling of rearing up godly seed. Often the worship service is not as Christ-honoring as we would like, the Sunday school teacher isn't as prepared as he ought to be, the church supper leaves much to be desired in culinary excellence, the prayer service becomes lip service. The preacher may deliver a topical talk instead of a stimulating exposition; the music may be off-key and uninspiring. But still in my heart is the desire to come before the Lord with thanksgiving and to enter His courts with praise in the house of the Lord.

My parents were not in ministry, but they were and are committed to minister in Christ's name in whatever humble ways they can. I love and honor my parents. Even if I were not in ministry (and several of my siblings are not), I cannot imagine dishonoring the faith of my parents, not to mention the divine mandate, by not honoring the Lord's Day through corporate worship—not just a family tradition but a core value passed to me from my parents. No parents ever poured themselves into their children any more than mine. They sacrificed their own pleasures for me to have opportunities.

Perhaps ministry kids should be as proud of and devoted to their parents' ministry as their parents are to their activities. Let's consider first the basics for corporate worship in Sunday morning worship and the Sunday school or Bible study hour (three hrs.), Sunday evening church training and worship (three hrs.), Wednesday meal and prayer service (three hrs.)—nine hours for church activities out of 168 hrs. in a week. For some ministry families, transportation to and from church would add another two or three hours weekly. Of course, there are parties, intramural sports, choirs, retreats, camps, missionary and evangelistic outreach that can be added. But when the complaints come about church activities, all too often the protest begins with the core gathering of the church.

What would I offer to ministry moms for consideration?

- *Make the Lord's Day special from start to finish. Begin the day with joy, move through with delight, and end with thanksgiving (Ps. 122:1).*

- *Don't feel guilty over encouraging and even insisting that the family support activities on the Lord's Day and midweek—not just because your husband is a pastor but because regular gatherings of the Lord's people are clearly described in Scripture. Your spiritual commitment to participate in gatherings of the Lord's people is part of your family esprit de corps and not just the terms of ministry employment. Perhaps you need to go through the Old Testament and the many feasts and festivals Israelites added to their weekly Sabbath gatherings. Supporting husband and father in his work/ministry is not a bad thing! Don't expect your children to spend all day every day at church—but a total of from ten to twelve hours per week—that is nothing!*

- Take time to explain to your children and teens why the Lord's Day and corporate worship are important. Let your discussion arise from Scripture. Consider especially the Book of Psalms. Yet beware of suggesting to your children that Scripture is a compilation of proof texts to justify commonly accepted practices. Rather the Bible should be presented as a total picture of an individual's life set apart unto God. The whole of Scripture is the pattern to which you look. You must take your children through the Old Testament to find foundations for corporate worship and varied ways of instruction in spiritual matters. Then move to the New Testament for a continuation of that emphasis as Christ portrays the gathering of believers as His Bride—the church.

- Challenge your children to take pride in the ministry of their father. If he were a football coach, would the family want to attend his games? If he were an entertainer, would the family be interested in his performances? I have heard my husband preach some sermons repeatedly in his itinerant ministry, but I still am his most eager listener.

- Have enough flexibility to know that there are times when you, or your child, are so physically worn out that you need a Sabbath of rest and renewal that cannot come in a public setting.

Missing in Action

If a minister is confronted by church members regarding the absence of his sons or daughters from an activity, service, seminar, or whatever event, he does not need an explanation. That would fall in the domain of parenting, which is no business of the church. Of course, he may choose to offer an explanation, but it is not required. The pressing concern of ministry parents must be that their offspring live their lives according to the standards of Scripture, that they try to emulate the ways of the Lord Jesus Christ, and that they behave as responsible adults. How church attendance plays into these goals is a family matter and not a congregational concern. Better that he participate in a few activities with a good attitude than to participate in all of them with a bad attitude. When I was forced to do things for which I saw no solid backing in Scripture, I came to resent everything, even things that might have been good and enjoyable otherwise.

For a child or youth whose heart is spiritually sensitive and who wants to pattern his life after biblical principles, you must be careful to move away from attempts to answer every question with an isolated verse. Resentment can easily arise if your child does not see what you see. In his view, Scripture is suddenly either bypassed or augmented or reshaped to fit your objective. As a ministry parent who happens to be a theologian, I am acutely aware that you may come from many years of studying Scripture and perhaps be equipped with formal theological training. What you accept as carefully fashioned presuppositions are not even considered by your child. Not only is a prophet without honor in his own country, but often a ministry parent is without honor in his own household. You should indeed put aside cultural standards, your traditions, and all but the most carefully formulated presuppositions (realizing that everyone has some presuppositions), and consider what is actually stated in Scripture, its proper context, and the whole of Scripture.

You may find that some passages of Scripture appear very different with the light of a new study. However, never throw out the baby with the bath water. Having lived more than a decade on the East Coast where in preceding decades liberalism had reigned in the seminary training leaders for its churches, I discovered that one of the major differences in dead or declining churches in contradistinction to growing congregations was that the former had done away with corporate worship on Sunday evening and had abolished midweek prayer services. As the seminary became solidly conservative, churches were revived, accompanied by more corporate worship. The seminary even sponsors a fall revival on campus, in which many local churches participate.

You cannot emphasize Scripture and then take it out of context, twist it, add to it, or otherwise misuse it and still maintain the respect and attention of a thinking teenager. They think and analyze the things you say. Many will do as you say and go to Scripture so you had better be interpreting and quoting it properly.

The main reason I did not want to go to most of the additional classes, activities, and seminars related to youth was that they bored me terribly. In addition to that, I doubted the credibility and integrity of some of those conducting various youth events. Much of what some youth leaders wanted me to do was pointless and nonedifying at best, and ridiculous and sometimes even infantile at worst. I was encouraged to participate in some activities that neither helped me to learn more about Scripture, to draw closer to God, to worship God, nor to help those in the world who needed help.

When you think of the degree to which you expect your sons and daughters to be involved in additional activities, services, and classes, consider what is required of them and of you by Scripture. Do not think of your job or position in the church or of what meddling parishioners think or say.

Armour has given ministry parents a clear message worthy of consideration. I encourage you to make this issue an important one in your family:

- *Determine the biblical guidelines for your family's participation in the church. Don't ignore the support you would want to give to husband and father whatever his professional track.*
- *Make your participation hearty unto the Lord and not merely a duty to your parishioners.*
- *Protect your children within the boundaries you as a parent set.*
- *Never forget that ultimately you are accountable to God for preparing your children spiritually—whatever it takes and regardless of whether you will be "Minister of the Year" or even "Father of the Year"!*

A Matter of Education

A pastor must educate his congregation, and that includes what information his parishioners may need on the boundaries protecting his family. You need not be confrontational unless someone gives you no other alternative, but you can and should teach them the standards and requirements of Scripture regarding the responsibilities of believers to the church and its ministries. You can, in so doing, make it clear to them that there is no reason for your sons and daughters to be any more involved than other young people. You may even find a need to redirect the vision of the church to decrease extracurricular activities and to elevate the role of family time as an important spiritual investment.

The subject of church attendance, how often you go and how much time is spent there, should be considered. The church should always be open to those who want to pray and worship. What should be considered, however, is how often young people—PKs or others— should be forced to go, and how many extracurricular church activities they should be expected to participate in. Remember, if you leave a bitter taste or create a slow fire of anger and resentment within them, those memories and that anger can remain for a long time afterwards.

As a teenager, I had to go too often and be involved in too much. In fairness, I must note that I did not have to do as much as some PKs or as some young people who were not PKs. I had to attend many church services and activities, but my parents stopped short of making me attend some of the extracurricular activities, classes, camps, and seminars. The fact that I was the preacher's boy may have played a part, at least subconsciously, in their desire that I attend, but I cannot say so for certain. I know they thought that these events and activities would have been good for my spiritual development, or they would not have encouraged me to participate.

Counting travel to and from, I usually spent six or seven hours minimum in church. For me, the only thing restful about the whole day was my two-hour afternoon nap before I got ready to head back to church.

On Wednesday nights I had to go either to a church service or to RAs, a missions-oriented class for boys and young men. I enjoyed RAs because I liked listening to missionaries, learning about other places, seeing their pictures and crafts, and eating their food, and I enjoyed the additional RA activities, namely sports, fishing, camping, and going to football games. I do not think I should have had to go, but I did like it. Had I not been forced to go, I probably would have gone most of the time anyway. There were times, though, when I would not have gone for the church service or for RAs because I had homework to get done. Being at a Christian school, we supposedly were never assigned homework on Wednesday nights, but there were a few teachers who figured a way around this school policy. While claiming that nothing was due on Thursday, they then assigned twice the normal load of work on Tuesday and said it was due Friday. So I did often have homework on Wednesday nights.

In my home, though, having a large amount of homework, being tired, or feeling bad were almost never an excuse to miss a church service, especially any service or class that convened at any time of the day or night on a Sunday. Aside from Sunday and Wednesday, there were other activities related to church. Some I had to go to, some I did not. Very few interested me.

Going to most of these services and activities prior to my teen years was reasonable. My parents had to look out for me and my sister, and it would have been ridiculous to have to hire somebody else to do it. It was more practical for us to go with them. Once I reached my teen years, though, I should have been able to make more choices. Having to go to Sunday morning church and Sunday school was fine and right—honoring the Sabbath and not forsaking our assembling together. Anything beyond that, as I see it, should have been my choice, PK or not.

On the one hand, I was expected to behave and act like a young adult. I agreed. My father expected me to behave as an adult, which I usually did, and I was given some adult responsibilities. I was honored that my mother and father considered me an adult and gave me those responsibilities, but I wanted adult privileges and choices to go along with the responsibilities. I have not remained angry about what seemed to me an injustice, nor do I harbor resentment about it. I share the matter in this forum to prompt thought and dialogue among those who will train up the future generations. If you think it through thoroughly and conclude that I am wrong, then you will not be any worse for having heard my position. Parenting comes with no guarantees, and there will always be some who go their own ways no matter how good a job their parents do, but I do not believe this exodus from the church and its influence has to happen to the extent it has.

The Trouble with PKs

PKs have quite a reputation for rebellion, engaging in the various pleasures of the flesh and finding creative ways to get into trouble. This reputation tends to be somewhat exaggerated and not wholly true. However, stereotypes generally do have a basis in fact, even if they are overstated. The stereotypical image of PKs is no exception. This observation would be difficult to blame on genetics for a number of reasons. Therefore, there must be social factors, and perhaps even environmental considerations, which tend to cause or exacerbate those reactions and behaviors in the PK stereotype.

Any pressure brought by parents—whether to follow in their ministry track, to be more active in church and church activities than their peers, or to be held to a different standard of behavior than their peers because their father is a minister—is the most serious problem. First, home ought to be the main refuge from hardships and difficulties of life, but young people live with their parents in that home. If there is pressure from parents, they will feel it both at home and in their activities outside the home. If a young person starts to feel smothered without relief from constant pressure, especially when this pressure might be felt from others in the church as well, the results are usually not good.

Second, despite anything young people may say, especially when angry or in an argument, they do love their parents, and they do care what their parents think. PKs have expressed to me how much they love their parents and wish to get along with them even after severe disagreements and arguments, and also in the midst of trying periods of struggle and disagreement and after having said some terrible things about their parents.

Despite some rebellious behavior and irresponsible words, the loving bond between parents and children remains. Because of this, any parental pressure that young people feel is not fair is going to be more hurtful. Furthermore, parents have the moral authority and the capability to deflect pressure or criticism coming from sources outside the family. Parents can make clear to sons and daughters that they do not care what others think or expect of them, and thereby take much of the pressure off their sons and daughters.

The minister can also help to educate meddlers in the church as to why such pressure is inappropriate (Prov. 20:3; 26:17, 21). I was always encouraged when my father said, "Don't worry about what they say or think. I don't care about that. You're doing fine, and I'm proud of you." If parents are supportive, then young people can discard or ignore the pressure coming from other sources. They can listen to what is said, and in their own minds be saying, "Get lost," and then laugh it off. I perfected this art as a PK, but it only works if parents are supportive and if they reaffirm to their sons and daughters that they have to please God first and their parents secondarily and not everyone else.

I felt pressure from some church members and from others outside the church—direct and deliberate, indirect and inadvertent, and direct but inadvertent. These disruptive experiences bothered me earlier in my life, but as I got older, the effect was diminished and eventually faded into insignificance. This relief was due in part to my parents who, in most cases, were supportive in letting me know that I did not need to please everyone. The other factor that diminished the effects of any outside pressure was the change in my own attitude and mind-set.

There was a point early in my teen years where I decided that I was not going to be a carpet for anyone to walk over. I would respect and honor Scripture, and I would respect authority, but I would not be beat upon or walked over, figuratively or physically, and I would not cower or submit to condescension or insult. I would walk away from such behavior, so long as the perpetrator did not follow me for too long, but I would not sit quietly and take it. I developed a toughness, from which ensued a peace of mind and spirit. I knew that I would not be the one starting trouble, instigating strife, or meddling in other people's affairs. I was not telling them how to live their lives or how to bring up their kids. I was not trying to be their Holy Spirit.

This toughness and peace of mind and spirit allowed me to brush off any criticism or pressure coming from other people. I learned much from the rhinoceros in this challenge. Rhinos have a thick, tough skin. They are not worried or bothered by much. They mind their own business. They are happy just to eat, sleep, copulate, roll in the dust, and take long walks through the bush or across the plains. They do not set out to hunt you down, kill you, or eat you. If you invade their personal space, the definition of which seems to differ a bit according to the individual animal, they may give you a clear but courteous warning, or a black rhino may come after you. If you are going to attack a rhino or its young, then you had better kill the animal quickly, for when so approached that rhino is ready, willing, and able to ruin your day.

Passing on job skills to their sons and daughters is something that all parents should do, but doing so has special and beneficial implications for those in ministry. Many of these kinds of skills can and should be taught in childhood. If a child or young adult questions why he has to learn these things, you should make clear to him that you are not suggesting that he do one thing or another. What he does for a living or what career he pursues once he is out on his own will be his business. What you are doing with him now is fulfilling your obligations as a parent to make certain that he has the knowledge and the skills to survive on his own no matter what hardships or challenges his life may bring. If he does not like that answer, you have grounds to tell him that he better get busy anyway and start working on whatever your project is. This training is not just about him; it is about you and your obligation before God.

As parents, my husband and I found it quite natural to pass along the skills we have to our children, regardless of what they would decide to pursue on their own. We are academicians as well as kingdom servants. We know the best methods of research and study; we are considered good communicators from the public platform and through the printed page. We find tools in interpersonal relationships indispensable. Whatever our children would do on their own, they could certainly find any "ministry skills" passed on to them to be helpful and adaptable even in other professional pursuits.

The Bad and the Ugly

Given the PK stereotype, this chapter would not be complete without a brief discussion of vice: the bad, the ugly, and the wicked. Some believe that PKs try to behave badly just to prove that they can be as bad as anyone else, but they often feel compelled to do more because they are perceived by their peers to be "holy rollers" due to their father's role as the "preacher man." I find this notion far from being a universal truth. In many, if not most, of these cases, there are contributing factors other than that the young person is a PK.

Vice, wickedness, and sin have been and always will be a part of our world. PKs will be drawn toward and tempted by various forms of sinful and generally unwholesome behavior. The question for PKs and for all is not if you will be tempted by sin but how you will respond and conduct yourself when you are tempted.

The scope of this book does not cover much of what happens once young men and women reach the age of eighteen and leave home for school or work. Tobacco is illegal until age eighteen and alcohol is illegal until age twenty-one by US law. When the law of the land speaks, the answer to a young person's request for the forbidden is no. There is much you could talk to them about if you like; but to keep it really simple, the answer is no.

Narcotics (I do not use the word *drugs* because so many drugs are legal) are illegal no matter what your age and the answer is again no. The most persuasive thing my father did to keep me from ever having a remote interest in drugs was to put me in the presence of drug addicts and former heavy drug users. I did not want to look or act like that. I wanted to be strong, fast, and quick in mind and body. I did not want the droll, bony, reeking, needle-marked body or the blackened teeth of a druggie. A few of them were well dressed and well groomed, but I did not want their perpetually wandering minds, their inability to focus, their medical bills, or the disaster that had come upon their personal and business lives. It was not a tough choice for me. Be sharp, strong, and quick and make the most of your life, or turn yourself into a blathering, stinking, mindless human specimen, spend time in the hospital, risk ruining your personal and professional life, imprisonment, and death. Put to me in this way, it worked well.

What, then, of the wide world and vice and sin? In particular, how does a minister approach the subject with his sons and daughters? Such confrontation can be more difficult for a minister in that there are some who seem to think that the minister should never speak of certain subjects unless he is blasting them from the pulpit.

There are three ways in which you can deal with the subject. One is to learn from experience. No one of sound mind and genuine spiritual convictions could think this idea good.

A second way is to try to avoid any specifics of the subject and try to act as if it does not exist, at least not in any way that can affect you. You can make frequent, general warnings to avoid all sin and wickedness, but you do everything you can to shelter your children and young adults and to keep them from witnessing any of this evil.

The third way is to take an honest and open approach in which you educate your sons and daughters through Scripture, instruction, dialogue, and exposure, within reason, to the wickedness that is around us. By exposure I do not mean participation.

My father chose the third method. From the earliest time I could understand words, he read Scripture aloud, expounded upon it, and explained it. He gave instruction and answered questions. Everything was based upon Scripture, and very early in life I understood the basics of what was right and what was wrong and the reasons for the distinction.

My father never set out to "show" me sin and wickedness in the world. For example, he did not say, "Son, I'm going to show you violence today, so let's get in the car and go look for some." Rather, we went to the places we planned to go, did what we planned to do, and interacted with the people in our paths. He merely allowed me to observe the business of sin. The effect upon me was profound. Whatever morality would not have kept me from doing at a given point, the images and knowledge of such heartbreaking waste would have. Spiritual convictions did play a part, but my father wanted me to learn and understand the harsh lessons of reality as well as of spiritual truths and to understand their linkage.

To his credit, my father never took the approach of telling me that sin was not fun. Anyone who tells young people that sin is not fun is either ignorant, incredibly naive, or dishonest. It is fun; for if it were not fun and enjoyable, there would not be such demand and desire for it. True, it is pleasurable only for a season, however long the season may last until the consequences become manifest; but many of the sinful acts themselves are enjoyable, or if not enjoyable, at least bring to the perpetrator some benefits or satisfaction.

Aside from the fact that you would not be telling the truth, you should never tell a group of young people that sin is not fun because some of them may know from experience how wrong you are. What little credibility you had will then be lost.

My father never denied that sin was fun, but he pointed out that it would only be so for a season. He focused more on the consequences, both physical and spiritual. He was less likely to harangue me about certain sins and more likely to ask if I was ready to bear and give an account for the consequences.

Allowing PKs to learn and understand what vice and sin really is, its effects upon individuals and society, and its terrible, long-term consequences, may take away some of the novelty and the light-hearted appeal of the sterilized image of a few and the gratification placed in their minds by advertising and entertainment mediums. Violence and death in real life do not look, smell, taste, or feel anything like what you experience on your television or at the movies. How can I say that with all the great special effects and acting we have now? For one thing, people who have to live with violence and death do not look for popcorn and a soda to sit down and enjoy in the midst of it.

To be in the presence of hunger and disease hurts, sickens, and angers your heart in a way that seeing such rendered on cable news cannot approach. You never view corruption, injustice, and oppression with the same reluctant but patronizing acceptance again.

To shelter your sons and daughters can only be effective if you can guarantee that you can keep them sheltered for their entire lives—a tall order in modern society. Too, you must be sure that they will have no inclination to go out and explore things for themselves. Otherwise, you may want to think of things in a different way. It does not seem to me that Jesus was shy about where He went and with whom He talked.

PKs will sometimes feel resentment in regard to certain aspects of their lives, and this resentment or anger is easily directed toward their parents, the church, or even toward Christianity in some cases. Given this possibility, one aspect of training a child or young adult often overlooked is the matter of Christian education. It is very easy for the views and understanding of Christianity formulated by children and young adults to be limited to their own churches and communities. They learn about the stories and people of the Bible and about the nature of God, yet often understand little about the cultures of the Bible and the histories of the civilizations that dominated the regions of biblical record. Furthermore, they understand little about the spread and influence of Christianity and the profound impact it had upon the world. They know little of how it has been misinterpreted and misused for personal and political gain and why that misuse reveals more about those individuals and governments who misused it than it does about the principles of Christianity itself.

Your sons and daughters need to understand that Christians are a very small part of something much bigger and more significant than themselves and the activities of their churches. When you undertake an objective study of Christianity in history, you cannot help but see that many of the things that come to your mind and the forms that shape your understanding bear little resemblance to your own church and community. This conclusion does not mean that your church family is doing anything wrong or that they are not doing great things for those in need in their respective communities and throughout the world. Rather, the point to be made is that you are but one small part of the diverse and influential history of Christianity. If a PK gains a clear understanding of the worldwide impact of Christianity historically and of the many positive ways it has improved the lives of individuals and altered cultures, he is less likely to view Christianity as merely a localized or family practice in which little or nothing is accomplished other than to make his life more difficult and to give people a social event to attend on Sundays and Wednesdays.

Your children must learn the principles of Scripture and be a part of the church; but they must also learn about Christian history and understand the distinct differences between Christianity and other religions. They will gain understanding and perspective that not only will help them later in life but also will give them a greater appreciation of the work done by their father in the local church and an understanding of why that work is important. Your youth must see Christianity in its full context, understanding it as a spiritual force that has changed the world and brought light when there was darkness—not just a local cultural practice with limited impact.

This information and learning are not difficult to come by. It takes only the time and effort on the part of you and your sons and daughters. Teach them the Scripture and whatever else you can. Put them in the presence of educated men and women who can teach them more and who are open to their questions. Go to the library or the bookstore and get the writings of other religions and the books that detail their beliefs and practices. Despite the ridiculous claims by many that all religions are basically the same, the fact is that there are glaring differences through which you can best evaluate the validity of the claims of truth in each.

If you are having difficulty in motivating your young people to read in this day of teen lethargy and obsession with electronic entertainment, try sweetening the pot. To my father, some books were worth twenty dollars, some fifty, and some a hundred. Some were worth an extra fishing trip, a trip to another desirable location, or a new football. I was as stubborn and hard-headed as any kid from the human womb, and there were books that my parents wanted me to read in which I was not interested. I said stubborn and hard-headed, however, not stupid and unreasonable. When there was money, fishing, new pigskin, and any number of other desirable things at stake, I grabbed the book and headed to my favorite couch. I had only to read it and pass my father's query on its contents afterwards to verify that I had done the reading.

You have to work within your means, of course, and the things that motivated and interested me may not be the things that motivate and interest your sons or daughters. Maybe they would like a new bike, skateboard, computer (worth several books, I would think), stereo, clothes, or a trip to the beach. You know what makes them tick. As you educate them, be creative in using this knowledge in a way that benefits both you and them. Do what you need to do to make sure that your kids have both a global and historical understanding of Christianity that doesn't stop at the steps of the church auditorium.

Finally there are two things that parents should never say to a child or young adult. To quote Churchill, "Never, never, never, never,

never . . . ." One, "God called me so He also called you," or a variation, "Because God has called us, you have certain responsibilities." The problems with this are covered in the discussion of the pressures and expectations put upon PKs. Suffice it to say, God called you, not them. If He is going to call them, it will be later in life.

Number two, and perhaps the most inflammatory thing a parent in ministry could possibly say to a child or young adult when having a disagreement or misunderstanding and trying to persuade him to comply: "People pay us good money for our advice and counsel . . . . They pay us to come to their churches and teach them, so you had better listen." This reasoning is terrible for a number of reasons, which I do not think need to be related.

Even when you are completely in the right and your child or teenager is in the wrong, he is neither asking for, nor offering to pay for, your advice or counsel. This fact does not mean that you should not give advice, counsel, and commands when needed, but you do need to be wise and prudent in how you do so.

CHAPTER Eight

The Sacred Seven

VIRTUES MUST BE PRESENT in the lives of those walking in the ways of the Lord, and principles must be incorporated into the lives of those who honor Him. Seven vital and sacred principles, when embodied, incorporate all other virtues and principles by which believers must live their lives. These principles must first be embedded by parents into their own lives and then taught to their children by example and instruction. Teaching by example is more important because your sons and daughters are not likely to heed or give credibility if your actions are at odds with what is spoken.

Whether teaching children or adults, lessons are better learned when things are simple. To teach a child adherence to one principle by which he embodies nine others, is better than asking him to focus on ten principles. Living by these seven principles should become second nature. Parents and children will fail at times, but they should not become discouraged or allow their spirits to be broken. Nowhere in Scripture is perfection required; rather commitment and all-out effort are the key ingredients. When your sons and daughters seek to attain these principles, they will not achieve perfection, but they will live a life pleasing and honorable in the eyes of the Lord.

Truth—The Cornerstone

Jesus Christ is the cornerstone of our faith (Eph. 2:20). You cannot read the four Gospels and be unaware of the enormous emphasis Jesus places upon truth (John 14:6). Nor can you read the rest of Scripture and be unaware of the importance of truth and of the requirement that believers be seekers of truth in all things (Isa. 65:16).

Those who lie or withhold truth do much damage. They hurt individuals, families, businesses, societies, and other nations in countless ways. The damage may be small or devastating. Being truthful may save innocent lives, but lying or holding back the truth can bring death to the innocent (Prov. 14:25).

Anyone who reads a daily newspaper has seen this principle demonstrated in current events. If you as a sinner are sickened, you can imagine how such is viewed by a holy God. People have lost money, possessions, their reputations, their livelihoods, or their lives because others lied or held back the truth. To be truthful is not an option or merely a good thing; it is a mandate throughout Scripture.

Love—The Imperative

Paul penned 1 Corinthians 13, a beautiful and definitive chapter revealing the nature of love. You can have all the gifts of the Spirit and do only good and noble deeds, but you profit nothing from those deeds without love, according to the apostle. No word is any more misused, misunderstood, and carelessly tossed about in modern culture than is love. Young and old alike do not seem to know the difference between love and lust, love and obsession, love and favor, or love and the desire for money, comfort, or whatever is wanted from another. The words, "I love you," used frequently and freely without the depth of conviction and understanding, are meaningless.

Love does not have conditions or demands. Its requirements are the same whether in difficult or good times. A young man who truly loves his wife will express passionate devotion to her when the sight of her face and hair could make a freight train take a dirt road while she throws up in bed at two in the morning and he has to clean it up, just as he would when she is looking good in a short skirt and heels. A young woman who loves her husband is devoted and loyal to her husband for who he is and what he stands for, not for who she wants him to be or for how high a credit card limit he can give her. Loving God's way is truly caring for others who cross your path in life and showing concern for their well-being. Whenever they need help and you have the capability to grant that help, you do so, expecting nothing in return. When they are hurting, you hurt with them. When they are rejoicing, you are happy for them.

When I tell someone "I love you," I am saying that I care for you, I want the best for you, and I am here for you. In my eyes you are my brother or my sister, my father or mother, my grandfather or grandmother, my uncle or my aunt. What is mine is yours. If you need anything that I have or can provide, I am at your service. If you ask me to check on your aging mother, I will treat her as if she were my own. If your child is sick, I will care for him as if he were my own. If anyone tries to hurt you or your family, I will stop them or die trying. Whatever I have to give is yours.

Of all the virtues believers pursue and all the principles by which they live, the most distinctive virtue should be love (John 13:34–35). They should be easily recognized by nonbelievers by their love for one another and for all people.

You cannot be serious about walking in the ways of Jesus Christ without demonstrating a genuine love for others. You do not have to agree with other people or approve of the things they do, but you must love them. To contemplate Christianity apart from love would be like thinking of McDonalds without hamburgers. You cannot, for love is the definitive characteristic of those who follow Christ.

When the lawyer tried to ensnare Jesus through verbal mendacity, he asked the Lord to define the greatest commandment in the Law (Matt. 22:35). Jesus defined the greatest and foremost commandment and the second in terms of love (Matt. 22:37–40).

Your sons and daughters have to know what is required of them. They must love God with all their hearts, souls, and minds, and they must love other people. This assignment is not easy; that is probably why Jesus placed such importance upon these two commandments. Only when you love can you serve God and your fellow man with a willing heart. Only when you love can you forgive.

Only when you love unconditionally, serve willingly, and forgive readily can you begin to emulate the ways of the Lord Jesus Christ.

To choose whether hatred or greed is the most destructive force in the universe may be difficult, but to identify love as the most powerful force is an easy choice (Song 8:6–7; 1 John 4:18). True love has no fear, succumbs to no force, and is the imperative for those who follow the way of Jesus Christ.

Ministry parents ought never to lose sight of the importance of this powerful weapon in fighting against the evil one for the spiritual life and success of their children. When all reasoning fails, when no instruction will be heard, when even the most consistent discipline fails, when your sacrificial investment of time and energy and resources means nothing, still you have the love of Christ in you—a love He will channel through you to your child. What an awesome force!

Honor—That Which Has Been Lost

Honor cannot be defined with a few words. The various definitions given in the *Merriam-Webster's Collegiate Dictionary* cover nearly a quarter of a page. "A good name, public esteem, reputation, a showing of merited respect, recognition, a person of superior standing, one whose worth brings respect or fame, a greater deference, chastity, purity, a keen sense of ethical conduct, integrity, your word as a guarantee of performance, and social courtesies or civilities extended by a host" are definitions given for the word as a noun. As a verb the word includes "to regard or treat with respect, to live up to or fulfill the terms of, and to confer deference upon."

Honor as found in Scripture is all of these things, yet more. When you have honor and live by honor, that honor infuses your manner, your ethic, your mind-set, and your worldview; and it manifests itself in your relationships, in what you say or will not say, and in the actions that you take or do not take. When you do not have honor, you cannot live by honor, and the absence of honor is equally clear and is manifested in the same ways as would be found in one who lives by honor.

Honor has been lost in the modern culture, not by all, but by many, if not most. To ask randomly selected individuals what honor means to them and requires of them would be interesting. Most of the

definitions and explanations given would be laughable—if not for the fact that the implications therein are serious. Likewise, when you live by honor and come into the presence of those who have none, you are quickly aware of its absence.

The word *honor*, in its various forms, is used throughout Scripture. Interestingly, though, it is not defined or characterized to any great extent because Scripture was written in a time and culture in which people understood honor and the expectations accompanying it. Even when used to condemn those who fail to show honor, the word is not defined or explained because it was so well understood. Those without honor needed to be told they had done wrong, but they did not need an explanation. They understood honor, how they had failed to show it, and what they could do to restore honor.

The writers of Scripture used the word often with the logical expectation that those reading or hearing the spoken word would understand what it meant, and, in fact, the vast majority of them did. The same was true in our culture until relatively recent times. Honor had certainly vanished in the 1960s but probably had started to slip before that—aside from a relatively small number of individuals in each generation. Perhaps the only group in the 1960s and 1970s among whom honor was consistently conspicuous and unflinching included the soldiers who did the fighting and the dying in the Vietnam War.

In this understanding of honor, you cannot delineate between Christians and non-Christians. While I know Christian men and women of honor, I know and have been with others who have no honor. Conversely, I can look back and realize that I have encountered non-Christians who conducted themselves with honor, or who at least had some sense of honor. There are many soldiers who are not Christians; yet most know what honor is, and they live and die by it. If I had to depend on someone in any serious situation, I would rather depend on a non-Christian who understands honor than upon a Christian who does not know what honor is.

The concept of honor is now absent to such a degree that men, considered by those around them to be committed and exemplary

Christians, will say words or do things without a second thought for those principles for which men have fought, killed, or died in other times and places and for which a few still would put their lives on the line even today in some cultures and locales. You cannot dismiss the importance of honor, considering the number of times it is mentioned and implied in Scripture. You cannot ignore the fact that, given the lack of description and definition as well as the examples of behavior and conduct revealed in Scripture, the people in biblical days understood honor, while most of those in our culture do not.

People mention honor from time to time in reference to Scripture (Exod. 20:12; 1 Sam. 2:30). Strangely, they seldom speak about what it means to honor parents, to honor God, or to live with honor, and even less do they try to put the concept into action.

If one insults or speaks rudely to the wife, sister, father, mother, daughter, or son of another without provocation, then he has no honor. If he calls another man a liar while having no proof of such an accusation, then he has no honor. If he attacks, threatens, insults, or is disrespectful of a minister of God or accuses him of wrongdoing or of moral, ethical, or scriptural violations without proof, he has no honor. If he speaks disrespectfully to an elderly person or slights him with his manner, he has no honor. If he acts condescendingly toward the poor or knowingly and deliberately increases his wealth at their expense, he has no honor. Furthermore, he taunts his Maker (Prov. 14:31). If he slights or is indifferent to those who can neither help him nor hurt him while being generous and cordial to all others, he has no honor. If he sucks on a lollipop, drinks soda, or smacks his bubblegum during a church service, he has not committed any great sin, but he clearly has no understanding of honor or of what it means to come before or to give honor to a holy and omnipotent God. If he leaves his wife and children destitute and without support by taking unnecessary risks with his money or by engaging in illegal or unethical acts that bring shame upon his family, associates, and sometimes his church, he has no honor.

I have stopped far short of listing all of the ways in which I have seen the absence of honor. More astounding is that, except for the few cases in which individuals ended up in the penitentiary, the standing of people as pillars of the church and community remains virtually unchanged even in the shadow of dishonor. It is difficult for me to understand how anyone with rudimentary skills of observation could argue that honor, by any of its definitions, is understood by more than a few.

Men and women of honor are generally quiet and soft-spoken (Prov. 17:27). They think before they speak (Prov. 4:7b–8). They contemplate their words and the words of others, for they know that words poorly chosen can be the cause of hurt, pain, strife, violence, and broken relationships (Prov. 18:7).

Men and women of honor are polite and kind. They are generous within their means (Prov. 3:9). They seek understanding and wisdom, knowing that their value is far above money and earthly possessions (Prov. 3:35). Being quiet by nature, they are humble before God. They fear Him and seek the wisdom of His Word (Prov. 22:4).

Inasmuch as it depends on him, a man of honor avoids strife and conflict (Prov. 20:3). A man of honor does not cower or flee when violence or war is forced upon him (Prov. 24:10, 5–6). A man of honor, therefore, hears the counsel of his elders, and of those who are wise and knowledgeable.

A man of honor will honor his father and mother because to do so is God's only commandment with a promise. When he is young, he obeys his parents and carries out their instructions. At all times and for all his life, he loves, respects, and protects, does all that he can to meet their needs when necessary; he is kind and gentle with them; he converses with them and seeks their counsel. When it is prudent to do so, he shows respect for their accomplishments, is kind and respectful toward their friends and associates, is sensitive to their feelings, forgives them if needed and does not hold grudges for matters of the past, and does not speak disrespectfully or dishonestly of them. Inasmuch as it depends upon him, he has a cordial and harmonious relationship with them.

I have witnessed cases in which parents made this discipline very difficult for their older sons and daughters. I have seen parents, for their own reasons, turn on a son or daughter and refuse to have a relationship of any substance with them. Even in a worst-case scenario, a man or woman of honor should call or visit that parent regularly to check on their well being and to see if they need anything. Sometimes, unfortunately, this ritual is all that can be done.

One of the strange species I have encountered, and also one of the most difficult with whom to reason, are those Christian parents who believe that their children are obligated by the command of Exodus 20:12 to obey them blindly for as long as they are alive, believing that if they do anything against the wishes of the parent, even if it is not something clearly forbidden by Scripture, they, even after they are fifty years old, are in violation of God's command to honor father and mother. This interpretation seems ridiculous and absurd, and I cannot find it supported by Scripture. These parents may be beset with some serious personal issues stemming from childhood or with marital problems kept below the surface. Whichever the case it is sad and unfortunate; and they need help and support—whether medical or spiritual.

Anytime you are living in someone else's home, you are certainly going to be subject to their rules. When a child becomes a man or woman, his relationship with his parents changes. He doesn't need their nurture physically or spiritually in the same way he did in childhood, but he still honors them by listening respectfully to their counsel and giving careful thought before going against their values. Whenever a child leaves his parents' home and can survive and make his living on his own, he makes his own decisions. To suggest otherwise is to cripple him and insulate him from the realities of life.

Once your sons and daughters have gone and are making their own way, at the very least they should have moved from parent-control to self-control, and hopefully they have moved already to God-control in making the decisions of life. They are under an obligation to obey God and to honor you, and they ultimately will give an account to God for their activities. Your children—whatever their ages—must honor you, but, presuming that they are not living in your home and are not dependent upon your support, for them to make choices contrary to your wishes or counsel would not necessarily constitute dishonor. Were they to engage in criminal activities or other kinds of conduct that violate the principles of Scripture, then they would be dishonoring you. Their obedience to House Rules until they leave your home and make their own way is expected, but after that they must make their own decisions. They are to honor you, but they do not have to look to you for their daily life choices. Accept the honor they show you, but do not try to run their lives.

Honor is but one word, yet it encompasses so much and is manifest in almost everything you do and say, or it will not be present in any of your actions and words. If you cannot live and act with honor among men, it is doubtful that you can honor the Lord. Your child must learn honor and understand its virtues, attributes, and qualities, which, when woven through actions, words, demeanor, commitment, and spirit, interlace to form the whole of what constitutes honor. Then he can walk with honor among men and ultimately bring honor to God (see 1 Sam. 2:30). Honoring your parents becomes a boot camp, so to speak, for learning to honor your Heavenly Father.

Courage—An Attribute or an Obligation

Is courage an attribute or an admirable quality of character, with which only some are blessed? Or is it an obligation for all who follow Jesus Christ? Courage seems to come more naturally for some than for others, so an argument could be made for the influence of genetics. However, to suggest with any veracity that courage comes easily to anyone who is fully sober is doubtful. The *Merriam-Webster Collegiate Dictionary* defines courage as "mental or moral strength to venture, preserve, and withstand danger, fear, or difficulty." If it were easy or enjoyable to persevere in the face of danger, difficulty, and fear, then courage would not be needed. Standing firm amid danger and difficulty would be something that anyone and everyone could do, and no word of distinction would be needed. Since many will not stand firm and because withstanding danger, difficulty, and fear is neither easy nor a desirable task to face, the word *courage* rises to denote those who do stand.

There are two kinds of courage: moral and physical, although you cannot separate physical courage from its mental, moral, and spiritual components. People often will exhibit one kind of courage but not the other. Some will stand strong for their beliefs and convictions amid the harshest criticism and threats of others to harm their financial livelihoods or reputations, yet will not be bold or courageous in a physical conflict or in the face of battle. Others will stand strong, cool, and unflinching under a hail of bullets and artillery or boldly step into an armed confrontation, yet do not have the courage to make a pronounced stand for their beliefs and convictions when they come under heavy criticism or risk losing their jobs or being shunned by people. This fact is admittedly odd, as one would think that a man who had the courage to face violence and the terror of modern weaponry would be unfazed by anything less.

Those who are fortunate may live their lives and never be faced with a situation that demands physical courage. On the other hand, for any committed Christian to go through life without having to stand firm for his beliefs and convictions is difficult to imagine. The degree or severity of the challenge will be more difficult for some than others. Christian leaders may have to withstand intense media pressure, the criticism and hatred of the masses, the loss of a job or position, or even threats upon their lives or those of their families. Other Christians may have to withstand the criticism and pressure of a local school board, of other parents in their child's school, or of their peers. Their challenge may not be widely publicized or bring intense personal attacks, but courage will be demanded of them all the same.

Christians have been persecuted from the earliest centuries. Before the brutality of Rome, the prophets of God were persecuted and killed. Even today, in the Sudan, Saudi Arabia, Egypt, China, and elsewhere, Christians are persecuted and killed.

Given the facts of history and of the modern world, coupled with the commands of Scripture and the examples of those men and women of faith and sacrifice who went before us, courage is a virtue required of those who follow Christ (Deut. 31:6; see Josh. 1:7). These commands to the children of Israel required that they be courageous in their adherence to the law of God and in warfare.

In the New Testament there are also commands for believers to be courageous in their faith (Acts 23:11). Indeed, to stand firm in the face of hostile governments, religious establishments, and masses of people and preach the gospel as Paul did cannot be done without tremendous courage (1 Cor. 16:13). The word *courage* is not used in the NASB translation as it is in some others, but clearly courage is one of the qualities of character mandated by Paul. Be strong and stand firm in the faith. If it were easy or if you were unchallenged, there would be no need to be strong and to stand firm.

Without question, courage is required of all who choose to follow Jesus Christ. The very nature of the commitment to follow Christ and to live by the precepts and commands of His Word implies and cannot be separated from courage. A few may be fortunate enough never to have to demonstrate courage in battle, in confronting violence, or in standing firm on principle before a hostile community or group, yet even in some of the lesser battles within your own heart and soul, courage is required. When a Christian businessman knows that by doing something unethical, a violation of Scripture but not of laws of the land in which he lives—such as demanding usury or being deceptive in his business deals in order to gain the advantage and make more money, thus providing greater financial security and wealth for his family— courage will help him choose not to do so because of his convictions and his commitment to Christ.

The businessman would have nothing to fear from the law, and he could reason that he was not doing anything that many others were not doing. Besides, he could be a better steward of his money, giving much of it back to God. It is quite natural for a man to want to make as much money from a deal as he can; and assuming he has no retribution to fear from the law, it is natural for him to be unwilling to give up any of the profit that he could make. He has family, business, and financial obligations. It therefore takes some courage for him to say, "No, I will not expect or take any more than what I can by keeping my dealings within the boundaries set by Scripture." He may have wanted to use the extra money to send his children to college or to pay for medical care for his aging parents. Even those smaller decisions not noticed by others require courage.

You can be a Christian and be bereft of courage. I have seen many examples prove the point. You cannot, however, be wholly committed to the precepts of Scripture and walking in the ways of Christ without courage. You cannot embody the principles set forth in Scripture without courage. You cannot be a leader among other believers or one upon whom others can depend without possessing great courage (Prov. 25:26).

Your sons and daughters must understand that courage is required of them. They should see that quality of character in you, especially if you are in the ministry. To be a minister without courage is like being a soldier without a weapon. Whether in small problems and personal decisions or in the most serious trials and hardships of life, you must have courage to complete the journey down that narrow path in a way that brings honor to the Lord.

Protection—An Option or a Mandate

The protection of the children that the Lord places in your care is twofold. One is spiritual protection and the other is physical protection. Few would disagree on the issue of spiritual protection.

When you teach your children the principles of Scripture—the things they should do and the things they should not do, the things that are good and the things that are harmful to them—you are teaching them to live in a way that brings honor to the Lord, but you are also granting them spiritual protection. To see the point more clearly and to better understand the importance of it, think of the situation of your children if you did not teach them the principles of Scripture and if you did not teach them why certain things were edifying and why other behaviors, habits, and practices were harmful. Sending a child or young adult out into the world without instruction and knowledge leaves him spiritually vulnerable and exposed. It would be like sending a man into combat without protective gear or weapons.

Few would disagree that providing spiritual protection for their children and young adults is necessary, but the embodiment and teaching of scriptural principles might be taken more seriously if parents would think of doing so not only as "teaching the Bible" but also as providing a shield of protection for young people as they prepare to make their way in the world. Some ministers think they can do most of what needs to be done from the pulpit, but this assumption is not wise. There must also be instruction and parental example, and to fulfill these two requirements adequately, a minister must be willing to invest his time. From his example and instruction a child acquires wisdom and understanding. He also learns discernment and discretion. Solomon spoke of a father's instruction (Prov. 4:5–6) and of the value of discretion and understanding (Prov. 2:11).

Most Christian men feel obligated by Scripture, decency, and common sense to provide physical protection for their families, and most believe that their obligation also extends to protecting those who are innocent and cannot protect themselves. However, there is certainly more disagreement on this issue among Christians than there is on that of the obligation to provide spiritual protection.

Parents must train their sons to take seriously the physical protection of their loved ones. There have been many women who have courageously defended both themselves and their children from the hands of the wicked. Their bravery and honor is to be commended. However, men have been given the primary obligation to protect, which in no way diminishes the honor with which women have protected themselves and their children. There is an instinct within women, at least within those not adversely affected by a torrent of narcotics or feminism, and within the females of almost all species, to protect their young; and that instinct is there for good reason. Many women have done so admirably.

In justifying their positions, pacifists generally abandon the Old Testament and consider it irrelevant except for a few favorite verses that are always used without regard for context. Some quote, "Thou shalt not kill." Of course, there is no such command in Scripture. The accurate translation of the Hebrew text of Exodus 20:13 is "You shall not murder." If the command had been never to kill, then the Hebrew word for "kill" would have been used. Swords, slings, stones, bows, arrows, and honor are far too prominent to be to a pacifist's liking, so he spends more time in the New Testament. Even there, though, without the stories of battle, they still have problems, and verses or concepts are taken out of context; and, more importantly, certain verses seem to be missed completely.

Pacifists invariably claim that Jesus held this position. Is this the same Jesus who with a whip drove the money changers out of the temple in John 2? Striking the flesh of another with a whip is not a passive act. Whips hurt. They can cut the flesh and leave nasty wounds. Interestingly, too, Jesus proved Himself adept with improvised weaponry. In John 2:15 Jesus fashioned the whips (or scourge as it is translated in the NASB) out of some cords that he found lying about in the temple. Weapon improvisation is not something learned in Sunday school over donuts and juice.

This incident is significant because it shows that some of the disciples carried swords. Jesus had to know about this. You cannot habitually carry a sword, even a short sword, without those closest to you knowing about it. Besides, Jesus was a bit more perceptive than the average man. He knew, yet He never made a general prohibition against His disciples carrying swords. In special circumstances He told them not to carry them, but there was never any general prohibition against being armed. These disciples were not arming themselves as a fashion statement. There are two noble and justifiable reasons to be armed: to go into battle and to protect innocent life and property.

The disciples were not in the army and were not going into battle. No one would tell someone to arm himself if there were no situation or circumstance in which he could justifiably employ his weapon. An order to carry a weapon is tantamount to an order to use it if a situation necessitates defensive action.

There are certainly times when it is best, or necessary, to go unarmed. If you are going to a location or region strictly for the purpose of sharing and preaching the gospel, especially if that region is in a country and culture with which you are unfamiliar, it is probably best, and maybe necessary, that you do so unarmed. If you are going into any federal government building, you definitely do not want to be armed. Jesus Himself, however, never made any prohibition against being armed or against taking action in defense of innocent life.

Pacifists frequently point to Jesus' arrest in Matthew 26 as grounds for pacifism, but what they miss in this account is more telling than what they point out. When Judas came with the crowd of chief priests and elders who were armed with swords and clubs, Jesus' disciples knew instantly why they had come. Peter drew his sword and sliced off Malchus's ear with a strike undoubtedly meant for the slave's head or neck. Fortunately for the slave, either he was quick or Peter was inaccurate.

Jesus then restored Malchus's ear and told Peter to put his sword back into its sheath. Note here that Jesus did not tell Peter to drop the sword or to throw it way. He did not say, "What are you doing with a weapon? Throw it down and never pick it up again!" Such words would have been the responses of a pacifist, but they were not Jesus' response. When you tell another to put a weapon back in its place, as opposed to telling him to forfeit the weapon or to throw it away, you clearly know that the weapon could be used again. Would a pacifist leave such a possibility to chance?

Now comes the pacifist's mantra, the statement that makes them giddy, bringing about a mild intoxication of delight. After telling Peter to return his sword to its place, Jesus said, "For all those who take up the sword shall perish by the sword." I do not pretend to be able to explain fully what Jesus meant by this phrase, but I can say what clearly was not meant. The statement cannot have been the words of a pacifist simply because Jesus did not admonish Peter against having the sword and did not tell him to throw it away; rather He charged him to return the sword to its sheath. Furthermore, it does not and cannot mean that everyone who takes up a sword, or whatever weapon of choice, will die by violence, although this interpretation is the way most pacifists understand these words.

Pacifists often use the variation of this phrase, "Those who live by the sword will die by the sword." Profound truth is found here. A man who lives by the sword is not one who takes up the sword only to defend the innocent or to fight in a just war. Rather, he is one who uses the sword, or any other weapons, to attain anything and everything he wants. A man who acts in this manner does greatly increase the chances that he will die by the sword. Besides the fact that by his actions he merits no divine protection, he plays a dangerous game in which he steadily lowers the odds of his survival. As the number of his enemies grows, he becomes a marked man in the eyes of more and more men; he becomes more widely and intensely hated, and there is always another man who is better, faster, stronger, or just lucky on a given day. Teach your sons not to live by the sword but to be protectors who take up the sword only as a last resort in defense of innocent life.

Pacifists then fail to understand the significance of Jesus' words to Peter after having told him to put away his sword. In verses 53 and 54, Jesus said, "Or do you think that I cannot appeal to My Father, and He will at once put at My disposal more than twelve legions of angels? How then will the Scriptures be fulfilled, which say that it must happen this way?"

How then would the Scriptures have been fulfilled if Peter had his way? Jesus admonished Peter for his failure to understand and accept the will of Almighty God. Jesus had told Peter and the other disciples that the day was coming when He would be delivered to the chief priests and scribes, whipped, crucified, killed, and raised up on the third day. He explained to them not only that these things would come to pass but that they had to come to pass in order for Him to fulfill His purpose and to carry out the will of His Father. Peter's mistake was in placing his feelings, desires, and will ahead of the will of God. He did not want to accept that purpose for which Jesus Himself believed He had been sent.

Jesus did not chide Peter for noble inclination and desire to protect an innocent one whom he loved. Nor did Jesus condemn the inclination of the others who were with Him to draw swords in His defense. Clearly others of Jesus' disciples and followers were armed and ready, willing, and able to bring their blades into action (Luke 22:49). The only difference between Peter and the others was that the others asked Jesus for instructions. Peter, being more aggressive and a decided man of action, responded on his own. In Luke's account as in

Matthew's, Jesus reprimanded Peter, but He did not rebuke Peter or any others for having swords or for their inclination to protect.

The other notable pacifist favorite is found in Matthew 5:39, "Whoever slaps you on your right cheek, turn the other to him also." Sadly, pacifists misinterpret this wonderful verse and rip it from context. Given what has been established from Scripture to this point, the pacifists who take this verse to mean that defensive action is never justified have missed the mark.

I have been slapped a few times, as the reader could by now probably imagine. Some of those slaps were probably justified, another point that the reader can likely appreciate. Slaps do not feel very good, and some of them hurt, yet they are neither a life-threatening blow nor one that can cause serious injury.

When considering the wording of the verse and taking into account the totality of Scripture for context, seemingly Jesus was making a clear distinction between blows meant to kill, cripple, or maim versus those meant to humiliate, embarrass, provoke violence, or even to enhance the ego of the one doing the slapping. In the case of the latter examples, a Christian would be wrong to respond with strength. These are cases in which you should turn the other cheek or just walk away.

A Christian has no grounds to take up the sword or to otherwise engage in violence when either his own life and health or that of another is not being threatened. When a man can avoid conflict or violence by taking a slap or two, or an insult, and then walk away, he must do so in order to bring honor to God. I know Christian men who have avoided conflicts by swallowing their pride and taking such action, even when they knew they could have easily won the fight. Turning the other cheek is not about pacifism; it is about being willing to take insults and blows that do no serious damage without resorting to violence, which is to be used only if you must defend innocent life from the hands of the wicked.

Most parents are committed to protecting their children. The Bible is full of examples of righteous men protecting themselves, their families, and nation. Likewise, your sons must learn that they are to be the protectors of the family. God gives them responsibility to protect those in their path who cannot protect themselves.

Some, too, will go on to be the men who protect our nation and our streets and cities.

Faithfulness—To the Lord, Loved Ones, and Calling

Of all the many attributes of God, His faithfulness is most prominent and precious. That faithfulness is unbound by time and change, independent of the sin and spitefulness of men, as certain as the rising and setting sun, and that which brought the gift of a sinless Son as the sacrifice and atonement for all. God is truly faithful (Deut. 7:9; Ps. 36:5; Isa. 25:1; Lam. 3:23). How better to honor a faithful God than to be faithful in all things—a minister to his calling and to those in his church, a husband to his wife and children, a wife to her husband and children, children to their parents, and all believers to loving and caring for one another, and to bringing comfort, help, and hope to those who have so little. Faithfulness in action is among the loveliest of attributes.

Because you are faithful, you honor and obey the Lord and bring the light and gentleness of His grace to the darkness of a harsh world. Because you are faithful, you love the Lord as well as your brothers and your sisters without conditions or expectations. Because you are faithful, you can forgive, not seven times but seventy times seven. To fall away is to be faithless (Ps. 101:3; Prov. 25:19).

The faithful, though, are precious in the eyes of the Lord (Prov. 101:6; 28:20). Faithfulness is among the fruit of the Spirit listed by the apostle Paul (Gal. 5:22). Children make mistakes as they grow and mature. Adults make mistakes as they seek to balance obligations of family, work, and church or community leadership with the inner search for the will of God and the wisdom and understanding that come only from Him. Perfection, though, is not your goal. You strive only to do the best you can and always to be found faithful.

Loyalty—It Has No Price

Some tout that loyalty can be bought. Prices will differ according to whose services must be purchased; but if you can pay any price, then loyalty will always be within reach. During the empire days after years of hard and costly fighting in Afghanistan, the

British said of the Afghans, "You never buy their loyalty. You can only rent it for a while."

Perhaps these words are not only true of Afghans. The first definition of the word *loyal* given in the *Merriam-Webster Collegiate Dictionary* is "unswerving in allegiance." If you take this definition in its present form, seemingly any loyalty bought with money, gifts, or privileges and not stemming from dedication based upon conviction, faithfulness, and a devotion of heart, soul, and mind to principle or cause, would only be rented. If you are renting something, is it really yours? You can have it, use it, or live in it for a while; but if it still is owned by someone else, it is not yours.

You could say that a person is loyal to one team for five years, or to a company for ten years before he moves on and changes his loyalties due to a better offer, but consider the differences in a more absolute sense. Unswerving in allegiance means allegiance that does not swerve or waver—not allegiance that does not swerve so long as conditions are favorable but allegiance that does not swerve regardless of conditions.

When you think of the nature of the loyalty you should have to God; to principles of His Word; to your children, your parents, your family; and to your calling to bring the love, compassion, and message of Jesus Christ to this world, that loyalty must not swerve or waver. It is not dependent on conditions but is founded upon conviction, fortified by the truth and message of Jesus Christ, and by faithfulness and devotion of heart, soul, and mind; and strengthened by the timeless tenets and wisdom of His Word. Such loyalty has no price.

CHAPTER Nine

The Tripartite Way

As I LOOK BACK ON MY YOUTH, the lack of attention to the Books of Proverbs and Ecclesiastes in the teaching and counsel I received at church and in a Christian school is puzzling. I have no memory of any lessons or Bible studies being done from Ecclesiastes. In counsel and advice I was given on various matters, I cannot remember anyone ever pointing out verses or principles from Ecclesiastes and how they might be relevant to my life.

Proverbs was not ignored. Certain verses were quoted often, especially Proverbs 3:5–6. However, its wisdom for life application goes far beyond these verses. You can gain new learning and understanding from the book, even when you have read it many times.

More emphasis should have been put upon Proverbs among young people. You cannot read the book once or even a few times and take in all of its knowledge and wisdom. You would be challenged to do so with many readings over a lifetime. Learning and understanding come gradually over years of prayerful study and contemplation interwoven with experiences, good and bad, over a lifetime. Not only do new experiences and challenges open your eyes to instruction and observation you might not have noticed before; but as your own understanding and knowledge grows, so does your capacity to recognize wisdom and your ability to differentiate between edifying counsel and human desires.

For years I have tried to include reading a chapter from Proverbs in my daily devotional time. Since there are thirty-one chapters, you can easily work your way through the book on a monthly cycle. Its subject matter is practical with helpful principles for everyday living. Even after decades of this discipline, I find myself encouraged and edified by new insights gleaned and better understanding received. Proverbs is truly an old book that is fresh with every reading. When Armour left home to attend the university, I asked him to do two things if for no other reason than "for love of your mother":

(1) Read something from God's Word each day (and I recommended the Book of Proverbs because it can be profitable in brief snatches of a few verses or chapter by chapter).

(2) Gather with God's people for worship each week.

Perhaps these proverbs, for varying reasons, make some people uncomfortable, so they move to verses with which they are more comfortable or avoid them. The worst gossips in a church would be hesitant to say much about Proverbs 20:19. The man who lives with a contentious wife might be reluctant to talk about Proverbs 21:9, especially when she is in the same Sunday school class. A man who could not button his coat due to ever-increasing girth would not want to spend much time on Proverbs 23:20 or 25:16. Those known for cowardice would have good reason to avoid Proverbs 25:19 and 26. Those who talk incessantly would avoid discussion of Proverbs 17:27.

Young people should not only be encouraged to read Proverbs regularly, but there should be a greater focus upon the book in Sunday school and Bible studies. When verses are read in a class, service, or around a dinner table, much of their relevance and life application will be missed, especially if you are not interested in the first place. Better to read a few verses and explain the meaning, context, and application than to read an entire chapter with little or no explanation.

While the reasons for the lack of thoroughness in teaching the Book of Proverbs is uncertain or open to question, the lack of attention given to the whole of the Book of Ecclesiastes is not. I became familiar with Ecclesiastes after my teenage years. I had read through it rapidly, as other seldom-mentioned books of the Bible. Once I studied the book and contemplated its instructions and observations, I was dumbfounded that it had not been given emphasis during my teen years.

As I look back on those years now, an unspoken taboo against extended discussion of the book seemed to exist. Certain verses were read, yet seldom would I find these verses to be encouraging, meaningful, thought-provoking, and profound. Discussion, explanation, or a series of lessons on the book itself did not happen.

Paige and I have considered Ecclesiastes special. I prepared study notes on the book for The Baptist Study Bible *and* The Woman's Study Bible *and was challenged to find good commentaries on the book. Even though I had personally enjoyed study and translation of this unique book, I was surprised that the book had such fascination for Armour. I began to give him helpful resources on the volume. You as ministry parents would do well to be sensitive to the Bible books in which your children have an interest to provide resources for them to pursue that interest.*

Bringing Perspective to Life

After giving the matter some thought, I asked my father why no one wanted to preach, teach, or discuss Ecclesiastes. "First of all," he said, "I have preached on it and will do so again." To be fair and to give credit where it is due, his response is true. "What is the response when you preach that it is better to go to a house of mourning than to a house of feasting, or that sorrow is better than laughter?" he continued.

People are uncomfortable with the harsher realities of life. For this reason, Ecclesiastes is often avoided, but as is often the case, the things you do not want to hear are those you most need to hear and think about.

Ecclesiastes is considered to be negative and depressing by those who do not like its contents. I never saw it that way. To me it is uplifting, edifying, and encouraging. Yes, there are some unpleasant realities observed and expounded upon, yet I realized that refusing to think of, discuss, or acknowledge these truths would not make them go away (Eccles. 9:3). I do not particularly like reality, but I cannot change it. I found it to be refreshing and encouraging to read the words of a man who was not afraid to speak truth and contemplate things that lesser men tried to keep far from their minds.

Young people are told to enjoy the days of their youth (Eccles. 11:9–10, 12:1; see also Eccles. 3:12–13; 9:7, 9). God has given them the time, and they should make the most of it. Some insinuate that to follow the desires of your hearts and eyes will always lead you to act in a way contrary to Christian principles. Ecclesiastes affirms the opposite.

"Follow the impulses of your heart and the desires of your eyes." What counsel could be more welcome by young people? If you have saturated your heart with the Word of God and have adopted biblical guidelines for making your choices, your impulses will be godly and your desires will be set apart or sanctified unto the Lord. After being urged to live life to its fullest and enjoy your time under the sun, you are reminded of your accountability before God and of days that will come in which you have no delight. No one relishes the thought of giving an account to God for wrongdoing. Nor do you look forward to the difficulties of advancing age, but these are the realities of life.

The best you can do is to enjoy the life you have been given. Enjoy the love and experience shared between husband and wife, between parents and children, and among friends. Celebrate what is lovely and beautiful in this world. Take pleasure in the simple things and marvel at the magnificent. Delve into the mysteries, conquer the challenges, bask in the pleasures, but in all things remember your Creator; for ultimately you must give an account to Him for your deeds.

A young person in church and especially a PK may begin to think that Christianity is all about the "Thou shalt nots." Young people are constantly told what not to do—that is, do not do this because God or your parents forbid it. Lessons or sermons can easily move to focus more upon the sin and evil to be avoided than on the good to be accomplished and the pleasures to be enjoyed, or at least it can seem so to young people.

Ecclesiastes approaches matters in a different way and in a way much more pleasing to the ears and hearts of young people. Rather than focusing only on what not to do, its readers are advised on what to do. Enjoy yourselves and make the most of the time God gives you. Follow your hearts and the desires of your eyes, but remember the One who gave you life. Do all that you do in a way that honors the Lord and is pleasing in His eyes.

Ecclesiastes is not a negative or morbid book; it celebrates life and embraces what is beautiful and pleasurable. It acknowledges the harshest of truths and expounds upon the most troubling realities. This emphasis is essential, even if unpleasant, for it brings perspective. The words in Ecclesiastes must be taken in the context of the book as a whole and in the fuller context of the whole of Scripture.

When you consider the preceding Book of Proverbs, note the emphasis on the pursuit of wisdom, understanding, and discernment—the Tripartite Way (Prov. 2:2–3; 3:13–15). Through experience, study, contemplation, observation, the counsel of the godly, and knowledge of and adherence to Scripture comes wisdom. From wisdom flows understanding. A man of understanding can act with discernment.

You can be knowledgeable but not wise. You can be educated and highly esteemed, yet lack understanding. You can be successful and receive the awards and commendations of men and know nothing of discernment.

All wisdom and understanding comes from God and has been made manifest through His Word and through His Son (Prov. 3:19). The ability to act with discernment comes with the acquisition of wisdom and understanding. Thus all must strive for wisdom, understanding, and discernment. Young and old, women and men, must seek to walk in the Tripartite Way, bringing honor to the Lord and light to a world darkened by sin and wickedness.

The process of acquiring wisdom and understanding is much like building muscle or mastering a martial art. The sooner you begin the more you can accomplish over a lifetime and the less vulnerable you leave yourself to the attacks of the wicked. For this reason, the acquisition of wisdom, understanding, and discernment should begin in childhood and youth. The Tripartite Way is never fully achieved. Rather, gains are steadily made over a lifetime.

What of Ecclesiastes then, where the same wise man who gave us most of Proverbs expounds upon the futility of wisdom and all human endeavor? The point of Proverbs is the pursuit and acquisition of wisdom, understanding, and discernment. Chief in Ecclesiastes is the emphasis on perspective. What is it worth to gain wisdom, discernment, and understanding without the balance of perspective? Only through perspective can you realize the value of wisdom, understanding, and discernment, and only through perspective can you know how to employ these tools.

Why is it better to go to a house of mourning than to a house of feasting? Some argue that Solomon was being poetic or using symbolic language. No, he wrote exactly what he meant. It is indeed better to be in a house of mourning than feasting because there you start to gain perspective. You face the truth concerning the end of earthly life and weigh truth in the deathly silence of your own heart and mind. Most try to avoid the house of mourning and the troubling nature of the truth therein. They gravitate toward houses of feasting, where the mood is light and jovial and there is seldom any meaningful thought, contemplation, or dialogue concerning the ultimate reality of things—where perspective is largely absent. Solomon knew that no one spends all or even most of his time in houses of mourning, nor are you meant to do so. The rarity of that occasion must be used in gaining the necessary perspective.

Likewise, sorrow is better than laughter, because therein you understand tragic consequences and the end result of your sinful nature. You gain perspective regarding the sacrifice of God's perfect and beloved Son, understanding both its magnitude and the reason the sacrifice had to be made. You understand which things are ultimately of value and importance. When you touch the cold hand or face of a beloved brother or sister resting in the Lord's arms, you realize the unimportance, irrelevance, and frivolity of so many concerns and worries, which only days or moments before seemed matters of paramount importance. The house you wanted but were unable to afford, the job you lost or did not get, the anger from being slighted by another, the vacation you did not get to take this year, the petty strife and conflict with other people—the seeming importance of all is suddenly gone at the moment you look into the lifeless eyes of one you love. The tears that fall upon the deathbed extinguish the fires of frivolity as a river would snuff out a candle flame.

When perspective is gained and you understand which things are truly of ultimate importance, you will live your life in a different way. Your goals and priorities will not be what they were before. Your mind-set will differ as day from night. You will see the gift of life in a new light and consider the hearts, souls, and plights of your brothers and sisters and fellowman in another way. All this you will do and understand when the time of mourning and sorrow comes. You open your heart, soul, and mind to the voice and truth of the Lord and allow yourself to be confronted with ultimate truth. Many take another option. You can fortify the walls of your heart and mind and turn a deaf ear when confronted with ultimate truth. In so doing you give yourself a false insulation to the ultimate realities and avoid the troubling confrontation with truth and the gaining of perspective, but you have not really avoided these. You have merely put them off. If not before, in another house of mourning, you will confront them when that bed soaked with tears is the one upon which you lie and wait.

When perspective is gained you realize that happiness is not found only in the activities you enjoy and the achievements you value. Nor is happiness always manifest with smiles, laughter, and the celebratory mood of parties and feasts (Eccles. 7:3b).

The houses of mourning and feelings of sorrow are necessary. If you avoid them, you fail to attain perspective; and all wisdom, knowledge, and understanding without perspective is of no value. Avoidance is not an option. You can engage truth now, or you can wait until you reach the river's edge and your time is short.

The Futility of Human Endeavor

A second point of Ecclesiastes is the futility of all human endeavors. This point would seem dichotomous to some, for Solomon even speaks of the futility of wisdom after having implored his readers to acquire it. There are, however, no contradictions. His words must be taken in context with perspective.

Except for that done specifically to reach the souls of men for Jesus Christ, all human endeavor is futile. Alexander conquered most of the known world of his time quickly and at a young age; yet he died a young man, and his empire was split into four parts and ultimately disintegrated. Napoleon was one of the greatest military minds ever to don a uniform. He accomplished incredible things, yet lost everything and died in exile.

All human endeavor is futile and your accomplishments will be enjoyed for a brief time. Then you go to the grave while others take over the work of your hands and enjoy the fruit of your labor.

What, then, of the futility of wisdom? To seek wisdom would seem a more noble endeavor than to seek wealth, possessions, and a prominent status (Eccles. 1:17–18). These words must be taken in context and with perspective. To seek wisdom only for the sake of being wise is futile. The purpose in seeking wisdom should be to bring greater honor and glory to God and to acquire understanding and discernment that allows you to live in a way more pleasing to Him. In using wisdom to spread His truth, to bring love, compassion, and help to His children, and to see that righteousness triumphs over wickedness whenever possible, you honor Him and do what is pleasing in His eyes.

At some point, Solomon lost track of what is and is not ultimately important. He lost perspective. The search for wisdom became intertwined with the pursuits of pleasure, glory, and power, making that journey futile and pointless. By the time Solomon put forth the words of Ecclesiastes, he had regained perspective. He could look back with painful clarity upon the years of sinful disobedience to God; futile endeavor, the pursuit of glory, wealth, power, and pleasure; and the striving after the wind.

With his perspective renewed, Solomon could see what was of ultimate importance and what was frivolous and mattered not. He could see his end as clearly as he could look back upon his youth and his prime. You can see that he does not say that wisdom is useless or that it should not be sought (Eccles. 2:13).

The pursuit of wisdom is neither folly nor futility, but it must be undertaken with perspective for reasons that are right and good. To pursue wisdom for the glorification of yourself is futile. To do so even for noble reasons, if you assume that in so doing you can change the ways of man and of the world, is futile and is striving

228 | A Handbook for Parents in Ministry

after the wind. In Scripture and in the realities of life, most will choose darkness over light in their earthly sojourn.

Your wisdom will not alter the course of the world or change the nature of human disposition, but it might make the lives of some better and bring others to the saving grace and love of Jesus Christ. In this pursuit, you will have honored the Lord; you will have done what is good and righteous, what carries through to eternity; you will not have been striving after the wind. The pursuit of wisdom is futile only if it is without perspective or for the wrong reasons. In much wisdom there is grief, yet this does not mean that you should not pursue wisdom. You must accept this reality of life. There is much sorrow and grief in wisdom simply because you can see clearly the ends of folly, wickedness, and sin. Those ends are ugly; they are troubling; they bring sadness, even hopelessness, to the heart. To accept the harshness of all truth and reality is neither easy nor pleasurable.

The Pursuit of Wisdom

The fact that sorrow can come with much wisdom and that truth is often unpleasant is not reason for you to refrain from the pursuit of wisdom or to avoid the acknowledgment and contemplation of truth. I hate to see, or even to think of, human suffering and death. Nothing about it is pleasant or comforting; yet it is still the truth.

Wisdom sought for the sake of self-glorification is futile. Wisdom sought with perspective and for the right reasons makes stronger and wiser men and women of God and brings honor to Him. All human endeavor for its own sake is a futile striving after the wind. Thus you should enjoy and take pleasure in the life God has given you in your time under the sun, but in all things you must remember your Creator and Lord. You must keep your focus upon what is eternal rather than on that which is passing (Matt. 6:19–21).

That there is a time for everything (Eccles. 3:1) is important first of all for the profound truth of life it conveys. It is important because some Christians, for reasons that I have never been able to understand, cannot or will not understand and acknowledge this basic truth.

In Ecclesiastes 3, the pacifist inexplicably and continually misses the point that there is a time for war (v. 8) and a time to kill (v. 3). The prudish and the legalistic miss the point that there is a time to dance (v. 4) as did David in his joy before the Lord. Those who chatter incessantly miss the point that there is a time to be silent (v. 7). Those who think that sappy expressions of love, outward affection, and the happy, universal acceptance of everything and everyone can resolve all problems miss the point that there is a time to hate (v. 8) and a time to shun embracing (v. 5). Those who think Christians must be happy and that if they are sad or brokenhearted they are living outside the will of God, miss the point that there is a time to weep and a time to mourn (v. 4).

Truly there is a time for everything. The opening verses of Ecclesiastes 3 became very precious to my heart as a young man, and they still are today. While hardship, trials, and tragedy are recognized as unavoidable realities of life, allowance is made for things that are beautiful, pleasurable, and lovely. You must face what is difficult, unpleasant, and frightening in life with courage and righteousness, yet you are free to enjoy what is pleasurable and beautiful. You will face the hardships and consequences of your sin and that of others, but God in His lovingkindness, mercy, and grace has granted to you many blessings by which the consequences of your sin are softened. For amid ugliness you see beauty; amid death you witness the miracle of life; amid hatred you live in love; amid faithlessness you remain faithful as your God is faithful; you experience sadness, but joy comes in the morning (Ps. 30:5). There is a time to die but then a time to rest in the arms of the Beloved in the place He has prepared.

Cultivate the pursuit of the Tripartite Way with your children and young adults. Teach them that there is an appointed time for everything. Let them know the futility of all human endeavor. Encourage them to enjoy the pleasure, blessings, and beauty of young manhood and womanhood, but remind them that they will give account to God for their actions. Help them to acquire perspective, to understand the importance of maintaining perspective, and to realize that when perspective is lost, all else to which they put their minds and hands will amount to a futile striving after the wind.

Conclusion: Recognize Their Independence

THERE COMES A TIME when parents must let go and recognize the independence of their sons and daughters. If you have sons or daughters who still want to live in your home after they are considered legal adults, you and they must work out the nature of your relationship. To look over their shoulders and inquire as to their whereabouts and what they are doing, unless they want to tell you or it comes up in the course of adult-to-adult conversation, is not wise. If they are staying in your home or asking for your money, technically you could lay claim to ask what they do with their time, but this inevitably breeds confrontation. Certainly whatever house rules are appropriate should be thoroughly understood and agreed upon by all parties before arrangements are set in concrete. In any case, the matter is between you and your offspring and not a subject to be addressed here.

Ministry parents do have some considerations beyond the usual concerns. For example, if the choices of a young adult reflect in a hurtful way on the personal testimony of his parents, parents and child must review whatever house rules exist and determine what boundaries are necessary. This matter would extend to vehicles owned by parents and to how money parents are supplying is spent. For example, I would feel very uncomfortable and in violation of my own commitments to the Lord if I supplied knowingly or unknowingly resources to be spent for alcoholic beverages or tobacco to be consumed by my children or their friends.

What is addressed here concerns those eighteen-years-old and older who are leaving home to live, work, or go to school. Once they leave and are making their own way and are not asking you for support, it is time for you to let go—not to let go of being a parent, for a parent you will always be, but to let go of being the prime authority in their lives. For some parents this decision will not only mean letting go but also backing off.

Parents who already have a peaceful, easy-going type of relationship with their teenagers have only to let go. Parents who have a more tumultuous or uneasy relationship with their teenagers will need to back off.

If your sons or daughters come to you for counsel, advice, or an opinion, then give it to them. This responsibility is part of being a parent. If you have a good relationship with your adult children and if they do not think you are intrusive or that you have been intrusive in the past, they will probably welcome your advice and opinions anytime. If, however, they feel you have been intrusive upon their adult lives in the past or if they feel you are invading what they perceive to be private areas of their lives now, many of them will not welcome your unsolicited advice, personal opinion, or parental instruction. For these parents the best alternative may be to back off from the everyday choices of your sons or daughters unless they ask for your input.

Giving your children and the Lord time may bring lasting changes more quickly than would your willful intervention. One encouraging promise from the psalmist has been a helpful reminder to me of who is really in charge: "Hope in God, for I shall YET praise Him [emphasis mine] . . . " (Ps. 42:5). Missionary Amy Carmichael suggested these words from the Heavenly Father:

> *One of the ways the soul*
> *is supplied with delight*
> *is by seeing Me*
> *Work in the events of those*
> *you love. Wait and see!*

I have shared this thought with many parents who have spent, are spending, and will yet spend agonizing hours in God's waiting room as He works in the lives of their children. Waiting is never easy, but it is God's plan for fashioning and molding us—and our children—into His likeness.

In an earlier chapter I urged caution in how you deal with young adults. I advised against the in-your-face approach: "You can do whatever you want when you turn eighteen, but now you're going to do it my way, and don't ask me to explain." As I cautioned, you may get what you suggest. They may learn the in-your-face technique from you and send it back at you when the eighteenth birthday rolls around.

Also I have observed that the more peaceful the relationships of parents with their sons and daughters in high school years, the greater the chance that their relationships in adult years will be open, with the parent being able to speak freely and be heard at any time. To be less intrusive or dogmatic with your teens does not suggest allowing them to violate laws or to debase your values (such as, using your house for drinking parties). What I suggest is that parents think twice before intruding when there has been no violation of law or Scripture. If you are intrusive after they turn eighteen and they have a strong and independent will, your counsel will probably not be sought, welcomed, or heeded.

If you have a relationship with your adult children in which you are free to speak your mind to them any way and any time, you already know that. If you are not sure or if you are sure that you do not have this kind of relationship, you may choose to back off and reserve your counsel and opinions for request.

When you have disagreed on a matter in the past and your adult child knows your opinion and you know his and you still disagree, carefully consider the wisdom of bringing the matter to the floor prematurely. Unless your child brings it up to you, you may do well to back off and let the matter rest. Otherwise, you may increase resentment within your adult child and build a bigger wall between you and him than is already there.

I am aware that there have been cultures in which fathers, through their lifetime, exerted almost total authority over their sons, but very few of our readers will come from this tradition. So I stay with the realities as they are observed in the culture in which most involved on either end of this book live and will die.

Unless you are certain that your adult children want you to speak up whenever you disagree with them or that because of their respect for you and their deference to whatever wisdom you want to share they want your input, then you may be better served to move forward with your lives and let your adult children do the same with theirs. If they really want to hear what you have to say, they will come to you. From my perspective, when parents go forward with their own lives, keep control of their emotions, and are not unduly invasive in the lives of their sons and daughters, their adult children will be more likely to come to them for counsel.

When I see parents who are at peace with others, who are in control of their emotions, who center their energies on the orderliness of their own lives, and do not tell others how to live their lives, I see stability, contentment, and happiness. Regardless of who they are or where they are from, I can learn something from them. Sometimes I watch such a couple and think they have something to teach me, even if I do not yet know what it is. If I stay around them long enough, observe them, and talk to them, I find out what it is. Conversely, when I see a couple that is constantly telling others how they should live their lives, be it their adult children or anyone else, and who are prone to emotional outbursts (see Prov. 25:28), be it rage or crying fits, I perceive that they are not sure how they should be living their own lives and might need the help of others to put their lives in order.

I do not know if problems between parents and adult children are any more common in ministry families than in others. I know some PKs who would be happy to make the argument that they are. I also know many ministers and their wives who have very close and congenial relationships with their adult children.

Be open to your adult children but respect their independence and their right to choose their own way. Respect their right to make their own decisions. You do not have to agree with them, but you do have to accept the fact that they no longer recognize your exclusive authority. You had eighteen years to be the authority in their lives and to tell them what and what not to do. Now that time is past. You must let go and accept them as they are.

However, never underestimate "knee power"! You as parents can fall on your faces before God—not once or from time to time but all the time. You can put before the Heavenly Father your burdens and concerns. Children can reject your involvement in their lives, especially your guidance or wisdom, because they feel they have outgrown it or have more wisdom themselves. But God is the Father always in charge. They can reject Him as well, but He has ways you don't have of getting the attention of even the most rebellious child. More than one erring child has been returned to the Shepherd by the tears and prayers of a godly mother who refused to give up her child to the clutches of the evil one (see Luke 18:1–5). God fashioned the mother's heart after His own, and I believe He is sensitive to her petitions.

Often in my parenting classes on the seminary campus, I am asked by a ministry mom, "What would you do differently in rearing your children?" Actually, not a whole lot.

- *I would again walk away from a lot of "ministry" opportunities to be available to my children and pour myself into their lives 24/7. I firmly believe quality time doesn't happen without spending a quantity of time with your children.*

- *I would again have Scripture in accessories throughout our home, Bible reading and prayer as part of our family routine, regular worship and fellowship with a body of believers, and I would attempt to interweave godly principles into everyday life as I walk, stand, sit, or lie down.*

- *I would spend more time in biblical instruction of my children, especially in preschool and early school years. I would probably opt for homeschooling to allow more time for educational enrichment.*

- *I would spend more time before God interceding for my son and daughter. I routinely went to the room of each as soon as they left for school and fell on my face before the Lord. I knew that Satan was in an all-out offensive to snatch away my precious ones or at the very least to neutralize them for any good they might do for Christ. I would spend even more hours in prayer.*

You will always be the parents of your children, but they also have the right and the obligation to choose their own way.

Ultimately, they are accountable to God, not to you. Remember, though, that by respecting their individuality and independence and by not intruding inappropriately in their affairs, you create a situation that is more relaxed and free of the barriers created by frustration or resentment—one in which they are more likely to ask for, listen to, and consider your counsel.

Parenting remains among the most challenging of all human endeavors. It is arguably more difficult today in Western culture, due to a variety of external factors, than it has ever been. To strive to be a good and godly parent challenges one physically, mentally, emotionally, and spiritually. All who undertake this challenge are due the deepest respect and admiration.

There are often no easy answers or solutions to difficulties that arise, and there is certainly no universal formula for success. You can only trust in the Lord, adhere to the principles of His Word, and then do the best you can. That is all God requires of you.

Never give up hope or underestimate or forsake the power of prayer. Love remains the most powerful force in the universe, and by love others will know that you are followers of Christ. With children or young adults, keep all of your senses sharp, including that critical sixth sense—your sense of humor.

May the peace and blessings of our Beloved Lord rest with you and yours.

Endnotes

1. Victor R. Fuchs, *Women's Quest for Economic Equality* (Cambridge, MA: Harvard University Press, 1988), 111.

2. Sara McLanahan and Gary Sandefur, *Growing Up with a Single Parent: What Hurts, What Helps* (Cambridge, MA: Harvard University Press, 1994), 2–3.

3. Sylvia Ann Hewlett and Cornel West, *The War Against Parents* (New York: Houghton Mifflin, 1998), 250.

4. Federal Interagency Forum on Child and Family Statistics, *America's Children: Key National Indicators of Well-Being, 2002* (Federal Interagency Forum on Child and Family Statistics, Washington, DC: U.S. Government Printing Office, 2002), 10–11.

5. Emphasis added.

6. Jerry Pipes, *Family to Family* (North American Mission Board, 1999), 50.

7. *Mothering*, Spring, 1988.

8. "Home Truths" in *The Family in America,* Rockford, IL: The Howard Center for Family, Religion & Society, vol. 17, no. 1 (January, 2003), 4–5.

9. See Dorothy Kelley Patterson, *A Handbook for Ministers' Wives* (Nashville: Broadman & Holman, 2002), 113–15.

10. Dorothy Kelley Patterson, *The Family: Unchanging Principles for Changing Times* (Nashville: Broadman & Holman, 2002), 154–61.

11. Two excellent books on the subject are *The Koehler Method of Dog Training* by William Koehler and *The Dog: A Child's Best Friend* by Gunter Huth.

12. David Alan Black, *The Myth of Adolescence: Raising Responsible Children in an Irresponsible Society* (Yorba Linda, CA: Davidson Press, 1999).
13. David Bakan, "Adolescence in America: From Idea to Social Fact," *Daedalus* 100 (1971), 979.
14. Bakan, 981.
15. Black, 15.
16. Bakan, 981; and Black, 15.
17. Bakan, 981.
18. Black, 61–62.
19. Ibid., 23.
20. Robert H. Bork, *Slouching Toward Gomorrah* (New York: Regan Books, 1996), 252.
21. Ibid., 255.
22. Ibid.
23. Ibid.
24. See Dorothy Kelley Patterson, *The Family* (Nashville: Broadman & Holman Publishers, 2002), 25–52.
25. Dorothy Kelley Patterson, *Where's Mom?* (Wheaton, IL: Crossway, 2003), 19–22.
26. See Brian Mitchell, *Women in the Military: Flirting with Disaster* (Washington, D.C.: Regnery Publishing, Inc., 1998).
27. See John Piper and Wayne Grudem, *Recovering Biblical Manhood and Womanhood* (Wheaton, IL: Crossway, 1991); and A. Strauch, *Men & Women: Equal Yet Different* (Littleton, CO: Lewis and Roth, 1999).
28. Steven Goldberg, *Why Men Rule: A Theory of Male Dominance* (Chicago: Open Court, 1993), 39.
29. Victor H. Matthews, *Manners and Customs in the Bible* (Peabody, MA: Hendrickson Publishers, 1988), 21–22.
30. Ibid, 174.
31. Ralph Gower, *The New Manners and Customs of Bible Times* (Chicago: Moody Press, 1987), 65.
32. Glenn Stanton, "Divorce: Bible Belt Style," *Focus on the Family*, June 2000, 18–20.

Index